| THE KINGDOM

THE KINGDOM

Kerry Football: The Stuff of Champions

JOE O'MAHONY

Gill & Macmillan

Gill & Macmillan Ltd
Hume Avenue, Park West, Dublin 12
with associated companies throughout the world
www.gillmacmillan.ie

© Joe O'Mahony 2010
978 07171 4667 3

Index compiled by Cover To Cover
Typography design by Make Communication
Print origination by O'K Graphic Design, Dublin
Printed and bound in Great Britain by MPG Books,
Bodmin, Cornwall

This book is typeset in 12/14.5 pt Minion.

The paper used in this book comes from the wood pulp
of managed forests. For every tree felled, at least one
tree is planted, thereby renewing natural resources.

A CIP catalogue record for this book is available from the
British Library.

5 4 3 2 1

CONTENTS

Chapter 1 ∾

FROM EVOLUTION TO REVOLUTION

C an the success of Kerry football be attributed to the scrotum of the bull? And did the Kingdom invent Australian rules football? It's a common belief that when the GAA was formed, in 1884, football immediately came into being. Not so: for it was 1887 before a Gaelic football championship was introduced. Also, ball games had already been in existence in Co. Kerry since earlier in the nineteenth century.

There's an oft-quoted thesis of the 1840s, credited to a Father Ferris of Glenflesk. It pertains to a code of football that was exclusive to the area encompassing the Dingle Peninsula. This code was called *caid*, or Kerry *caid*. In this thesis the characteristics of this game are described. Among them are that players were allowed to use their hands and feet to control the ball; that they were not permitted to throw the ball—they had to hand-pass or kick it; and that they were required to bounce the ball after covering a certain distance. The ball for these games is said to have been made of animal skins, with an inflated natural bladder inside. The word *caid* refers to the ball used, made of the scrotum of a bull.

There were different forms of *caid* around Co. Kerry, with different features. The object in the crosss country game, according to Pat O'Shea in *Trail Blazers: A Century of Laune Rangers, 1888 to 1988*, was 'to take *an chaid* home. This game was played in the winter and at Christmas time, particularly when the crops were cleared off the ground.' For the field game, trees at opposite ends of the venue were used as goals, and games often lasted from dawn till dusk. Teams drove forward, just like the rugby ruck, but they could also kick the ball forward in order to gain ground. O'Shea adds: 'Both games were played in Dingle, whilst in the

Tralee area they played the field game. Many tournaments, which aroused much enthusiasm, also took place on the Cork-Kerry border.'

The historian T. Ryle Dwyer feels that there would have been a strong social aspect to games such as *caid*.

> I would have thought it was the participatory element to it, that it was what people could take part in, but I wouldn't think it was organised in any functional way as we would later look on it. I'd say these things started off impromptu; there wasn't a special game organised six weeks in advance—maybe during the week of a game.

The game was by no means limited to certain areas, as the GAA historian and author Eoghan Corry discovered.

> What is showing up is different types of football throughout the entire county. I would imagine the contact between various parts of the county was even closer back then. Because the distances were so vast by land, people would be in contact a lot by water, so somewhere like Waterville and Cahersiveen would be in very close contact with Dingle. *Caid* also shows up in Killorglin and Killarney. Also, there are reports in newspapers, such as the *Cork Examiner* in 1870s, where the results give *Cúls* as opposed to tries or goals. Rules did not differ much between the regions, with the game being something between rugby and Gaelic, but it appears more a carrying game than a propulsion game like modern football. We'll never really know what *Caid* was like, but we have hints.

Some believe not only that *caid* ultimately became the modern game of Gaelic football but also that it evolved into Australian football. Hypotheses abound regarding the exact origin of Aussie rules, and there appears to be no definitive answer. It is argued that only in Dingle was a specific type of *caid* played, and that its characteristics are identical to a type of football that appeared in Victoria, Australia, in 1853. This date could be significant, as it coincides with the big gold rush down under. It is therefore not inconceivable that Kerrymen invented Australian football.

William Webb Ellis is credited with inventing rugby. Legend has it that Ellis's father was once stationed in Ireland, where he could very well have encountered *caid*. The Welsh, however, will argue that *caid* was derived from a sport of their own called *cnapan*.

So, who invented the game the others took and turned into their own? Nobody really knows. O'Shea in *Trail Blazers* traces the birth of ball games much further back than caid, 'to the dim and distant ages.'

The historic founding of the GAA took place on 1 November 1884 in Hayes's Commercial Hotel in Thurles. Among those present was a member of the Royal Irish Constabulary, Thomas St George McCarthy, a Kerryman, who at that time was based in Templemore. He had played rugby for Ireland, and there has since been debate over the reason for his presence at the meeting. Eoghan Corry feels he was in attendance to support an old friend and one of the GAA's founding fathers.

> Everybody has been stabbing away in the dark as to what he was doing there at the meeting. Was he there spying, was the GAA founded by a sub committee of the IRB (Irish Republican Brotherhood) to monitor and find athletic young men? Was it a sporting organisation, which the IRB attempted to take over afterwards? The jury is out on that. McCarthy was one of Michael Cusack's past pupils, a friend and went along to the meeting to support him. McCarthy didn't have much of an involvement afterwards.

The *Cork Examiner* reported that hurling and football weren't mentioned at the formation meeting of the GAA, adding that the meeting was concerned with discussing athletics.

T. Ryle Dwyer believes that the GAA was an ideal way of promoting Irishness.

> I don't think organised sport was that high on the agenda. You had the politics of course, and politics were an all-consuming passion with some people. I would think such an Association would be an extension of showing we're Irish and we're proud of it. Politics permeated the GAA afterwards and I'm sure it did at the start as well.

A few months after the founding of the GAA the *Kerry Sentinel* published an advertisement of sorts.

> The parish of Ballymacelligott is still prepared to play a match of football, 21 each side according to the Gaelic Rules or in rough and tumble, with any parish of Munster.

In his book *An Illustrated History of the* GAA, Eoghan Corry writes that Maurice Davin, one of the founders, may have been responsible for bringing football into the GAA. This, Corry believes, was a result of Davin's awareness of the growth of rugby clubs throughout Munster, significantly in the future GAA heartland of Co. Kerry, where Killorglin was among the early affiliates.

At almost every turn there's a link to Co. Kerry at landmark moments in the history of the GAA. Marcus de Búrca's book *The GAA: A History* recounts a defining moment that centres on the Tralee sports of June 1885. Michael Cusack fixed the GAA sports for the same date as those of the Amateur Athletic and Cricket Club. When the day arrived, more than ten thousand people attended Cusack's fixture, while his rivals presided over an almost empty venue.

> For Cusack the Tralee episode was much more than a local victory, he regarded it as the turning point in the GAA's first struggle to stay alive. Not only did it prevent the IAAA (Irish Amateur Athletic Association) from gaining a foothold in the South; it also convinced his opponents in Dublin that the GAA was not intended by Cusack to have political undertones.

The book *Munster GAA Story*, published by the Munster Council, lists the promoters of this sports meeting as Moore Stack (father of Austin), B. O'Connor-Horgan, Michael Power, Maurice Moynihan and Patrick Clifford, with Michael Cusack as the starter. According to O'Shea in *Trail Blazers*, the GAA in Co. Kerry was launched by IRB men, among whom were Maurice Moynihan, Tom Slattery, Paddy Power and Moore Stack.

The Kerry County Board was established on 7 November 1888, as recounted in the *Kerry Weekly Reporter and Commercial Advertiser* of 10 November 1888.

> Mr Maurice Moynihan (for the purpose of the meeting) took the chair, he said he could not but feel a certain sense of congratulation

when he saw the very good attendance present, and comparing the standing of the Gaelic Association in the county at present to what it was twelve months ago, nay three months ago. Then there were but one or two clubs affiliated in the County, but now he was glad to say, they could be numbered by the score.

It is also worth noting that the inter-county competition that exists nowadays can be traced back to Co. Kerry and in particular to hurling. The rule in the early years was that the champion club in any given county could only select players from their own club. Eoghan Corry, however, in *An Illustrated History of the GAA*, explains:

Two Kerry clubs had changed the GAA's All-Ireland Championship for ever. For the 1891 hurling competition, the Kilmoyley club disbanded altogether and re-registered with Ballyduff so that eight of their players could represent Kerry in the All-Ireland. One of their best defenders was P County (in fact P Quane who gave a false name because he was from Kilmoyley). The following year the Cork County champions, Redmonds, selected three players from Blackrock and two from Aghabullogue. The GAA consequently decided to change the rules. Henceforth, the team could be picked form all the clubs in the County, not just the club which had won the County Championship.

It is ironic, given Kerry's success in football, that the county's first all-Ireland championship, in 1891, was in hurling. That was one season before the Kingdom contested its first all-Ireland football final.

Laune Rangers were the club that represented Kerry on that occasion, losing to Dublin. Among those involved was one J. P. O'Sullivan, father of the legendary Kerry trainer Dr Éamonn O'Sullivan, who was active in that role from the 1920s to the 1960s. JP, however, was to make a significant contribution of his own to Gaelic football in Co. Kerry and has long been seen as the forefather of GAA in the Kingdom.

Rangers were one of the leading lights in Kerry football at the beginning of the association. Jerome Conway, chairman of the Kerry County Committee, himself a Laune Rangers man, explains the background.

The club was formed in 1888, towards the end of the year. At that time there was a thriving rugby team in the town, football was not really played at all, and the captain of the rugby team was J. P. O'Sullivan. Three teachers who had won the Dublin county championship with Erin's Hopes came to Killorglin and they helped form Rangers. It was they who convinced the likes of J. P. O'Sullivan to turn away from rugby and join the new association, the GAA. Rangers were very successful in the beginning, won the County Championship of 1889, and represented the County in the Munster Championship—lost to Middleton. The following year, they won the county championship again, with JP the captain. Unfortunately they ran up against Middleton again and lost after a replay.

In 1891 O'Sullivan took part in the athletics championships, and he became all-Ireland champion.

He won the high jump, also the slinging the 56 pounds shot, was third in the 100 yards sprint, then first in the long jump, first in the 16 pounds shot, second in the 120 yards hurdles and he was first in throwing the 56 pounds hammer. He also came third in the quarter mile flat race and second in the one-mile flat race. Ever afterwards he was known as 'the Champion'.

After serving as vice-chairman of the county board, O'Sullivan went on to become its chairman. He was also a selector for the Kerry team that won the 1903 all-Ireland title. Kenneth O'Sullivan, a great-great-grandnephew of JP, is secretary of the Fitzgerald Stadium in Killarney, continuing the O'Sullivans' association with the GAA, one that stretches back further than a century.

Co. Kerry had the highest annual rate of emigration in the twenty years up to 1911. The census of 1841 recorded a population of 300,000; within fifty years this had been reduced to less than 180,000, and by 1901 it had declined even further. In the last census before Kerry won its first all-Ireland senior football championship the county had a population of 165,726, of whom 84,427 were male. That might seem like a sizeable number from which to select a squad capable of competing on the national stage in football; but a breakdown of this number shows that fewer than a quarter were between the ages of twenty and thirty-five. If one were to assume that the members of the Kerry squad that brought home the all-Ireland honours in the 1903 season were within this age bracket, the Kingdom won its first title with players from a county that boasted only 20,538 males of football-playing age. And how can one gauge what percentage of the 20,538 actually played football?

No records exist to give us a breakdown of the number of players in each club at the time. The Kerry County Board had just been re-formed, following a two-year lapse, and it had more pressing matters to consider. In fact the only sources for much of the information about the early decades of the GAA in Co. Kerry are those that appeared in the local papers at the time. This means that it is almost impossible to determine the size of the pool of players Kerry were choosing from. We do know that sixteen teams participated in the county championship of 1902, and that eighteen teams took part the following year. For teams with an average of twenty-five players it can be determined that between 400 and 450 players were available to the county selectors for the 1903 and 1904 inter-county campaigns. At the time the best players from the various lower-grade clubs found themselves called up by the senior teams. So, the Kerry side would be made up of players who participated in the senior county championship. Nowadays the Kerry squads are generally made up of players not only from senior clubs but also from intermediate and junior clubs.

As the county champions of 1902, Tralee Mitchels had earned the right to represent Kerry for that 1903 campaign, but they could also call on members of other clubs if they wished. When Kerry won the 1903 all-Ireland final, Mitchels boasted eight of the starting seventeen, Killarney Crokes had seven and Castleisland two. One player each from Laune Rangers, Tarbert and Cahersiveen had lined out for the Kingdom in the earlier stages of the campaign.

Can anything encapsulate the feeling of a county—or a country—in the same way that a sporting event can? That's certainly how it is in Co. Kerry for the progress of the county football team. The web site of the National Archives contains a telling piece of information. Under the heading 'What was Kerry like in 1911?' there is a line that sums up the power of football for the people: 'It might even be considered that the only real unifying force in the county was the emergence in Kerry of the top Gaelic football team in Ireland.'

There is no one reason for Kerry being the most successful county in the history of Gaelic football. A sense of tradition is often suggested as a contributing factor—not only a tradition of winning all-Irelands but also that of a deep-rooted association with ball games. Did the early and widespread playing of ball games in the county lend it a distinct advantage in the playing of such a game? It makes sense that if Kerry people played the games before others they would benefit from it, but not necessarily straight away.

What cannot be disputed is that the Kingdom have for more than a century been the standard-bearers of Gaelic football. It's a proud tradition, one that helps to define the county. Each generation is merely continuing the traditions of its forefathers.

The journalist Dónal Keenan, a regular visitor to Kerry, says:

People in Kerry might not understand what it means to me to go to Kerry and watch what goes on. I meet the young lads down in Kerry. I have a nephew who plays for Rahillys in Tralee. Those guys follow everything, but they *play* football. Football is still number 1, and while that may seem natural to everybody in Kerry, it's not natural outside Kerry. My own son is playing rugby, and follows soccer. He'll follow Dublin, but he's not playing Gaelic, because it's just not the same thing. In Kerry, Gaelic football is number 1, and everything else is a distance away . . . I was stopping with a friend of mine and he was introducing me. The minute he'd say Keenan from Roscommon they'd know the history. Young men in their thirties could tell me that my father won two all-Irclands with Roscommon—that's the difference. It's something that is very special, and it'd be very sad if Kerry ever lost it.

ı UP KERRY!

The twentieth century was five years old—but only three seasons old—when Kerry secured its first all-Ireland senior football championship. The Tralee Mitchels won the Kerry crown, after a 1902 county championship that had descended into farce: Tralee won the title by getting three walkovers, including one in the final, and by winning a single match.

The 1903 all-Ireland championship is best known for the three matches with Kildare and for the emergence of one Dick Fitzgerald. Over the years much has been said of the young Killarney man's contribution to this first crown for the Kingdom. His age at the time has been disputed, with some believing him to have been a mere teenager during the games. However, Father Tom Looney made a startling discovery when researching his biography of Fitzgerald, *King in a Kingdom of Kings.*

> I went to the Cathedral in Killarney and found out the date of his birth, 2 October 1882. Everyone thought he was born the year the association was founded (1884) but he was two years older than always granted . . . In local folklore he was still down as the youngest person ever to win a Senior All-Ireland which is not quite true. Even his family, when he died, put down the wrong date on the monument. He was born in 1882, not in 1884 or 1886 . . . Dick was a very humorous kind of guy and he never corrected those little misconceptions about his date. He didn't mind being regarded as younger than he really was. I didn't want to explode the myth, just tell the truth.

In an interview with the *Irish Press* in 1963, Denny Breen of Castleisland stated that he himself, at the age of twenty-one, was the youngest member of that season's winning side.

The 1903 championship began for Kerry on 12 June 1904 and ended on 12 November the following year. (It was common at the time for the championship not to be run off in its calendar year.) It was also in the early years of the century that the 'Up Kerry' chant came to prominence, thanks to a poster backing James Baily of Ballymac, a Kerry County Council hopeful, which proclaimed 'Up Baily.' Having spotted this poster, supporters of the future green and gold adopted it.

Waterford were brushed aside, 4-8 to 1-3, in Kerry's championship opener. Clare were next for the Kingdom and went down, 2-7 to 2-0. The *Kerry Sentinel* published the following brief match report:

> Kerry pressed and, with the wind in their favour, scored 2 goals and 5 points to Clare's nil. In the second half the Clare men pulled themselves together and seven minutes after resuming play scored two goals. The match then became a give and take one, and at the final whistle the score stood Kerry 2 goals 7 points Clare 2 goals.

As illustrated by this report, the press coverage afforded to the GAA in the early 1900s was vastly different from what we've become accustomed to in more recent times. More often than not the games were given only a few paragraphs, although this increased as the season progressed. However, on occasion there were no reports of games, merely the results. Also, records were not kept as readily as they would be in later years, leading to discrepancies in accounts.

Cork succumbed to the Kingdom in the Munster final. Kerry led by 5 points to 1 at half time, going on to win, 1-7 to 0-3. Kerry's next match in the championship, their semi-final with Mayo, did not take place until 7 May 1905, when Mayo were despatched with ease, 2-7 to 0-4.

Eoghan Corry believes that Kerry's futuristic approach to the 1903 season lay behind their qualification for the decider.

> What Kerry did in 1903 changed everything, because they introduced the notion of collective training. They gathered the players in Tralee and in Killarney and there was one player from Castleisland who cycled down to Killarney for twice a week training. The Tralee boys played the Killarney boys. By the time the all-

Ireland final came around they had a pretty strong cohesive unit.

The home final for the all-Ireland championship saw Kerry meet Kildare, semi-final victors over Cavan, in Tipperary in July 1905. The GAA historian Father Tom Looney says there was a host of reasons for championships of that era to run behind schedule.

> I think a lot of the reason would be administration. The association had very little money in those days. They hadn't the money to organise things, you had a lot of objections; objections held everything up. There was trouble in a lot of county boards, including our own county board. It was the club team that represented the county, and if the county championship wasn't finished you didn't have a representative for the county team. Things weren't as tightly organised as they are now; maybe it was an easier-going age as well.

For the final, Kerry were represented by a selection from Tralee Mitchels and Dr Crokes, in addition to Denny Breen and Rody Kirwan of Castleisland. Kirwan, from Co. Waterford, was a bank clerk in Castleisland.

Paddy Foley, better known as the legendary PF, recounted in his book *Kerry's Football Story* the supporters' struggle to make their way to the encounter and to get there on time.

> All carriages were packed, even the Guard's van, for the railway people, never anticipating such a contingent, had made no adequate arrangements to cater for the huge throng. The train broke down between Ballybrack and Killarney, and a special relief train had to be sent from Tralee. There was a further long delay at Limerick Junction. Hundreds of people left the train and proceeded to walk into the town. The Kerry train did not reach Tipperary Town till 3.20 and the match was already in progress when the Kingdom contingent arrived in the field.

Kildare, affectionately known as the Lilywhites, even had their boots painted white for the occasion. Kerry wore the colours of the county champions, Tralee Mitchels: red, with green cuffs and collars.

Kildare led by two points to one at half time, Jim O'Gorman the Kerry scorer. Kerry edged ahead in the second period with points by Charlie Duggan and Dick Fitzgerald. A controversial Joyce Conlon goal put Kildare back in front. The *Kerryman* went into detail regarding that Conlon strike.

> Kildare, with dashing play along the sideline, carried the ball right up to the Kerry goal, and after some smart passing, Conlon sent home. Kerry disputed the score on the grounds that the ball was out of play at the time, having gone into touch, but the referee allowed the goal.

That goal gave Kildare a two-point advantage with ten minutes remaining. They soon made it a three-point game. A John Thomas Fitzgerald score for Kerry brought the gap back down to two. Paddy Foley's book *Kerry's Football Story* best describes a highly dramatic conclusion to the proceedings.

> Two minutes to go, Kerry attack in desperation. Up the wing they came. A Kerryman was fouled in possession and his side got an angle free. Dick Fitzgerald kicked the ball; the leather sped straight and true to the mark. It seemed as if the ball would drop on the bar but it fell underneath. The Kildare goalman held it safely, but in doing so, pulled the second leg behind the line. The goal umpire raised the fatal green flag.

It was Kildare's turn to dispute a goal, but the referee was having none of it. Kerry fans, in excitement, flooded the pitch. The referee attempted to clear the supporters, but he blew his whistle in vain. After failing to get the match restarted he declared Kerry the victors and all-Ireland champions. It finished at Kerry 1-4, Kildare 1-3; but this was not the end of the matter. Kildare, who had protested vigorously after Kerry's goal, still refused to accept the outcome. The Central Council met immediately after the match. Paddy Foley recalled that Kerry were not represented, as they had no notice of the objection. Despite the match officials standing by their decision, a re-fixture was declared.

Meanwhile, according to Foley, the Kerry train after the match did not get back to Tralee until 4:30 a.m. John Barry and Éamonn Horan, in

Years of Glory: The Story of Kerry's All-Ireland Senior Victories, recount that the special train left at 6:15 sharp, with most Killarney people left behind.

'Bravo Kerry!' read the headline in the *Kerryman* of Saturday 29 July 1905, the week after the final. Its 'Kerryisms' column proclaimed that it didn't believe that a more magnificent exhibition of Gaelic football had been witnessed since the inception of the GAA. The writer enthused: 'We believe that the match could claim to be one of the most sensational that was ever played.' The mood changed, however, as the paper lashed out at the decision to call for the counties to meet again.

> The action of the Central Council in ordering the match to be replayed, on account of Kildare's objection to the Kerry goal, will not induce greater respect for the GAA nor more confidence in its decisions. The referee awarded the match to Kerry and one of the most stringent rules of the Association, or what is supposed to be so is that the referee's decision is final. When the Central Council deliberately breaks such a rule, passed at the annual convention it is of course acting *ultra vires*. It has neither the power to make rules nor to violate them.

Leading up to the rematch, the mood of the paper had not changed.

> Pay a visit to Cork tomorrow and see your county men play as they never played before to demonstrate the correctness of their recent victory robbed from them by the incompetent rulers—it would be a violation of good language to call them administrators—connected with the Gaelic Athletic Association.

Kerry and Kildare had well and truly captured the imagination, as much for matters off the pitch as on. Special trains were put on from Tralee, Killarney, Cahersiveen and Castleisland for the replay, which was to be played in Cork. Foley described the Killarney and Tralee groups training separately and then being brought together for trial matches in the two towns, as well as in Listowel.

In the replay Kerry were ahead by 0-5 to 0-3 at half time. Further points from Billy Lynch and Charlie Duggan seemed to put Kerry out of reach. However, they were held scoreless to the end. Kildare pointed, then that man Joyce Conlon goaled as he had done in the first fixture. Kerry and Kildare couldn't be separated, the game finishing 1-4 to 0-7.

The *Kerry Sentinel* attributed Kerry's concession of the equalising goal to 'carelessness and overconfidence.' The *Kerryman* was also less than impressed by the game-saving goal.

> Disappointment is no name for the feeling of most intense disappointment experienced. Kerry had won all over the field for three quarters of an hour and was leading comfortably three minutes from time when Kildare scored a most unaccountable and lucky goal. The goal was by no means a fluky one but the Kildare man should not have got a chance of scoring. The Kerry backs, having played a marvellously excellent game up to this, seemed suddenly to lose their heads and go to pieces. Even the Kildare followers had to acknowledge that their idols had met their masters. Kerry proved conclusively the last day they were superior footballers, even though luck did go against them, but they must now rise superior to luck and Kildare.

A third meeting between the two teams was now required. This was not Kildare's only triple contest of the season: earlier it took them three games to dispose of Kilkenny in Leinster.

Unknown to the players, they were cementing the future of the GAA. The renowned commentator and legendary broadcaster Mícheál Ó Muircheartaigh describes how that series of games was becoming a hot topic of everyday life.

> Up to then, it wasn't a big public topic, talking about football. It didn't get a lot of coverage in the newspapers, which was the only means of communication at that time. But those games caught the imagination of the public. They began to talk about them.

And so to meeting number 3. The second replay saw the sides return to Cork, where another massive crowd turned out. Eoghan Corry explains its impact: 'The third game drew a very big crowd of 18,000 into the Cork Athletic Grounds. That gave the GAA money, it gave it a little bit of status. People started taking it seriously.'

Constant rainfall that morning and before the throw-in made

conditions difficult, with many believing that such wet weather would lead to Kerry's downfall. It's always dangerous to write off the Kingdom, however! Kerry had worn the green and red of Tralee Mitchels for game number 1 against Kildare; however, come game 3 the Kingdom were wearing their now-famed colours. For the second replay against Kildare the *Kerryman* writer J. J. McC. reported that 'from a corner of the field a handful of men, dressed in green and gold jerseys and trim white knickers, walked on to the grass. A roar greeted them, a roar that made the nerves tingle, for there was a sting in it.'

Kerry held a slender advantage after the conclusion of the first period of that second replay, three points to two. Two points apiece from Jim O'Gorman and Billy Lynch, plus another by Dick Fitzgerald, finally put Kildare to the sword. Kerry had won by eight points to two. The *Kerryman* proclaimed: 'A magnificent triumph for the Kingdom— the scene at the Killarney and Tralee stations on Sunday night was simply wild enthusiasm. It is all over; the great football struggle has ended in favour of Kerry.'

The *Kerry Sentinel* was also rich in its praise of the Kingdom. 'Never before in the history of the GAA has any team fought so hard and stubbornly for the premier gift of the association. The matches will live ever in the memory of those who were fortunate enough to witness the contests.'

The GAA owes much to those efforts of Kerry and Kildare, a fact not lost on Ó Muircheartaigh.

> It was said at the time it was the biggest crowd that ever watched a sporting event in Ireland. Rugby internationals were in vogue that time and soccer internationals. It got the people talking about football, it got the balladeers writing the penny pamphlets, distributing them at race meetings and fairs all over the country. That was the moment that made Gaelic football a part of the national identity.

Eoghan Corry too is quick to point out the impact of this famous triple contest between Kerry and Kildare.

> There's a real 'what if?' What if the crowd had not spilled on the field. What if that goal had been allowed and Kerry won the match

by a point and there would not have been those huge crowds and the huge attention. A lot of people learnt a lot in those few months. The notion of collective training, an urban thing, was introduced by both counties. They worked out tactics, perfected techniques that can only be done on a training field by a group of people. These matches elevated the game into something else altogether, and Dublin papers started taking note. The GAA learnt that they had nowhere capable of staging an all-Ireland final that attracted real interest. It's probably where the idea of buying Croke Park came from.

Father Looney believes this triple contest set Dick Fitzgerald on the road to stardom, and in the process it made him the first superstar of the GAA.

> He was a brilliant exponent of the game, he was a classy player, very articulate and a very good mind. He did write the first manual on playing football in 1914, and often chaired County Board meetings while still playing. He was a superstar on the field and also very important off it as well.

Eighty-one years later (remember that the 1903 final was not played until 1905) it was revealed that a nine-year-old boy aided Kerry's cause against Kildare. In the period leading up to the all-Ireland final of 1986 a *Kerryman* reporter, Éamonn Horan, uncovered how the Traleeman Billy Mullins played his part in that triple contest against Kildare. Mullins explained that the house he and his parents lived in was too big for them and that they kept five lodgers, including two Kerry players, Johnny Buckley and Denny Kissane.

> As I was going out the door with my father to the train for the replay, the old lady called me back and handed me a brown paper parcel and told me that it contained one of Johnny Buckley's football boots, which he had let fall from his bag when departing the house. 'Be around when he wants it' . . . The team had gone upstairs in the hotel to tog out to go to the field. We heard fierce ructions in the room, with Johnny Buckley being abused for only bringing one football boot. I hammered on the door with the boot. It was opened

and I said, 'Did anybody lose a boot?

Billy Mullins's brother Dan won two all-Irelands with Kerry, both times as goalkeeper, in 1913 and 1914.

Kerry may have defeated Kildare in the home final, but there was still work to do, with London to be faced in the final proper. From 1900 to 1903 there was a home and also an away all-Ireland final, in which the home all-Ireland winners would each year play London. It's said that strangers are but friends we are yet to know. Well, in the final against London the Kingdom first met a friend who was to become one of its fondest and most frequent visitors in the coming decades. The London captain in that decider was a certain Sam Maguire, who two-and-a-half decades later was to lend his name to the most famous trophy in Irish sport.

Kerry were comprehensive winners against London. Having registered eight points, they kept London scoreless in the opening half. London had chances but failed to avail of each of them. The sides shared six points in the second half, with the match finishing 11 to 3.

The Kerry Association in Dublin would not be formed for nearly another half century. However, even in the 1900s the bond between exiled Kerrymen and the team of their birthplace was evident. The *Kerryman* recalled how, on the night of the Kerry v. London final,

> the Kerrymen resident in Dublin entertained the Kerry team and their friends at a banquet—there were present men from every part of the County, from Dingle to Rathmore and from Kenmare to Tarbert, all to do honour to the famous Kerry seventeen. The spacious hall was full to overflowing and at times it was hard to believe we were a couple of hundred miles from our native Kerry hills.

Two of the winning team of 1903, Dick Fitzgerald and Austin Stack, have given their names to Kerry's county grounds: Fitzgerald Stadium in Killarney and Austin Stack Park in Tralee.

12 November 1905 goes down in the history books as the date on which Kerry won its first all-Ireland senior football crown. For the 1904 season their backbone was the core of the squad that eventually got the better of Kildare in 1903. However, by virtue of the fact that they had yet

to face London in the 1903 final proper, the Kingdom didn't begin their 1904 championship campaign as all-Ireland winners!

Two weeks after their defeat of Kildare in the 1903 home final, and a fortnight before taking on London in the 1903 final proper, Kerry met Cork in their 1904 Munster championship opener. Kerry cruised to a 1-4 to nil victory—justice, considering the circumstances surrounding the original fixture. The *Kerryman* of 22 July 1905, reporting on the fortnightly meeting of the Kerry GAA County Board, reported Kerry receiving a walkover against Cork, who then appealed. The paper was not impressed by the actions of their near neighbours, accusing them of 'resorting to their old discreditable and unsuccessful dodge of lodging an illegal and frivolous objection.'

The Kingdom went on to scrape a draw against Waterford in the provincial final. Despite making numerous changes for this game, Kerry went into the tie as raging-hot favourites. They were the defending Munster and all-Ireland champions and were among the fancies for the 1904 national crown; but they were to receive the shock of their lives.

The score at the break did not reflect Waterford's superiority in that opening half. They held a slender advantage, 2 points to 1. Waterford extended the lead to 3 points to 1. Kerry brought it back to 3 points all. The issue was well and truly in the balance as both sought to find a winner. A nervy finish ensued, but the sides couldn't be separated, finishing at three points each.

When the teams reconvened the following month, Kerry had seven points to spare in a 2-3 to 0-2 win. Half time arrived with Kerry leading by 1-2 to 0-1. Strangely, the match reports carried no description of Kerry's first-half goal. Many reports of that era also omitted the names of the scorers. It was noted that Lynch goaled for Kerry in the second period.

On the beaten Waterford team was Percy Kirwan, a brother of the Kerry defender Rody Kirwan. Rody missed those games against Waterford but returned to the Kerry defence for latter stages of the championship. Legend has it that Rody was not keen to line out against his native county. However, the records show that he played against them in the 1903 season.

The *Kerryman* meanwhile was likening this Kingdom side to one of the most famous names in sport.

If we take the Kerry victories for some considerable time back, one is justified in designating the team the All Whites, the opposite colour being that applied to the invincible New Zealanders. The All-Ireland champions have obtained yet another victory, and this so soon after the Christmas holidays. This is a demonstration that they are still in the best of form, and will continue to sustain that form so long as good health and unity are evident.

In a postscript to the Kerry v. Waterford replay, the *Kerry Sentinel* reported that before the game the Kerry players had a meeting and had adopted a resolution to send their best wishes to the president of the county board, Eugene O'Sullivan, for his forthcoming contest for the representation of East Kerry in the British Parliament. (He was unsuccessful.)

Over the years it has been claimed in many quarters that Kerry received a bye to the 1904 final. Not so! Some papers at the time rather confusingly had the Kerry v. Cavan match billed as the 'Inter Provincial tie of the All-Ireland Championship.' Well, this semi-final did take place, on 6 May 1906. Kerry railroaded their Northern opposition, a goal by Dick Fitzgerald giving them a 1-3 to 0-1 half-time advantage. An early second-half goal courtesy of P. J. Cahill put the game beyond Cavan. Kerry finished with a tally of four goals and ten points, with Cavan registering only a single point all afternoon. Mission accomplished for Kerry: another all-Ireland final appearance secured.

The Kingdom were to meet Leinster opposition once more. This time, however, it was not Kildare they would face but Dublin. Dublin had accounted for Mayo in their semi-final, 0-8 to 1-3.

Denny Breen, in his interview for the *Irish Press* in 1963, described the training regime of his era.

Players were expected to get themselves fit and never failed. Many is the time I went into one of the fields at the back of the town and did a couple of laps. That, with gymnastic exercises, was as much as the individual did. We kept ourselves fit by match practice. Approaching a big game our employers would allow us to leave work early on Tuesday and Friday evenings. The team then travelled to Killarney where the probables played the possibles.

Unfortunately for Denny Breen, he was one of four members of the 1903 winning side who were omitted this time for the decider. Denny Kissane and Billy Lynch were two of the others. The fourth was Thady O'Gorman, captain during the previous campaign's triumph. Thady may have been denied a second all-Ireland medal, but his legacy would be seen in the coming decades. His son Jimmy became a multiple all-Ireland medal-holder, while Thady's nephew Bill scored the goal that saved Kerry in the 1926 final.

The thirteen others from 1903 each started that 1904 decider. As with Kerry's all-Ireland victory of 1903, the 1904 decider took place two years after its official date.

Dublin, the surprise Leinster champions, were now all that stood between consecutive all-Ireland crowns for Kerry. As with the Waterford replay, the weather was not favourable to the men from the Kingdom, and it was feared that the inclement conditions would sour the spectacle; but they overcame it all.

At the turnaround, Kerry led by a double score, 0-4 to 0-2. As could be expected, Dublin took the game to their opponents in the second half. Kerry stood firm, however, keeping the men from the capital at bay. The sole score of the second period was a point by Dick Fitzgerald. A victory of 0-5 to 0-2 meant that Austin Stack was the second Kerry captain of an all-Ireland winning team.

Kerry's 1904 post-match celebrations couldn't begin immediately, however. Tom O'Sullivan had to retire early in the proceedings as a result of a leg injury. However, the extent of what he had subsequently to endure merits further explanation. The *Kerry Sentinel* recounted that

> he ought to have received more humane treatment than had been meted out to him. The accident occurred during the first five minutes of the match. The man was removed to the dressing-room in intense pain and there he was allowed to remain until the match was concluded, when he was removed on the shoulders of some of the members of his team. It was then proposed to put him in an ordinary hackney car for conveyance to the South Infirmary. Wiser counsels however prevailed and the Cork fire brigade ambulance was requisitioned and was quickly in attendance.

The *Kerry Sentinel* noted that 'Dick Fitzgerald played a particularly brilliant game; while Stack, O'Gorman, Kirwan, Cahill and Sullivan got through a lot of useful work.'

A final score of 0-5 to 0-2 in an all-Ireland football final was low scoring by today's standards. However, it was not so at the time, especially when two sides of the calibre of Kerry and Dublin met. Father Looney explains:

> A lot of the low scoring was because firstly the game was a lot slower than it is now. The pigskin was very heavy. I played with the leather pigskin. When that ball got older it got larger and heavier. On a wet day it was a ton weight.

That Kerry success of 1904 is rarely spoken of, being overshadowed by the previous season's victory and largely as a result of the triple contest against Kildare. Ó Muircheartaigh feels that's understandable.

> It was only a follow-up. There's something very special for any county to win for the first time. That one in particular is never forgotten. Let it be a good game or a bad game, it is the first and remains the first for ever. 1904 was certainly overshadowed. It was the same players more or less, they had established themselves by winning the 1903 title. 1904 was just another one added on to it. It was the beginning of a unique run. Every decade since then, Kerry have managed to win an all-Ireland.

The *Kerryman* went on to state its belief that if the Kerry side stuck together there would be no obstacle to the county winning again in 1905. They came within one match of being granted that particular wish but surrendered their title at the final hurdle, going down 1-7 to 0-5 against Kildare in that 1905 decider, played in 1907.

Nonetheless, the Kingdom's efforts of 1904 in securing its second all-Ireland laurels afforded the poets and balladeers the opportunity of honouring the county's heroes. Ó Muircheartaigh describes how such offerings were commonplace.

> They had no radio at that time. They had to wait until people came home from the matches to get an account of the game. There was a huge demand for the likes of the *Kerryman* . . . The ordinary

household did not get a daily newspaper in those days. They depended on word of mouth, let it be in song or in ordinary prose to get the accounts of the heroes and all that. Those ballads were very generous to the opposition as well.

Having lost the 1905 all-Ireland final, Kerry suffered a similar fate in 1908. They were defeated by Dublin in the home final of 1908, played in May 1909. Within seven months, however, they were to be all-Ireland champions.

The actual 1909 championship saw both Tipperary and Limerick despatched *en route* to a Munster final meeting with Cork. However, those opening victories weren't as straightforward as the results suggest. Tipperary went down by 2-10 to 0-5, after trailing by 0-2 to 0-1 at half time. Limerick were defeated, 2-18 to 1-2, but Kerry led only by the minimum, 1-3 to 1-2, at half time.

On to Cork, with the Munster title at stake in Limerick on 19 September. Against Cork, Kerry held a three-point advantage at half time, 1-6 to 1-3. However, the main talking point was the display of the referee, Naughton. Paddy Foley explained that

> the referee was from a Limerick hurling district and it became early evident that he knew little about football. First incident to rouse the ire of spectators was when Con Murphy, fielding a high ball, hopped it once and was whistled! Players caught and obstructed each other to their hearts' content. The second half became rough, the referee allowing every latitude.

The *Kerryman* was even less forgiving of the man in the middle, lashing out at his 'incompetence and an ignorance of the rules which were amazing and beyond a shadow of a doubt lost Kerry the match.'

One incident in particular irked the Kingdom, leading to a walk-off. A Cork player picked the ball clean off the ground, going on to score, to Kerry's disgust. The Kingdom men left the field in protest but were eventually persuaded to continue. Cork went on to win, 2-8 to 1-7, but their efforts were in vain, as an objection from Kerry about the validity of the Cork line-up saw the Kingdom awarded the title. A Kerryman by the name of Jerry Beckett had played for Cork. As Foley explained: 'While holidaying in his native Kilgarvan, he played with the village team, which was not affiliated.' So Kerry were awarded the championship, which they refused to accept, as they had not won it on the field. They requested a re-fixture, which was subsequently granted by the Munster Council.

The Kerry v. Cork re-fixture went ahead in front of the biggest crowd at the Cork Athletic Grounds since the famous Kerry-Kildare triple contest. The sides retired at half time with Kerry trailing by 0-3 to 0-1. Cork also held a two-point advantage with ten minutes remaining. Then came the decisive score, as described by the *Kerryman.*

> At this stage of the play one of the nicest bits of football that I have seen took place. Dick Fitzgerald received from a long punt from midfield, and centring the ball beautifully for Skinner, who receiving, and coming on with lightening speed, simply mesmerising the Cork custodian, scored a goal amidst thundering applause.

Kerry subsequently closed the game out, winning by 1-6 to 0-6.

Cork objected to the make-up of the Kerry team, claiming that four players were illegal. When the Munster Council met it was moved and seconded that the match be awarded to Cork. It went to a vote. After beating Cork on the field of play, Kerry also defeated them off it, by five votes to three.

Amazingly, this hearing took place a week after Kerry's all-Ireland semi-final victory over Mayo. Against Mayo, Kerry led by 0-5 to 0-2. Two goals before half time put the issue beyond doubt, as described by the *Kerryman.*

> Connor returned to Kennelly, who sent to Sullivan, the latter player being immediately responsible for a major. Rice was once more fouled and Tom Costello, taking the kick, sent the ball to the mouth of the goal, and Skinner put in Kerry's second major.

Those goals gave Kerry a 2-5 to 0-4 advantage at the break. The result was 2-12 to 0-6. On the other side of the draw, Louth won through to the decider with a 2-13 to 0-15 defeat of Antrim. The 1909 final against Louth was a rarity in that it was played in the actual year. The *Kerryman* painted the picture of all-Ireland final day.

Sunday was Kerry's day out . . . Familiar faces were to be met in nearly all the public thoroughfares, wearing their green and gold badges, and the general air of jubilation proved the boys were there for a purpose.

The first half was a classic nip-and-tuck affair. All that separated the sides was a Johnny Skinner goal for Kerry. It's worth quoting Paddy Foley's description of that strike.

A lengthy ball from O'Connor at midfield was clutched securely by Fitzgerald. Two Louth backs pounced upon him, but the irrepressible Dick swerved clear and short passed to Skinner whose shot shook the net.

It was 1-3 to 0-3 for the Kingdom at half time. Kerry scored six points to Louth's three in the second period. Victory and the all-Ireland were Kerry's on a scoreline of 1-9 to 0-6. The *Kerryman* reporter was in jubilant form.

Up Kerry—the old cry has taken on again and is now shouted out with as much spirit as it was a few years ago. The delight was great when it became known that our boys from the kingdom had once again annexed All-Ireland honours. When the tidings arrived on Sunday night the shout Up Kerry caught on like fire and before half an hour everybody knew that the victory was Kerry's.

Had Footballer of the Year accolades been in existence in 1909, Johnny Skinner would have been a leading candidate. His goals that year were vital: one in the Munster final re-fixture against Cork, another in the all-Ireland semi-final victory over Mayo, then the only goal of the all-Ireland final against Louth. It's impossible to document Skinner's scoring tally for the season. In addition to there being very little coverage of the earlier rounds of the Munster championships, there are also discrepancies in the reports of what Skinner scored in that season's final. Depending on the source, he scored anything between 1-3 and 1-7.

The title Champions of Ireland may have been won on the pitch, but it then had to be secured off it. Just like Cork when it came to the Munster championship, Louth objected to the make-up of the newly crowned national winners. The counts on which they based their objection were not dissimilar to Cork's. The Central Council met on 2 January 1910 to rule on the matter. Three of the points of objection were answered successfully, and Louth withdrew the others.

The manner in which Kerry were finally proclaimed 1909 champions seems almost surreal, following the objections by Cork and Louth that resulted in both Munster and all-Ireland titles being won at council meetings in addition to on the field. However, the way in which the Kingdom surrendered the title, without losing a game, is arguably the most bizarre, and most unfortunate, that the association has ever seen.

The defending champions, Kerry, reached the 1910 decider, where they were to play Louth once again. The Wee County were hoping and expecting to gain revenge for the 1909 final defeat, but they never got the opportunity: the Kingdom refused to travel for the decider following a disagreement with the railway company. Foley recounted how

> the Great Southern Railway company management of the time was regarded in Gaelic circles as hostile to the national games. Excessive fares were often charged and proper travelling facilities were not provided . . . In reply to strong representations, the Kerry team had been granted a through carriage for the 1909 Final.
>
> However, a similar request for the 1910 decider was rejected. Kerry were so displeased with the way they had been treated by the railway company that they opted not to travel for the final.

The *Kerry Weekly Reporter* noted in its issue of Saturday 19 November 1910 that the Central Council was to meet that evening and that subsequently

> a semi-official explanation issued practically exonerates Kerry for not travelling. It was arranged that the Kerry team, twenty in number, would travel by the 3.20 pm train from Tralee on Saturday but on receipt of the voucher on Thursday it was found that the provision of the reserved carriage was not forthcoming, no more than a voucher for twenty of their followers, who also wanted to travel on Saturday at excursion rates.

This reserve carriage was subsequently granted; but, as the paper reported,

> it was expected in Tralee that when the railway company granted the reserve carriage that they would go the whole hog and grant the terms asked for, to the reduced number of twelve, but the company did not do so and Kerry declared off then.

Opinion was divided over Kerry's stance. Paddy Foley's book describes public bodies in Co. Kerry endorsing the players' stance, as too did nationalist organisations throughout the country. However, Foley also reports the Dublin County Board condemning the action and calling for Kerry to be expelled from the association for five years.

The Central Council met twice on the issue. On the first occasion opinion from the various counties was split. According to the *Kerry Sentinel*, the Dublin delegate, after calling for the five-year ban on the Kerry officers and the players, asked that there be no compromise. That, he suggested, 'would open to any other county to act as Kerry had done.' Support came from a surprising source, given the recent acrimony, when 'a well known Cork Gael rejoined, "If Kerry go into the wilderness we go in with them."'

When the second meeting of the Central Council took place, on Sunday 4 December, Austin Stack of Kerry, according to the *Kerry Sentinel*, questioned whether Dublin's motion was in order, as Kerry had given the requisite three days' notice. The *Kerry Sentinel* reported that the rule Dublin were quoting could refer only to individuals. Dublin then asked for the team to be suspended. According to the *Kerry Sentinel*, 'the Chairman said they had no rule authorising them to suspend Kerry, and he ruled the motion and the amendment out of order.'

There was then a call to reschedule the match, but this was defeated by seven votes to six, and Louth were declared all-Ireland champions.

Because no final was played, no funds were available to buy medals for Louth. Foley quotes the *Kerryman* writer P. J. O'C. as stating that the Central Council should buy leather medals and present them to Louth, because 'paper champions' richly deserved such trophies.

That was not the end of the matter, as Foley recalled.

The entire incident had a disturbing effect in Kerry and threatened wider repercussions. A suggestion was made that the county withdraw from the Association and that a Munster body, independent of the Central Council, be established. A serious split in the Association once looked likely, but wiser counsels prevailed under the healing balm of time. Moreover, there came a revolutionary change in the attitude of the Railway Company to travelling Gaelic teams. If the Kerry players in our time can journey in comfort to Dublin in corridor carriages let them remember these concessions were only secured by the sacrificing of an all-Ireland. Through the arches of the years let all Gaels applaud Kerry's gallant 1910 stand down.

The immediate result of the dispute with the railway company and of Louth receiving a walkover in that 1910 all-Ireland final was that the Kerry defender Maurice McCarthy sensationally quit the inter-county game. His time would come again.

'Revenge' may be too strong a word, but Kerry would gain redemption against Louth three years later. They would do so in the famed Croke Memorial Final, a competition held to raise funds for honouring the memory of the first patron of the GAA, Archbishop Thomas Croke, a man with strong Kerry connections. The final, which saw Maurice McCarthy come out of retirement, was the foundation for all-Ireland number 4 for the Kingdom and was to have far greater ramifications for the GAA as a whole.

| THE WEXFORD TRILOGY

Kerry had a point to prove in the 1913 season. The three previous campaigns were memorable for all the wrong reasons: 1910 had seen Kerry refuse to play in the all-Ireland final over a dispute with the railway company; they failed to progress out of Munster in 1911, exiting in the semi-final to Waterford; and 1912 brought all-Ireland semi-final heartbreak and embarrassment, with Antrim brushing Kerry aside, 3-5 to 0-2.

For 1913, Kerry were backboned by members of their all-Ireland winning squad of 1909. Names such as Tom Costello, Tom Rice, Dick Fitzgerald, Con Murphy and Johnny Skinner were still feared on football fields throughout the country. 1913 was also the first season of fifteen a side; before this it had been seventeen a side.

Kerry's 1913 championship began with a low-key encounter with Clare. A victory by 2-2 to 0-1 set up a semi-final against Tipperary. Three weeks before that championship opener against Clare, Kerry had played Louth at Jones's Road, Dublin, in the final of the Croke Memorial. Father Tom Looney outlines the story behind the Croke competition.

There was always the idea that they should honour the late Tom Croke, the Archbishop of Cashel and Emly, a Corkman, whose mother came from Tralee. Ger Hogan's shop in the small square in Tralee was where Mrs Croke was born . . . He spent summers with his grandmother in her sweetshop. There's to be a plaque erected commemorating the Croke connection with that house. Dr Croke died in 1902 and the GAA always said they should do something to honour him so in 1906 they had a competition. Dick Fitzgerald was captain of a Munster team that won the Croke cup. They were hoping that they would make some money out of this but not a whole lot of money came, until 1913 and 1914. In 1913 that really peaked because you had the great classic series of games with Kerry and Louth. There was huge international interest actually because in 1910 there was that stand down by Kerry. Louth were awarded the all-Ireland title. They took it, and the Kerry lads said, 'Leather medals for paper champions.' That didn't go down so well in Louth.

Interest in the meeting with Louth was as widespread as that for an all-Ireland final. It was seen as something of a grudge match. Paddy Foley's *Kerry's Football Story* describes how trial matches were specially arranged for the Croke final of 1913.

The Kerrymen's P & B [Patriotic and Benevolent] Association in New York sent 81 dollars for the training fund. A Kerryman in Holyoke, Massachusetts wrote, 'Although far away from my native Kerry my heart throbbed when I heard our boys are pitted against Louth. Kerrymen, think of your brothers across the sea, and let the old war cry Up Kerry be heard once more at home and abroad.'

The match with Louth ended all square, Kerry 0-4, Louth 1-1. The sides reconvened at Jones's Road on 29 June. This time the honours went to Kerry, by 2-4 to 0-5. Foley reported celebrations at the final whistle akin to those at all-Ireland finals. 'Immediately the match was over, thousands of Kerry followers danced in over the pitch and the players, in spite of their protests, were seized and chaired to the sideline, amid scenes of indescribable enthusiasm.'

It was hoped that the Croke Memorial tournament would help raise funds for erecting a monument in Thurles. However, such was the enormity of the interest in those Kerry-Louth matches that the attendance on both occasions surpassed expectations: approximately 25,000 for the drawn encounter and 40,000 for the replay. On 18 December 1913 the money from the gate—aided by a bank overdraft—enabled the GAA to purchase the field at Jones's Road, which later became known as Croke Park.

It was the last day of August when Kerry were able to resume their Munster championship campaign, against Tipperary. The *Kerryman* reported: 'The match was looked on as a walkover for the men who so signally defeated the Louth champions.' However, it was anything but. Tipperary led by 0-2 to 0-1 at half time. It was an advantage they maintained almost until the final whistle. Recalling that equaliser, Foley reported in his book that

> Moriarty sent a long kick to Dick Fitzgerald near the corner. The old Kerry skipper got possession, but was pounced on at once. He slipped clear. At a difficult angle he steadied himself and took aim. The leather sailed straight and true between the uprights. The last whistle went almost immediately, a miraculous escape for Kerry!

That Dick Fitz point ensured a replay, giving the Kingdom a chance to redeem itself. The replay against Tipperary, which took place six weeks later, more than made up for the drawn affair. In a fast-fought contest there was only one score in the opening half, a point from Johnny Skinner of Kerry. Ten minutes into the second half Tipp goaled, a real shock to the Kingdom. *Years of Glory* credits Dick Fitzgerald, Denis Doyle, Con Murphy and Johnny Skinner with Kerry's second-half points, which saw them through on a final score of 0-5 to 1-0.

A fortnight after accounting for Tipp, Kerry took on Cork in the Munster final. They had an emphatic victory, with the game virtually in the bag by half time. The Kerry forwards were to the fore in that first half, after which a dominant Kingdom led by seven points, 1-4 to nil. It was the turn of the Kerry defence to shine in the second period. The Kingdom added only two more points but kept Cork to just one of their own. The result was a 1-6 to 0-1 defeat of Cork.

Having qualified from Munster, Kerry were to meet Galway for a place in the all-Ireland final. The *Kerryman* was quick to point out a few facts to the boys from the West.

> If I don't make a mistake I think it was the president of the Connacht council who was fixing a venue for Galway and Wexford after the latter's defeat of Louth. Apparently the dear gentleman must not have figured on Munster playing a part in the final stages of the All-Ireland. It may be news to him but I can assure him it's a fact that, leaving Kerry out, Cork or Tipperary could play ducks and drakes with his mushroom team. Fancy a county that could never

boast of an All-Ireland trying to belittle men who stand proudly in the front ranks of the GAA for years.

A dominant display by the Kingdom kept its title charge on track. A Dick Fitzgerald goal, as recalled in the *Kerry Sentinel*, gave the Kingdom the platform for victory. 'Keating fielded the goal kick beautifully, and sent to Clifford, who conveyed to close quarters and centred to Fitzgerald who found the net. This seemed to dishearten the Galway team.' Kerry were in control, 1-3 to 0-1 at the half-time break. The final whistle showed Kerry easy winners, 1-8 to 0-1.

That result set up a decider with Wexford. The *Kerryman* reminded its readers that Wexford, by their defeat of Louth, had jumped into prominence in a very pronounced manner and since then had trained conscientiously, with all-Ireland honours in mind. Wexford's 4-4 to 0-1 demolition of Antrim in the semi-final would also have put the Kingdom on guard. The man responsible for the training of Wexford that year was Jem Roche, the world heavyweight boxer.

The *Kerryman*, the day before the meeting of Kerry and Wexford, declared:

> The eve of the battle finds the Kerry fifteen fit and well. The men have undergone a light course of training for the past few weeks. Personally I would much prefer that the training had been more severe, but I also realise the fact that a good thing can be overdone. The team as it stands could not be improved on and I congratulate the selection committee on their pick.

In the same issue it hit out at the Kingdom's detractors, referring to the Croke Memorial Final.

> Kerry's whipping victory over Louth raised them to the highest pinnacle of football fame, but it also awoke an amount of envy in the breasts of make believe Gaels. They wondered that this out of the way County of ours could produce men capable of holding the premier football position in Ireland. The press were as eager in their endeavours to belittle Kerry's prowess—our men however could afford to treat them with the contempt they deserved. They had earned their laurels without fear or favour.

Years of Glory recounts how for the final Jacky Wade was the Kerry mascot, accompanying the side onto the pitch 'dressed in his team's regimentals.' Once play had begun it was Wexford who had the better of the early exchanges. The Kingdom posts survived until the seventeenth minute, though, when the first point of the decider arrived. Kerry then had the ball in the Wexford net, twice, as described in the *Kerry Sentinel*.

> The Kingdom lads were just now going best, and Healy sending to Fitzgerald the latter beat the Wexford custodian for a goal. Continuing, McCarthy and Kennelly were conspicuous for the southerners and Fitzgerald, getting possession, scored a point, which he followed a moment later with a goal, which was ruled offside, much to the disgust of the Kerry admirers.

Fitzgerald's goal separated the sides after a low-scoring half, 1-1 to Kerry and 0-1 for Wexford. The second half was also short of scores, although Kerry added a significant second goal, as described by the *Kerry Sentinel*.

> Healy took the free and after Rice crossed to Skinner, the Killarney man scoring Kerry's second goal amidst cheers . . . Once again Kerry had demonstrated her unconquerable prowess.

The *Kerryman* too was rejoicing in the county's first title since 1909, captured on a scoreline of 2-2 to 0-3.

> The battle is over and won and once more our Kerry footballers are dubbed the champions of Ireland—they have earned a position in the ranks of Gaelic football hard to reach and nearly impossible to emulate. Their victories in the year that is fast drawing to a close have been the most sensational ever witnessed since the inception of the GAA and when the history of the movement is written, Kerry's name will be found emblazoned in letters of gold.

The county awaited the return of its champions, as the *Kerry Sentinel* reported.

> On the result becoming known in Tralee much enthusiasm was

displayed, many of the thoroughfares and houses being illuminated. On the arrival of the train at midnight, which was awaited for by a very large crowd, loud cheers were raised, and Maurice McCarthy, who travelled down by that train, received a great ovation, being raised shoulder high and borne through the streets, headed by a torchlight procession. The team captain, Dick Fitzgerald, experienced a similar reception on his return to Killarney.

The only goal Kerry conceded during the course of the six games in 1913 was in the Munster semi-final replay against Tipperary. The *Kerryman* reported that the midfielder Pat O'Shea did some fine aeroplane turns in midfield, catching the ball at almost incredible heights. From that time on the nickname Aeroplane was bestowed on O'Shea. Ten seasons after helping their county to win the all-Ireland for the first time, Dick Fitzgerald of Killarney and Maurice McCarthy of Tralee had both captured their fourth title.

The Kerry squad for 1914 was not dissimilar to the championship-winning panel of 1913. Once again Killarney Crokes and Tralee Mitchels formed the backbone of the team. The championship opener was against Clare, and the Kingdom was expected to win with ease. It duly obliged, by 3-6 to 2-0.

Just above the *Kerryman's* report of this victory there is an advertisement for the forthcoming Kerry v. Wexford challenge match. The paper describes the encounter at the Tralee Sports Field on 5 July as a 'battle for football supremacy' and a chance in a lifetime for the many who missed the 1913 all-Ireland. Kerry went on to lose the match, heavily, which led to their all-Ireland prospects being written off in some quarters. This Wexford win, even though it was a mere challenge match, made them championship favourites for many.

Kerry meanwhile had to regroup for a Munster semi-final against Tipperary in September. Confidence was at least partially restored when Louth fell to Kerry, 2-5 to 2-1, in a further challenge match in August. The *Kerryman* reported that expectations in the Premier County were high before their tussle with the Kingdom.

Our Tipperary friends were confident of fielding a team this year, capable of playing rings round our champions. I had it early in the year that north and south Tipperary would supply the men capable of defeating the best team ever fielded by the Kingdom.

With the events of 1913 fresh in the mind, a more dedicated effort was required. In the previous season's winning campaign a late point saved Kerry from an infamous Munster championship exit at the hands of Tipp.

Any apprehension about the result against Tipperary did not filter its way through to the Kerry squad. The *Kerryman* correspondent, who travelled to the match with the squad, related that

> by the time we reached Killarney all thought of defeat was completely wiped out of my mind. Tom Costello, Jack Lawlor, Jack Rice, Con Clifford and some others were quietly playing a game of thirty-one. Pat O'Shea was busily engaged in explaining to Johnny Mahony and Martin Carroll the exact state of the war [the First World War, just begun], and the present position of the rival armies, and Maurice McCarthy and Dan Mullins were fighting old battles over again.

Maurice McCarthy, defensive hero of the first four all-Ireland victories, was not part of the Kerry squad, having retired for the second time.

Kerry weathered the early storm before going on to record a convincing 2-3 to 0-2 victory over Tipp. Denis Doyle of Killarney Crokes goaled for Kerry in both halves. Kerry hosted Cork in the Munster decider on 4 October. *Years of Glory* recalls that such was the interest in the Tralee encounter that special trains ran from Valentia Harbour, Kenmare, Castleisland, Castlegregory, Dingle, Waterford, Limerick, Cork, Youghal and Mitchelstown.

For the Kerry fans who had made the trek from the four corners of the county, the journey was a worthwhile one. The Kingdom faithful had to be patient, however. John O'Mahony of Killarney was responsible for the sole score of the first half. In the second half Kerry finally made their pressure count on the scoreboard, although a low-scoring period was the order of the day once again: Kerry had won by 0-5 to 0-1.

Beating Cork had secured Kerry another Munster title, but they were also into the all-Ireland final. Some weeks previously Kerry had won their all-Ireland semi-final!

Until 1925, if provincial championships were running behind schedule a county had to be nominated for the all-Ireland semi-final. Two years earlier, Dublin had beaten Roscommon in the semi-final but then lost to Louth in Leinster. Louth went on to win the all-Ireland championship.

Cork were nominated to represent Munster in the 1914 all-Ireland hurling semi-final, because of the provincial championship not being completed. Cork defeated Galway but lost to Clare in the Munster final. So Clare went on to beat Laois in the final that year, claiming their first all-Ireland hurling title.

In 1914, a week before playing Tipp and a month before taking on Cork, the Kingdom competed in the all-Ireland semi-final. On 6 September, Kerry overcame Roscommon, 2-4 to 0-1.

Qualifying for the final was not enough to appease one *Kerryman* reader, who, after the Munster final, expressed his feelings in the paper.

> I wish to draw attention to the very poor showing of some of the most prominent members of our team. Their display on the whole was disappointing. I understand that the Munster Council intend allocating a sum of 40 pounds for training expenses in view of the coming All-Ireland. It is therefore up to our men to go into training at once. Jerry Collins and Billy O'Connor have signified their intention of taking the men in hand, and the fault will be with the players if they don't defeat Wexford.

For the second successive season Wexford were to be Kerry's opponents in the all-Ireland decider. The Kingdom had prevailed in 1913, 2-2 to 0-3. Wexford had seen off Monaghan that year in the semi-final, 2-6 to 0-1. Kerry were trained by Jerry Collins and Billy O'Connor, while Wexford were once again in the hands of Jem Roche.

Leading up to the Kingdom's title defence, the *Kerryman* felt they seemed to be peaking at just the right time.

> For the past three weeks they have been under the hands of their trainers and their work during the present week has been highly satisfactory. They have gone through their daily routine of skipping sprinting etc. and while they have hardened up and improved in a

marvellous manner, none of the men have been weakened owing to their exertions.

A gusty wind on the day made matters unpleasant for players and spectators. Rain had fallen incessantly during the previous day. Two early goals put Wexford in pole position. Kerry registered one point in the opening period, after which Wexford led by two goals to that one Kerry point. *Kerry's Football Story* describes the game reopening in sensational fashion, with an equally dramatic conclusion to the encounter.

O'Shea, the Castlegregory aeroplane as Wexford called him, brought down a lofty ball which he swung into the safe hands of Fitzgerald. Fitzgerald was tackled at once but in the nick of time passed over to Breen. McGrath, Wexford's great goalie, never saw the ball till he retrieved it from the net. Con Murphy got the kickout and Kerry's noted midfielder, now appeared in the role of sharpshooter. From long range he let fly and the white flag reduced the Wexford lead to a point. Time was nearly up—Kerry went off in a last do or die rush. The forwards missed unaccountably, but the effort was repeated. Dick Fitz has the ball close to the Wexford sticks. He is thrown down. Pop goes the referee's whistle! Dick takes steady aim, gauges the crosswind, and gets his boot squarely under the greasy ball. He lets fly as the spectators gaze with bated breath. Like the arrow from the bow, the ball leaves his boot and crosses just above the bar.

That brought the teams level. Kerry outscored their opponents, 1-2 to nil in the second period. The game ended 1-3 to 2-0. A second meeting would be necessary to decide the all-Ireland champions of 1914. Despite that heroic second-half comeback against Wexford, not everyone was impressed, with one writer to the *Kerryman* calling for changes.

The forwards were unable to penetrate the Wexford backs, there was something also wrong with the centre-field. New blood must be infused, as it was apparent to everyone that there were several passengers on the team. I think these crocks should stand down of their own accord to younger and better men, and save the honour of the county.

Plans to regroup for the replay were a shambles, as recounted by the *Kerryman*.

Sunday's practice at Killarney was a regular fiasco, only 16 men out of the 36 notified turning up. Some of the men thought that their duties commenced and finished with their putting in an appearance on the field. They entered into the very little work they accomplished with a listlessness, and want of spirit . . . Their actions on the field were actually sickening. A large crowd assembled in the hopes of witnessing a first class match. Their disappointment must have been bitter, and from the expressions on every side, it appears to me that they were anything but favourably impressed with the showing of some of the players present. The comments on the absent members were anything but complimentary. There must be something more than mere apathy at the back of this apparent carelessness. It was whispered a week ago that some of our players funked in a most barefaced and cowardly manner in the All-Ireland game. I was loath to believe such a rumour, but the present showing of some of the members adds weight to the statement.

Matters improved considerably the following week. Changes were made for the replay. The Kingdom called on the services of the veteran defender Maurice McCarthy, who was part of Kerry's four previous all-Ireland victories. Father Looney believes McCarthy's return was pivotal.

The replay was on 29 November and this was a classic game. They convinced Maurice McCarthy of Tralee to return and play. He had retired a few times but they begged him to come back. He agreed to come back. Maurice McCarthy's return strengthened the Kerry squad for the replay with Wexford.

The pattern of the replay was strangely similar to the drawn encounter. Kerry went in scoreless at the break and were trailing their opponents by six points. Even though their prospects seemed bleak, they had shown when the sides met four weeks earlier that writing them off would be premature. Sure enough, the game was turned on its head. The *Kerryman* reported:

Maurice McCarthy cleared at the Kerry end, Shea and Murphy dominating the game at midfield. The forwards are in possession; we hold our breath as the sphere travels towards McGrath. But the Kerry time has not come yet and the Wexford goalie clears. Breen is again in possession and this time he gives McGrath no chance, the green flag proclaiming that Kerry are now but three points behind.

They were level moments later.

Kerry field in grand style, swing round and their huge kicking is telling on the defenders. The Wexford men are striving manfully to keep them out. But no; the Kerrymen cannot be held back now. A scramble around the goal gives Johnny Mahony a chance; his shot travels in at lightning speed, and the spectators are wondering what has happened. The green flag goes up. The Kerry supporters are mad with delight; every available article is thrown into the air, and pandemonium reigns for some minutes. The teams are level after four and a half minutes.

By the mid-point of the half the boys in green and gold were to forge ahead, courtesy of a Dick Fitzgerald point. Fitzgerald doubled the advantage, and Johnny Skinner put over to make it a three-point game. The victory was soon Kerry's, by 2-3 to 0-6.

Kerry's Football Story quotes Carbery in the *Gaelic Athlete*.

That Kerry are a wonderful lot, no one who ever saw them perform will deny. They have evolved a method of football which is ever a pleasure to watch and have brought the game to a pitch of popularity and perfection which looked an impossibility prior to their advent. And the beauty of it all is that they are sportsmen every one. Never have foul dishonest nor ungraceful tactics been associated with their name. On and off the field they behave themselves in a style which does credit to their county and the game they play. The perfect system of the trial games, with regular training practised by the Kerrymen, has given the lead to Ireland. Behind all that and perhaps the main factor in winning victory after victory is this great moral force—a big enthusiastic County's whole hearted support. Never has a team been so loved by their County.

What Gael is not familiar with the teeming train loads from valley, field and glen who throng to the Finals; and what Dubliner is dead to the wild war-whoop which greets the Kerry flags. With their County men's heart behind them, Kerry will long keep near the top of Irish football.

Having won the all-Ireland in successive seasons, Kerry were afforded the honour of keeping the all-Ireland championship cup, which had been presented by the Great Southern and Western Railway. The railway company then provided a second trophy.

The *Kerryman* sent its correspondent to the homecoming.

Kerry were welcomed home in Killarney by the brass and reel band. As the train steamed in the victors were loudly cheered, as the train departed the Tralee contingent was lustily cheered. A procession was then formed and marched through the town. Several houses were illuminated and bonfires blazed in various centres. In front of the town hall captain Dick Fitz spoke, the proceedings ended with ringing cheers.

That year Fitzgerald published his renowned book *How to Play Gaelic Football.* The book was seen as revolutionary. In it Fitzgerald expresses his belief that football is a scientific game. He also touches on a topic that to this day is one of the most divisive among the GAA fraternity.

Can anyone say that Gaelic Football is unscientific since the memorable Croke Final encounters between Kerry and Louth in 1913. It has been said on all sides that never in the history of outdoor games in Ireland have people gone home so well pleased with what they then saw. It is hoped that Gaelic Football will always remain as natural a game as it is today; and accordingly we trust that, while it will ever be developing on the scientific side, it may never become the possession of the professional player.

Fitzgerald covers many other topics, including the duties of each player, the role of the captain, the importance of the referee, advice on training and how to cope with playing in different conditions.

Mícheál Ó Muircheartaigh believes that the book was the template for many other counties.

> I don't know what spread books had at the time, how many books would have been sold for every edition but I'm sure lots of counties got a copy of it. Again, he paid tribute to people from other counties. I think Louth in particular, he mentioned people from Kildare in it and even in 1914 he was talking about professionalism. We should guard against it. The way he put it was, 'I hope the game of Gaelic Football will never become the possession of professional players.' He thought it would ruin it. He was far-seeing in many ways. Dick was a player that will never be forgotten.

In the wake of the all-Ireland final replay the *Kerry Evening Post* lavished praise both on the boys in green and gold and on their vanquished opponents.

> They are undoubtedly skilful, scientific and lithe players and well deserve the honour which they have won. Probably against any other team they would have achieved a greater success. In the Wexford men they found opponents of splendid mettle and stamina. Everybody who has witnessed the magnificent performances of the two teams will hope that in the final round they may again be the competitors next year.

The paper's wish came true: in 1915 Kerry reached the all-Ireland final once more. This time, though, the honours went to Wexford. The Leinstermen avenged the defeats of the previous two seasons on a score of 2-4 to 2-1.

The 1915 victory was Wexford's first of their subsequent consecutive four—a feat Kerry would equal in the 1920s and 30s. Reaching the 1918 decider meant that Wexford had qualified for *six* all-Irelands in a row. That achievement would take Kerry a little longer to emulate!

Chapter 4

THE BOND THAT CAN'T BE BROKEN

After winning their fifth all-Ireland title in 1914, Kerry went a decade without another, as events off the field took centre-stage in the Kingdom.

During the War of Independence period, 1916–22, only once—in 1919—did Kerry come out of Munster. That year they succumbed to Galway in the all-Ireland semi-final, 4-2 to 2-2, in a replay.

The Civil War hit the Kingdom harder than most. Kerry was a county and football fraternity divided. The anti-Treaty players were either imprisoned or on the run. The death toll in Co. Kerry was far above the national average, and the county was the scene of some of the worst atrocities, as the local historian T. Ryle Dwyer explains.

> Three of the major atrocities were in Kerry. [One was in] Ballyseedy where they took prisoners from Ballymullen barracks. They took them out to Ballyseedy and tied them around a mine and blew them up. They thought they had killed nine men but one survived. The same thing happened in Countess Bridge in Killarney, the same day. One survived there as well. The following week when they took five men out in Cahersiveen they shot them in each leg to make sure none of them escaped . . . This had a poisoning effect on the political life in Kerry for the rest of the century almost.

Eoghan Corry believes that people need to grasp the scale of these incidents.

> There is nothing as bitter as what happened in Kerry during the

Civil War. There is nothing as bad as Ballyseedy and Countess Bridge. These are war atrocities on the international scale of things that would cause outrage anywhere.

Team-mates were on opposite sides in the Civil War: on the one side republicans such as John Joe Sheehy and Joe Barrett, on the other side Con Brosnan, a captain in the Free State army. However, mutual respect was maintained. One particular incident, recounted by Eoghan Corry, demonstrates the bond of Kerry football that can't be broken.

Even during the war John Joe Sheehy was allowed play. In a Munster Final [1924], he went to the match and emerged from the crowd with his togs on under his coat. He threw the coat on the sideline, played the match alongside Con Brosnan. Con Brosnan is supposed to be one of the men who is hunting for John Joe Sheehy. He [John Joe] didn't go back to the dressing-room. It was too big an ask because players were being arrested in other counties. He did that and he had the courage to do that. Con Brosnan and the boys had the courage to do it on the other side.

Mícheál Ó Muircheartaigh describes how this was not a unique event, either for Sheehy or for other players.

I believe there was the respect between the players that were on either side. Even during the Troubles some of them went and played matches. They came in their ordinary clothes and stood amongst the crowd until the game was about to start and then they'd slip in and they'd be gone again when the game was over. They'd melt into the crowd and disappear again.

Despite the Civil War, Kerry won the Munster championship of 1923. Their progression came as a surprise. Paddy Foley, in *Kerry's Football Story*, reports that

Kerry were drawn to play Limerick. Only two players turned up for practice. In the match against Cork, Kerry could only muster a dozen players and three followers were called in from the sideline.

Kerry beat Limerick in that first round. They then disposed of Cork in the semi-final before accounting for Tipperary in the Munster final of 1923, which was held on 14 October. Paddy Foley's book recalls how, following the Munster final against Tipp, a number of political prisoners had been released.

> News had reached the outside world of the Kerry boys' prowess in the different internment camps. Teams sprang into activity all over the county; there were several in Tralee. The ex-internees issued a challenge to the Munster Champions.

The tide turned for Kerry football in February 1924, when the most famous challenge match of all time took place. The importance of these games, and of football in general in Kerry, is not lost on Dwyer.

> The game was played in 1924, just after they ended the Civil War. The challenge match in Tralee was between the Free State and the Republicans. It obviously attracted a lot of attention. The fact that they did play football helped to bind up some of the wounds between them. It helps to explain why the passion of the Civil War is put into football and why the Kerry team was so successful. It was the one thing that was binding the two sides who had fought so bitterly.

This game has gone down in folklore as the catalyst for one of the most successful eras of Kerry football. According to Ó Muircheartaigh,

> the greatest test of their character was when the whole thing was over, when those that were interned were let out, this famous challenge game in Tralee that ended in a draw between the existing Kerry team and the ex-internees. It ended in a draw, and I think it deserves a place in the *Guinness Book of Records*, because it was the only challenge game anywhere in the world that was replayed.

It was April 1924 before Kerry played their all-Ireland semi-final of 1923, against Cavan. Following those challenge matches in February and March the Kerry team that defeated Cavan was a mixture of ex-internees and Munster championship players. Kerry beat Cavan, 1-3 to

1-2, to set up a decider against Dublin. With the delay in the 1923 championship, it overlapped the 1924 campaign. By the time Kerry lost to Dublin in the 1923 final, which was played in September 1924, they had already accounted for Tipperary and Cork in the actual 1924 campaign.

For the 1924 championship Kerry were captained by Phil O'Sullivan. As team leader, the Tuosist man set about finding a trainer for the side. Kerry football expert Weeshie Fogarty explains the circumstances behind one of the most significant appointments in the history of Kerry football, that of Dr Éamonn O'Sullivan.

> Dr Éamonn was only a very young man at the time, only twenty-four, and when Phil O'Sullivan became captain of the Kerry team in 1924, believe it or not they had no trainer. There was no such thing as a manager. Phil O'Sullivan then asked Dr Éamonn would he train the Kerry team. Dr Éamonn agreed, and before he knew it he was training the team, and they won the all-Ireland.

No training was undertaken for Munster finals at that time, and sometimes the team went to all-Ireland finals without having trained at all.

> Éamonn was brought in when they were in trouble. He was busy with his own work in St Finian's Hospital, and he was writing books, so he was only brought in at times. When he did come in he was very successful. Because they had gone to school together and Phil O'Sullivan had seen him in action and spoken to him, he knew the great brain he had for football. Dr Éamonn of course had played with Munster at one particular time. He had been a very good footballer, and his father was the great J. P. O'Sullivan, known as the Champ.

In the 1924 championship opener against Tipperary, Con Brosnan played at midfield, with John Joe Sheehy in the half-forward line. 'Kerry's great football victory over Tipp' read the *Kerryman* headline after the Kingdom began the 1924 season with a 5-3 to 1-5 defeat of the Premier County. Goals by Jimmy Baily and Bill Landers helped Kerry to a half-time lead of 2-3 to 1-1. Landers goaled twice more in the second period, with John Joe Sheehy also netting. A semi-final with Cork was next.

Another Kerry goal-feast lay in store. Bill Landers had the first goal of his second consecutive hat trick five minutes into the clash. Landers goaled again before the break. Those two goals were the only scores of the first thirty minutes. The Rebels goaled early in the second half, but Kerry assumed control once more. After Con Brosnan goaled, Bill Landers rounded off his hat trick. Kerry won, 4-3 to 2-1.

The Munster final was against Clare. Paul Russell was making only his second appearance for the Kingdom. His debut came earlier that year, in the delayed all-Ireland final of 1923. Russell came to the attention of the powers that be in a challenge match, with Dick Fitzgerald the talent-spotter.

Clare were despatched in the Munster final of 1924, played in October. Kerry led by 0-5 to 0-1 at half time, and it would have been much more had the Kingdom taken the many chances that came their way. The second half saw Kerry gradually turn the screw. They goaled on three occasions, coming out the winners by 3-10 to 2-2.

The all-Ireland semi-final against Mayo was fixed for 7 December. Kerry made three changes for their meeting with the Connacht champions; among those called up was Jack Walsh of Asdee. Legend has it that Jack Walsh began playing football only a year previously. It's a tale with which Mícheál Ó Muircheartaigh is familiar:

> I don't know how accurate it is but someone told me that he had never played football until 1923 and that his house was a safe house and that he deserved a place on the Kerry team on account of that. He was brought for a trial match and apparently played well and went on to win six all-Irelands. There was no minor at that time. Some people believe that he had never played football until he had played for the Kerry senior team. Maybe there's a grain of truth in it.

The *Kerryman* headline spoke of 'Kerry vanquishing Mayo in a strenuous and vigorous contest.' Mayo registered only one score in the semi-final. Nonetheless, as the *Kerryman* report continued, it wasn't quite the cakewalk that such a statistic might suggest.

Kerry, though winning the toss, elected to play against a strong wind. The game resolved itself into a rare duel between the Kerry backs and the opposing forwards.

Despite being second-best in the opening period, Kerry were level at the break. The dogged performance of the Kerry defence was matched only by the incompetence of the Mayo front line. According to the *Kerryman*,

> when it came to locating the posts Mayo were hopeless—they possess the most erratic front line I have ever seen in a high class team. Time and again, when favourably placed, the Mayo forwards shot ridiculously wide. From all positions, at point blank range, they missed.

The *Irish Times* correspondent reported how the game-turning score arrived.

> Ten minutes of the second half had gone and the teams were still level, when Brosnan worked down on the left. Baily helped him and a crossing punch of Brosnan's gave Ryan a chance and racing in and drop kicking quickly his shot found the net and Kerry were a goal up.

Mayo then very nearly scored a goal of their own, the crossbar saving Kerry. The westerners continued to exert pressure but without result. Kerry, on the other hand, made their pressure felt and won, 1-4 to 0-1. Praise was lavished on the Kingdom captain, Phil O'Sullivan, but the *Kerryman* raised questions about matters at the opposite end of the pitch.

> One of the greatest defensive games I have ever seen played by a Kerry back was performed by the Kerry skipper on Sunday. He was the outstanding player for the kingdom. Of the halves, Jerry Moriarty played the game of his life. Kerry were weakest at forward. There is no proper understanding or cohesion between the inside men.

The *Irish Times* called Kerry v. Mayo a disappointing match, adding that the Kingdom would have to improve considerably to hold Dublin's forwards in the decider. Dublin had won their semi-final against Cavan by 0-6 to 1-1. For Kerry it was the chance of revenge not only for the previous season's final defeat to the men from the capital but also for Dublin's disrespectful treatment of the Kerry legend Dick Fitzgerald. *Years of Glory* describes how

Dublin objected earlier to Fitzgerald refereeing the Dublin-Cavan semi-final because of an incident in the 1923 semi-final between Dublin and Mayo when Fitzgerald was an umpire. Dublin team member Paddy Carey told a Central Council meeting that the ball went over the Dublin end line, struck the netting and rebounded into play and was finally sent into the net. Mr. Fay, the other umpire, said it was no score but Fitzgerald allowed a goal. Mr. Fitzgerald, Kerry's representative on the Council, stood up to reply. He said Mayo had scored a goal above board, Mr. Fay did not say it was not a score and he [Fitzgerald] would not be intimidated by Dublin.

Dick Fitzgerald went on to ref Dublin v. Cavan, and there was plenty of spice added to the occasion when Kerry and Dublin convened on 26 April 1925. *Years of Glory* quotes the Dublin captain, Paddy McDonnell, taunting Kerry that they hadn't got 'an earthly chance' of winning. But McDonnell would soon be eating his words.

Dublin were going for their fourth title in a row, Kerry for their first in a decade. The early stages saw both sets of defenders take the honours. Chances came and went at each end. A Con Brosnan free gave Kerry a 0-3 to 0-2 half-time advantage. Jack Sheehy of Dingle 'brought off some wonderful saves' in the early minutes of the second period, as described by the *Irish Times*.

The Dublin captain hit a beauty of a ball right up to the crossbar but Sheehy cleared brilliantly. Dublin almost goaled from their next rally for Madigan was inches wide with a rasping grounder. O'Brien drove a ball with great accuracy and power—it brought Sheehy to his knees in Kerry's goal but he cleared at the expense of a 50 and again fisted away a great ball.

The *Times* believed that Dublin's failure to put their superiority on the scoreboard at this time led to their ultimate downfall.

During this period of Dublin's aggression the magnificent work of

Kerry's back line roused spectators to a high pitch of excitement and I really think the game was won and lost during those hectic minutes. Barrett and Co. slashed back the invading tide as the Kerry cliffs brave the Atlantic's wildest storms.

Nonetheless, Dublin managed to draw the game level, at three points apiece. Kerry then had the ball in the net, but to no avail. From that same movement came the match-winner, as recounted by the *Kerryman*.

Excitement was intense when Kerry stormed the Dublin posts and Baily crashed the leather into the net. But the green flag, in spite of Kerry players' remonstrances, was not hoisted as the whistle had gone for a foul. The cheering, which half came to an abrupt stop, was renewed when the ball was placed for Kerry at 20 yards range. Brosnan, with great deliberation kicked over the bar, giving Kerry the lead. The cheering was now deafening.

When the full-time whistle sounded, Kerry had done it, by four points to three, and the all-Ireland was theirs, following a ten-year sabbatical. The *Kerryman* lavished praise on the men from the Kingdom.

On the whole Kerry clung on to their men like ivy on the old garden wall. They crashed into their men, bustled them off their game and Dublin craft went down before Kerry brawn. Dublin could not withstand the dash and vigour of Kerry's methods. Paul Russell was the brainy player of the 30—his hands and sidestepping were beautiful to watch. Kerry's victory was a triumph of purely Gaelic tactics.

Those tactics belonged to the man who was to shape Kerry football for decades to come, Dr Éamonn O'Sullivan. And the genius of Dr Éamonn was not witnessed only on the pitch: it was also his idea to introduce a scoreboard in order to keep spectators updated as the scores were registered.

Martin Bracker Regan, an all-Ireland winner of 1931, feels that the team's victory can be traced back to the dark days in the county.

All the stars, Jackie Ryan and all those, were in jail for four years.

They were brilliant. They came out, those internees. They played a Kerry team and slaughtered them, and they took over the Kerry team. They learnt their football in jail.

Paddy Foley, writing in the *Kerryman*, believed that

our victory over Dublin is sweet. They objected to Dick Fitzgerald as referee of the Dublin-Cavan game and some of their players insulted a man whose name will live in the annals of the GAA when meteoric footballers are forgotten.

Eoghan Corry feels that Kerry's success in 1924 was a just reward for leading by example in the aftermath of the Civil War.

Everybody said the GAA was a great unifying factor after the Civil War. And it was. It was the one forum where the two sides got around a table and talked. It was the one forum where the players actually played on the same field. Up and down the country there were different reactions to the Civil War within the GAA. I remember Martin Walsh, the 1932 all-Ireland medallist for Kilkenny, saying that anti-Treaty players didn't get picked on the Kilkenny team of the twenties. Clare ended up with two county boards, twenty-seven clubs in one, twenty-six in the other. They had two county boards and two county championships during the Civil War. We had situations where players were arrested, matches were stopped, and the Free State soldiers came in and arrested. We had a situation in Kildare where the county champions lost the title because one of the players had played under an assumed name. He was on the run and an anti-Treaty player. In Kerry you had the very famous amnesty given to John Joe Sheehy. Everybody could look to Kerry and say, If Kerry can do it . . . and Kerry got the reward for it.

For one all-Ireland winner of 1924, life was to head down an intriguing path. The *Kerryman* cryptically reported that

I am sure I voice the feeling of Gaelic Kerry when I say that in the weeks that are before us, Mundy may feel that we are watching, aye, watching patiently with our hearts and souls with him, that our victory may be an inspiration helping him along to reach the goal, to reach that charmed circle to which 'many are called but few are chosen.'

In *Kerry's Football Story*, Paddy Foley explains: 'In August Reverend Father Prendeville left for Perth, Western Australia. On his appointment as Archbishop of Perth, he was the youngest Archbishop in the world.'

The Kerry captain of 1924, Phil O'Sullivan, emigrated to the United States later that decade and was to die there some years later, a forgotten man. Fortunately, however, and fittingly, he was remembered later. Weeshie Fogarty explained that

> he went to America then with the Kerry team around 1926. They were at a huge banquet in New York one night, and there was a girl playing the piano, her name was Kathleen O'Sullivan. She was only eighteen. Phil O'Sullivan had a beautiful voice, so his team-mates persuaded him to go up and sing a song, accompanied by Kathleen. Out of that they fell in love, and he didn't come back but got married. He stayed in America and came home periodically on holidays to Tuosist. They had a tough life; they had no family, and they separated. Phil was working on his own, and he died in hospital with no-one around him. He was buried in an unmarked grave. Later on, in the early fifties, a group of his friends from the Tuosist area came together in America and put up a big headstone over his grave. He was remembered.

Kerry's defence of the title they won in 1924 came to an end at a Central Council meeting. The Kingdom had beaten Cavan to qualify for the 1925 final, but the northerners objected, claiming that Phil O'Sullivan was illegal. The objection was upheld, and Kerry were thrown out of the competition. Kerry then objected to a Cavan player, and the Breffni men were also ejected from the championship.

The other semi-final saw Mayo defeat Wexford, even though the Connacht championship had not yet been completed and Mayo had been nominated by their provincial council. When the Connacht decider was eventually played, Galway prevailed against Mayo and were subsequently declared all-Ireland champions.

Kerry had been given all the motivation needed to regain the crown they relinquished in such controversial circumstances.

The 1926 campaign began with a first-round tie against Clare. Many of the victorious side of 1924 were still involved, men such as Joe Barrett, Jack Walsh, Bob Stack, John Joe Sheehy and Jackie Ryan. Kerry opened with a less than convincing 0-6 to 1-1 triumph over the men from the Banner County. The *Kerryman* declared it to be

a very close call. Of the 6 points scored by Kerry, JJ Sheehy accounted for 4. Had this player been off colour, Kerry would probably have lost. Our chances of Munster honours are by no means bright while an All-Ireland is unthinkable in our present form. Changes are wanted—this game was the writing on the wall.

Cork were to provide the opposition in the Munster semi-final; but before that, Kerry played Tipperary in the McGrath Cup final. The prize on offer was a silver cup and medals presented by Pat McGrath, then secretary of the Munster Council. Kerry won by five points to two. Jerry Moriarty captained Kerry in that final.

So, the old enemy awaited in the Munster semi-final. The *Kerryman* felt that 'with a depleted, ill trained team Kerry will be set a hard proposition to win.' Kerry gave themselves a mountain to climb against Cork, conceding two early goals and trailing by six points after only twelve minutes. But they were level by half time, with a Paddy Farren goal proving the catalyst. At the short whistle it was Kerry 1-4, Cork 2-1. Cork failed to add to their tally in the second period, while the Kerrymen tagged on five more points. Seven days later Kerry were in action again, Tipperary providing the opposition in the Munster final.

It was feared that Tipp would pose a serious threat, with talk of a far superior team than the one that faced Kerry in the McGrath Cup. But any apprehension about the result was misguided: Kerry held the edge after the first period, six points to four. They outscored Tipp by five points to a goal in a disappointing second half. Kerry had won in Munster again, this time on a score of 0-11 to 1-4.

The Kingdom was now through to an all-Ireland semi-final against Cavan. The *Kerryman* had a warning for Kerry followers.

We can look forward to a dour determined struggle for supremacy.

Cavan are by streets a classier team than Tipperary, and far more dangerous. On the two previous occasions the teams met, Kerry won by a solitary point.

But Kerry were to prove superior almost from the outset against Cavan. 'A pretty even game for fifteen minutes,' according to the *Kerryman*, 'then a Kerry point and a goal—thereafter it was a rout.' The *Irish Times* described that Kerry goal: 'Brosnan's free reached the area, and after Kiernan saved under the bar Ryan flashed in and netted for Kerry with a grand drive.' The half ended with Kerry ahead, 1-1 to 0-1. Just as against Cork earlier in the campaign, Kerry outscored the opposition five points to nil in the second period. Cavan, beaten by 1-6 to 0-1, were well and truly put in their place. The *Kerryman* waxed lyrical about the outcome.

> Kerry were worth double the scores. Cavan are by this time sadder and wiser men—Sunday's defeat will cure their conceit of which they and their partisans seemed to have an overdose. To the men of the past is our reputation due. We are custodians of their great football traditions.

For the fourth season running, Kerry had qualified for the all-Ireland final. Kildare, 2-5 to 0-2 winners over Galway, were to provide the opposition.

The game against Cavan may have been relatively straightforward for Kerry, but the build-up to the decider was anything but. Matters both on and off the field threatened the Kingdom's challenge. Paddy Foley recalled yet another railway dispute concerning Kerry.

> A Saturday special was arranged to run from Tralee. North Kerry enthusiasts asked for a connection with Listowel and their request was supported by the County Board. The Railway Company did not accede to this demand and a public meeting of protest was held in Listowel. The North Kerry players were requested not to travel. More sensible counsels ultimately prevailed.

Listowel got what they had requested, but there was more sensation as the big game approached. The *Kerryman* reported that

Jerry Moriarty, the crack left half, met with an injury to his ankle which prevented him training, and his inclusion in the team was doubtful to the last. For a similar reason Phil Sullivan was long regarded as a doubtful starter. A phone message was received from Con Brosnan on the Wednesday before the match saying he was ill and unable to play, but that he would travel as sub.

The team selection for the final added to what had already been a dramatic build-up. The *Kerryman* was astounded.

> What a sensation that selection produced. There were drastic changes—[Johnny] Riordan was called upon to guard the net. Joe O'Sullivan and Bill Gorman, two players young and inexperienced, were introduced. Denis, better known as Rory, O'Connell was given the left wing position. Pat Clifford had injured himself in training. Would he be fit in the event of Phil Sullivan being unable to play?

In the end, Jerry Moriarty, Phil O'Sullivan and Con Brosnan all lined out, with Pat Clifford a used sub. With these mini-dramas out of the way, supporters could concentrate on the matter in hand. Kerry trailed two to one at half time, and it was felt that Kildare's domination merited greater reward. The *Irish Times* now expected the Kingdom to push on and exert its authority.

> It seemed that Kerry with their well known reserve power and resolve would, with wind and sun to aid them, fairly smother this team which they had held so well. Not a bit of it. So good were Kildare in the early part of the second period that the game seemed won by the beautifully polished football of Kildare.

The Lilywhites did put themselves in a game-wining position. With just seven minutes remaining, the Kingdom trailed by three points. The *Irish Times* knew better than to write them off.

> These Kerrymen are dour material. Fighting every inch of the way they refused to be beaten. Many men were leaving the grounds assuming that Kildare's position was unassailable. Fighting recklessly Kerry worked down. It seemed to me at this period that

Kildare were over confident, for they rested on their oars for a fatal moment. Walsh had a soft loose ball in Kerry's defence. He gripped it lightly and drove out to Russell. The guardsman fed O'Gorman and the newcomer in the Kerry team smashed that ball home to the net. It was a wonderful goal and a fitting result of Kerry's gameness. Sheehy almost won their game in the last minute. All honour to Kerry but I should consider Kildare the most unlucky losers of many championships had Sheehy swung that point truly.

At the full-time whistle the score read Kerry 1-3, Kildare 0-6. The Kingdom had got out of jail. The replay would take place six weeks after the drawn encounter. The selected Kerry team had Tom O'Mahony named in place of Denis Rory O'Connell. But a series of late dramas meant that the side initially selected couldn't take to the field for the replay. Paddy Foley explained at the time how

> misfortune seemed to dog the Kerrymen. Jack Murphy lay on his deathbed in a Tralee hotel. His loss could only be appreciated by those who saw his amazing display in the draw. Joe O'Sullivan took part in a 'friendly' for which trophies were offered and he was thus illegal. On arrival in Dublin, the players were greeted by Phil Sullivan, carrying a stick. He too was *hors de combat!* Three star players short—such was the situation which confronted the selectors as they picked the team at midnight on Saturday.

Pat Clifford replaced the injured Phil O'Sullivan in the full-back line, John Slattery came in at left-halfback, Jerry Moriarty moved to the centre and Jack Walsh dropped to the corner. In the forwards, Tom O'Mahony started, but so too did Denis Rory O'Connell after Joe Sullivan was ruled illegal.

Eoghan Corry, in *An Illustrated History of the GAA*, notes that in the wake of the drawn game Jack Murphy put on his clothes without bothering to take off his playing gear. Days later he was taken ill. The *Irish Times* meanwhile believed that Kerry's chances depended on whether or not the man they called 'the hero of the drawn game' was fit to play.

While Kerry's changes for the decider were enforced, Kildare altered their forward division in the hope of overcoming the Kingdom's match-saving defence of the drawn encounter. It was not to be, as Kerry's defenders once more stood firm, conceding only four points as the Kingdom claimed the honours.

Kildare did, however, hold the upper hand after the first half and led 3-2 at the break. The *Kerryman* felt that 'Kildare's front line was shaky, and erratic shooting deprived the all whites of a bigger lead.' Such squandering persisted in the second period. Goal chances were spurned at each end, before the telling moment arrived, as described in the *Kerryman*.

> Kerry cleared. Moriarty took the free and centred—the leather was punched by Sheehy across the sticks. Mahony sprinted in and boxed the flying ball into the corner of the net.

That goal, the first score of the second half, put Kerry in front, 1-2 to 0-3, and the Kingdom built on the strike. Tom O'Mahony and Bill Gorman raised white flags for Kerry, who went on to win, 1-4 to 0-4. Victory was Kerry's, and the plaudits were being handed out by the *Kerryman*.

> Weakened by the absence of three of their best payers in the replay, the selected team rose gallantly to the occasion and sheer pluck turned the balance in their favour. Without in any way detracting from the display of the Kerry 15 it was Moriarty's covering of Stanley and O'Mahony's forward play brought the 1926 all Ireland to the south.

Father Tom Looney concurs with that verdict on O'Mahony.

> There was a young player at that time from Moyvane called Tom O'Mahony. He stole the show. He scored a goal and a point. He was only ten stone and three pounds. He was the star of the replay.

The *Irish Times* didn't disagree that the better team won. However, its reporter also felt that the footballing gods were on Kerry's side.

> Kerry will stagger home, so wrote we here on Saturday. Kerry were lucky to stagger home, for the best men in Kerry were the defending

uprights. Three times in the last half the Kildaremen shook the railway posts—twice the upright next the entrance kicked back the fast Kildare attack and when the cross bar was hit at midway one felt that the luck was against Kildare. However, one must say that the better team won. And they won under great difficulties—Murphy and the Sullivan pair were off.

Kerry's all-Ireland championship win prompted the usual jubilation and celebration, but every now and again something happens that calls on us to put sport into perspective. The South Kerryman Jack Murphy, part of the Kerry team for the drawn game against Kildare, was prevented by illness from taking part in the replay, and tragically that same illness cost him his life. The 22-year-old Murphy died of pneumonia days after the replay.

Murphy's team-mates of 1926 formed a guard of honour at his funeral. One of them, Paddy Whitty, presented his all-Ireland medal to the Murphy family. Jack Murphy's legacy lives on: each year the winners of the South Kerry senior football championship are presented with the Jack Murphy Memorial Cup.

Kerry v. Kildare in 1926 saw the first radio broadcast of an all-Ireland football final. The same counties got to the final again in 1927, where the Kingdom surrendered its title, going down by five points to three.

| SAM FINDS A NEW HOME

Sometimes before a team can rise to their greatest heights they must fall further than ever before. That was the case for Kerry as the 1920s came to a close. In 1927 the Kingdom lost out to Kildare at the final hurdle, five points to three. Then 1928 saw Kerry—the all-Ireland favourites—suffer a surprise defeat to Tipperary in the Munster championship. Legend has it that most Kerry supporters declined to take in the match against Tipp, as they were waiting for the final!

Weeks before the Tipperary debacle Kerry had beaten the reigning all-Ireland champions, Kildare, in the league final. That win over Kildare in April occurred a month after Kerry had been suspended for six months, then reinstated, after walking off the field in a Railway Cup match following a dispute over a throw-in.

With a turbulent 1928 behind them, Kerry attended to the task of regaining respect in Munster. This side was also aiming to become the first Kerry team to get their hands on the recently introduced Sam Maguire Cup.

Only weeks before the provincial opener against Cork came the news that Austin Stack had died. A member of Kerry's first all-Ireland winning side of 1903, Stack was captain of the following season's victorious team. Off the field he served as chairman of the county board, as well as being on the Munster Council and Central Council.

Kerry's 1929 challenge opened away to the Munster champions, Cork, on 26 May. The *Kerryman* reporter was apprehensive and also bemoaned the inability of several of the Kerry players to last the hour in recent matches.

Kerry went into the encounter without Johnny Riordan, John Joe Sheehy or Jackie Ryan. They could still, however, call on seven of the team that downed Kildare in the 1926 final replay: Jack Walsh, Con Brosnan, Bob Stack, Paul Russell, James Baily, Joe Barrett, the team captain, and Denis Rory O'Connell. O'Connell was in goal against Cork. He had played midfield and half-forward when Kerry previously won the all-Ireland in 1926.

There was a sensational start to the game. Cork goaled in the first minute, then tagged on a point. Kerry responded and were on level terms before long, helped greatly by a goal by John Joe Landers. Kerry pressed but couldn't make their pressure count. The half ended with Cork ahead by 1-2 to 1-1. Despite Kerry passing up numerous goal chances, it was felt that the margin of Cork's lead should have been bigger. Early in the second period Cork fluffed further attempts to add to their tally. Kerry would make them pay dearly. They restricted Cork to a single point in that second half, scoring six of their own in the process. Kerry progressed on a score of 1-7 to 1-3.

Clare were now all that stood in Kerry's way to the Munster title. John Joe Sheehy was a welcome addition to the side. Kerry were relentless in that first period against Clare, a team on a mission. It was game over at the break: Kerry ahead ten points to nil. The second half was a mere formality, Kerry going on to record a 1-14 to 1-2 success.

That win against Clare meant an all-Ireland semi-final with Mayo. Before that fixture Kildare visited Tralee to play Kerry in a challenge match, a fund-raiser in aid of the Rock Street Club. The previous April, Kildare had travelled to Tralee for the same reason, but the untimely passing of Austin Stack led to the challenge game being postponed.

When Kildare and Kerry reconvened, Kerry won. The *Kerryman* explained that, with a potential all-Ireland final clash between the same counties in the offing, the match was used to try out new players and that both sides kept their cards close to their chest.

Kerry's meeting with Mayo was the first all-Ireland semi-final to be played in Roscommon. Fittingly, the men from the Kingdom were treated like celebrities, as reported by the *Kerryman*.

The Kerry team arrived in Roscommon at 10.30pm on Saturday— outside the railway station a torchlight procession had been prepared and headed by the local band, the team were escorted to Murray's hotel where the Roscommon council chairman read an address of welcome to the Kerry team.

Having been treated like heroes before and after the game, Kerry played like champions for the sixty minutes of the match. They simply crushed Mayo. Kerry's half-time advantage stood at 1-3 to 0-1. As the second half progressed, Kerry's advantage grew. They won 3-8 to 1-1. Kerry's win meant an all-Ireland final meeting with the champions, Kildare. The Leinster champions had accounted for Monaghan, by nine points to one.

Kildare had beaten Cavan in the previous year's final and had taken care of Kerry in the 1927 decider. In 1926 it was Kerry who had defeated Kildare in the final. This was therefore Kildare's fourth final in a row.

Kerry supporters are often derided for their poor turn-out at matches. Critics often choose to forget the journey that faces some of the most rural and distant football followers in the land. Not so in 1929. The *Kerryman* reported that

> from the uttermost confines of the county the fans began to collect in Tralee early on Saturday. They came from the extreme end of the Dingle Peninsula and Iveragh, from along the Shannon and the Roughty. Young and old they came, boys and girls, to cheer the Kingdom to victory . . . Half an hour before the big game started all attendance records were broken and the gates locked.

This was the first recorded attendance of forty thousand at a GAA match. The sizeable and noisy presence from the Kingdom made itself known before the throw-in, a fact noted by the *Kerryman* correspondent. 'The all white champions were first to appear on the pitch but the cheering was surpassed in intensity and volume as the green and gold jerseys gradually filed out.'

Early honours went to the Leinster champions, who raced into a 0-2 to nil lead. It's hard to believe, but Kildare didn't register another score until the second half. In the intervening period the Kingdom took over, first going in front by four points to two. Then came that all-important goal, best described by the *Kerryman*.

> Sullivan stopped Kildare and Kerry burst upfield. Ryan had a free, which bounded off Baily's hands across to Sweeney. Sweeney lashed at the ball, and a grand oblique shot hit the far upright and slithered through for a goal—the first to pass Reilly in this year's Championship. Scenes of the widest enthusiasm followed.

Kerry took a commanding 1-5 to 0-2 lead into the second period. They may have expected an easier ride in those remaining thirty minutes; Kildare, however, produced the kind of comeback that's associated with champions. While Kerry added a solitary point to their half-time total, Kildare in the meantime registered one goal and three points. This meant that, with ten minutes left, the score read Kerry 1-6, Kildare 1-5.

Kildare very nearly equalised, but the Kingdom had the final say. The two John Joes came up trumps: late points by Landers and Sheehy secured the win, Kerry coming good on a scoreline of 1-8 to 1-5.

The *Irish Times* credited John Joe Sheehy with getting the Kingdom over the finish line. 'Kerry found a new life when scores were all but level and Sheehy's aggressive tactics paved the way for a Kerry championship.'

The all-Ireland winners returned home on Monday. The welcome home, as witnessed by the *Kerryman* correspondent, was fitting for the Sam Maguire holders.

> The victorious Kerry team had a royal reception in the Kingdom last evening. Bonfires blazed from the first outpost at Rathmore and at various points to Tralee. At Killarney station the Dr Crokes club had organised a reception—the Pipers Band and a huge crowd had assembled and scenes of wildest excitement prevailed when the train arrived. In response to repeated calls Joe Barrett appeared at the carriage window with the coveted Cup, which he said, they hoped to hold for more than another final. At Tralee station a large and enthusiastic crowd assembled accompanied by St. Joseph's Brass band and Strand Street Fife and Drum Band. The Sam Maguire Perpetual Challenge Cup, value 150 pounds, which comes to the Kingdom for the first time, was borne aloft amidst great jubilation through Edward Street and Castle Street and thence to the Central Hotel where the bands in turn discoursed appropriate selections. Afterwards, the Cup was again carried in triumph through the Mall, Bridge Street, Russell Street and thence to Rock Street, to the home of the Kerry captain, outside of which the bands again played. Cheers were raised for the team and county and the names of the individual players were greeted with loud and prolonged applause.

James Baily won his third all-Ireland medal that year. He had won his first alongside his brother Johnny in 1924. The contribution of another brother, Denis, was just as significant, maybe even more so. Denis—or Den Joe, by which name he was known in GAA circles—served the county for more than thirty years. He first became secretary of the county board and then chairman. He's widely regarded as the man who held peace in Kerry GAA circles at a time when the Civil War and its effects meant that the association was at its most fragile in the county.

———

Kerry's all-Ireland success of 1930 is portrayed as one of the easiest. They had to play only three matches in that two-in-a-row success, scoring 7-24 and conceding just 1-8 in the process. That's an aggregate victory of fifteen points to four. However, that year's final very nearly never happened for the Kingdom. With only three teams competing in Munster, Kerry received a bye in the semi-final of the 1930 provincial championship.

The final was against Tipperary. Kerry had good reason to be taking nothing for granted against the Premier County. The game was to take place in Tipperary, scene of the infamous defeat two years earlier. Nonetheless, victory was expected, considering the make-up of the Kerry team. Such stalwarts as Joe Barrett, Jack Walsh, Paul Russell, Jackie Ryan and John Joe Sheehy were selected. The West Kerry defensive linchpins Joe O'Sullivan and Tim O'Donnell also lined out. The midfield maestros Con Brosnan and Bob Stack also took to the field that day against Tipp.

Conditions, as the *Irish Times* reported, made for an unpredictable afternoon on 10 August. 'A drizzling rain fell throughout the afternoon, rendering the ground and ball extremely slippery.' Such conditions contributed to a low-scoring first half. The *Kerryman* described the only goal of the opening thirty minutes. 'Kerry came again, and Fitzgerald punted into the square—Sheehy got under the ball and cleverly boxed over Weston's head into the net.'

At the short whistle it was advantage Kerry, 1-1 to 0-1. Kerry very nearly added to their tally early in the second half. It was Tipp, however, who made the first telling contribution of the period, a goal drawing them level. The sides were tied at 1-1 apiece with a quarter of an hour to go. Kerry finished stronger, and the old adage of 'goals win games' shone true on this occasion. Late goals from Ryan and Brosnan helped Kerry to an unconvincing 3-4 to 1-2 victory.

Kerry were to meet Mayo in the last four of the all-Ireland championship. On the other side of the draw it was to be Monaghan against Kildare. Many were already anticipating another Kerry v. Kildare final. Before that could happen, though, Kerry would need to see off Mayo.

The first half against Mayo gave no indication of what was to follow. Mayo held a slender advantage at the short whistle, four points to three. As the *Kerryman* reported, the Kingdom could very easily have been further behind at the break.

> Mayo is now attacking amid great excitement, and with the ball in the Kerry goalmouth, the Mayo attack is successful and Courrell finds the net—but the whistle is gone and the score is disallowed. This was disallowed by the referee, whose whistle, which few heard, had gone for a foul by Keating of Mayo.

Kerry drew level early in the second half, and the signs were ominous for Mayo as Kerry kept the pressure up. A goal by the boys in green and gold was not long in coming, the captain, John Joe Sheehy, doing the necessary. The goal had Kerry three in front, 1-4 to 0-4. Five unanswered points by the Kingdom followed. With Mayo failing to register a score in that second period, Kerry went on to win by 1-9 to 0-4. The Kingdom had scored an impressive 1-6 in the second half.

The *Irish Times* was in no doubt that the better side was progressing to the final. 'On the run of the play Kerry deserved to win and in the second half they completely outplayed their opponents.' However, the *Kerryman* disagreed.

> Mayo had the best of the play for 40 of the 60 minutes. It is not correct to say that the better team won. With more collective and individual training Mayo would have had a comfortable victory over Kerry. The display of football to which we were treated was of a standard which few other counties in Ireland could hope to attain.

While Kerry did the necessary against Mayo, Monaghan were busy shaking the GAA world's foundations with a spectacular 1-6 to 1-4 defeat of the raging-hot favourites, Kildare. Followers of the green and gold had been denied the chance to renew rivalries with their old adversaries. A showdown on 28 September with Monaghan was in the offing.

Thoughts of the all-Ireland final soon became secondary, however. Forty-eight hours before Kerry were due to face Monaghan, the Kerry legend Dick Fitzgerald died in a rooftop accident. Father Tom Looney relates the events of that tragic Friday afternoon in 1930.

> He was all set to go to Dublin with his friend 'Small' Jer O'Leary of Main Street, to go to Croke Park to the all-Ireland final. They were taking the afternoon train to Dublin. Dick climbed onto the roof of the courthouse to watch the people going on the early trains to Dublin. People came and asked him to come down. The Gardaí were there, as they were concerned about him. Small Jer got word and ran up. Unfortunately, as Dick turned to come down he stumbled and fell . . . That was Friday midday. The Fitzgerald family wanted to have the funeral on the Sunday. The county board had an emergency meeting; they asked the family would they mind postponing the burial until Monday. The family agreed.

In *Kerry's Football Story* Paddy Foley remembered how

> a deputation from Killarney motored to Tralee on Friday evening with the object of calling the game off as a mark of respect. A wire from Dublin expressed sympathy and detailed the arrangements that would be made on Sunday to honour Fitzgerald. A meeting of the County Board was hurriedly summoned on Friday night to consider the situation. Many held that the Dublin demonstration of sympathy would be the most effective tribute that could be paid. The Killarney delegates maintain that the game should be called off. Mr O'Keeffe, General Secretary GAA, was in telephone communication with the Kerry officials at the Ashe Memorial Hall but up to 10pm could get no definite assurance as to whether the Kerry team would play.

A further meeting of the county board on Saturday morning decided to go ahead and play the final. Many Kerry fans had by now begun their lengthy journey to Dublin, contributing to the decision. Fittingly, tribute was paid on the day of the match, as recalled in *Years of Glory*. 'The teams wore mourning armbands, the national flag flew at half mast and that morning there had been a memorial service in Gardiner Street Church.' However, perhaps the most fitting tribute of all on such an occasion is the performance of those in the jersey once adorned by the recently deceased. Kerry's display in retaining the Sam Maguire Cup was phenomenal, with Monaghan brushed aside in a 3-11 to 0-2 victory by the Kingdom.

The *Kerryman* reported:

> Kerry are awarded a free at midfield, which O'Donnell sends to Sheehy, who transfers to Sweeney. Excitement is now intense as Sweeney lobs to Landers, who bursts through the defence and boxes over Bradley's head for Kerry's first goal. The score now reads 1 goal 4 points to 2 points in favour of Kerry, who are at this stage having the better of the argument. Kerry are now playing marvellous football.

At half time the score stood at Kerry 1-6, Monaghan 0-2. The second half was notable only for two further goals. The match ended 3-11 to 0-2, with many Monaghan supporters departing long before the final whistle. The *Irish Times* summed the game up best.

> Rarely has Kerry played so brilliantly. Their goal man Riordan did not touch a ball for the hour and that fact tells in plain language the outstanding superiority of the team in front . . . There was not a weak link in the champions' chain of defence and attack. Landers, at full forward, snapped up all his passes with fine precision and he was as fast as lightning in netting them. He was well flanked by Sheehy and Sweeney whilst Doyle on the 40 yards mark was a great asset. Indeed I doubt if we have marked such a quartet in recent years. Kerry have all the attributes of a genuine champion team.

Kerry's Football Story later paid tribute to members of that champion team, calling John Joe Landers 'a football genius. One of the greatest forwards the County has ever produced.' Landers himself was in awe of the midfielder Con Brosnan.

> I used watch him, the way he used field the ball. I used to say to myself, Wouldn't I love to be able to do that! He'd rise, field, come down. He'd evade the tackle and kick the ball. His partner Bob Stack, he was a real tough man but not what you'd call a footballer. Not in the same grade as Con Brosnan at all.

Years of Glory quotes the Kerry captain, John Joe Sheehy, paying tribute to the late Dick Fitzgerald on receiving the Sam Maguire Cup in 1930: 'He was always there, encouraging us on, pointing out our mistakes and always urging us to do better'.

Given the untimely death of Dick Fitzgerald two days before the final, the customary welcome home for the all-Ireland victors was dispensed with. Instead the GAA fraternity gathered in Killarney the day after the final to pay their respects to the former Kerry captain, the man the world knows as the first superstar of the GAA.

Kerry's 1930 championship-winning season began and ended within six weeks. Their Munster final took place on 10 August and the all-Ireland semi-final on the 24th of the same month. The final was played on 28 September.

——

1931 proved to be a trophy-laden year for Kerry. Before securing three all-Ireland titles in a row they first won the National League, beating Cavan, 1-3 to 1-2. In *Kerry's Football Story*, Paddy Foley reports that the subsequent Cavan county convention said that while some might be jealous of Kerry, they were not, and they admired them both as a team and as a county.

National League success was followed by the capture of the Railway Cup. On St Patrick's Day, 1931, an all-Kerry team representing Munster defeated Leinster, 2-2 to 0-6. Next up for Kerry was the McGovern Brothers' Cup.

The National League and the Railway Cup are well known in GAA circles, but most would not be familiar with the McGovern Brothers' Cup. When Kerry toured America in May and June 1931 the promoters of the tour put up this trophy. *Years of Glory* points out that 'an all important consideration was that Tralee Sportsfield was to benefit to the tune of 500 pounds by the trip.'

So the tour went ahead, Kerry remaining unbeaten throughout. *Years of Glory* notes that Kerry played in front of more than sixty thousand spectators at Yankee Stadium, New York, then forty-five thousand in Chicago. Kerry also lined out in Philadelphia and Boston. Legend has it that the renowned boxer Jack Dempsey, said to have Mid-Kerry connections, put up one of his cups and a set of gold medals for one of the matches. The *New York Advocate* stated that Kerry were 'a credit to the Irish race—high class, intelligent young athletes, at home in any company.'

The Kingdom were proclaimed 'Champions of the World.' Parades were held for the players when they returned home; but bigger and more important tests lay in store.

Less than a decade before, Kerry was in the midst of the Troubles. Team-mates on the football pitch were on opposite sides in the Civil War. There were Republicans such as John Joe Sheehy, while Con Brosnan was a captain with the Free State Army.

For the 1924 Munster Final, which took place at a time when Sheehy was on the run, Brosnan guaranteed Sheehy a safe passage. It was neither the first not the last time that this happened, both with Sheehy and others. Brosnan and Sheehy played alongside each other in the Munster Final of 1924, as they did throughout that championship winning campaign.

Brosnan's actions were not forgotten. He was rewarded with the Kerry captaincy in 1931.

Joe Barrett was the man behind this most magnanimous of sporting gestures. His son JJ explains:

> Stacks had won the championship and they had the nominating of the captaincy so my Dad would be getting it and he decided he was going to hand it over to Con. Con had been a Free State soldier and my Dad would have been on the opposite side during the Civil War. My Dad gave it to Con and there was a lot of controversy. They overcame it anyway.

The historian T. Ryle Dwyer is in no doubt that Joe Barrett's gesture would not have been met with widespread approval.

> The Austin Stacks had won the County Championship so Joe, he was invited to captain the team again. But he thought the honour should be given to Con Brosnan. He offered the captaincy to Con Brosnan. I'm sure a lot of people on the Austin Stacks team felt they should be offered it before an outsider. They still weren't prepared to stand up and they were prepared to accept his choice. Joe Barrett felt that Con Brosnan deserved the recognition because he was a Free Stater. He had been a captain in the Free State army and he had provided the safe passage for Republicans during the earlier years. As a result Con Brosnan ended up captaining Kerry to their first three in a row.

Con Brosnan's son Jerry says he and his father had a good relationship with Barrett's club. He is glad his father was afforded the opportunity of captaining Kerry, an honour the Moyvane man was unlikely to gain otherwise.

> They made him captain. The Tralee team used come out here and we used to make a new field for them. We'd have to line the field three or four days before it and get the loan of it. When the match was over we'd have to pick everything out of it for the cattle. The Tralee team, they thought so much of him on account of him getting them out of jail. He was in the Free State and they were on the opposite [side]. When they were in jail, he used get a free passage to get them out and take them back in again. They thought so much of that they made him captain.

Kerry were scheduled to play Tipperary in the Munster final on 9 August 1831, with the victors to proceed to the all-Ireland semi-final three weeks later. Kerry fine-tuned their play with a comprehensive win over Dublin in a challenge match the week before their meeting with Tipperary.

When Kerry took to the field against Tipp they had eleven of the side that started the 1930 all-Ireland final. The forwards who the *Kerryman* were reluctant to put too much faith in came up trumps as the team posted a total of five goals and eight points to Tipp's two points. Some familiar faces were missing for the outing against Tipp, but there was a new star in the making: Martin Regan.

It was a stroll in the park for the Kingdom. Moreover, it was the debut of a lifetime for the man who was to become Bracker. The *Kerryman* wrote:

> Young Regan made an auspicious debut as forward and his early goals put the issue beyond doubt. Against the wind, Kerry's newcomer had 2 goals up in the first ten minutes, and the Kingdom thereafter swamped the opposition. When a long ball was finished by Landers for a goal the game lost all interest. Keane scored two minors for Tipperary. Regan replied with a goal for Kerry and half time arrived with the home team leading by 4 goals to 2 points.

The second half was along similar lines. Even allowing for the quality of the opposition, a 21-point victory by Kerry seemed ominous for the other teams.

A week after their easy victory over Tipperary, Kerry ventured north to meet Ulster. *Years of Glory* noted how keen the province was to see the all-Ireland champions in action.

> Kerry made the long journey to Monaghan to play in a football friendly in aid of Threemilehouse Catholic Church. Kerry's visit created widespread interest and all games in Cavan, Armagh, Fermanagh and Monaghan were cancelled for that Sunday. Kerry duly lived up to their great reputation, beating the Ulster side to earn themselves a set of gold medals.

Kerry won that game by 2-13 to 1-2 in front of an estimated crowd of eleven thousand.

It was now time to concentrate on the coming all-Ireland semi-final against Mayo. An early Jackie Ryan goal set the tone for Kerry to dominate the opening half against the westerners. With half an hour to go it seemed like game over for Mayo, trailing as they did by 1-5 to 0-1. But they stormed back. They goaled, then had the ball in the net for a second time, as reported by the *Kerryman*.

The air was electric as the Mayo forwards and the Kerry backs surged to and fro near the Kerry goal with almost 15,000 throats helping to put on the pressure. Then the ball was in the Kerry net and the Mayo supporters swarmed over the pitch waving banners of green and red and cheering wildly.

When order was restored Mayo were awarded a fifty as the ball had gone over the end line off a Kerry defender and was put back into play by the people who packed the sideline and end line and encroached on the playing pitch at times.

Kerry hung on to emerge victorious. The won by 1-6 to 1-4, despite putting over only one point in the second half.

The other semi-final saw Kildare edge out Cavan by 0-10 to 1-5. Another year, another Kerry v. Kildare final—the fourth between the counties in six seasons. Kerry led two to one going into the 1931 encounter.

With the defender Tim O'Donnell an enforced absentee for the final, the half-forward Tim Landers dropped back to the number 7 slot. John Joe Landers was drafted in at half-forward. The big shock, though, was the goalkeeper Johnny Riordan being left off the starting fifteen. The decision to omit Riordan was forced on the selectors, according to Mícheál Ó Muircheartaigh.

He was togged out in the dressing room to play in the final. He was told by the county secretary he was not playing. Dan O'Keeffe the sub goalie was going in. I pressed [John Joe] Purty Landers very hard to tell me what happened. All he would say is he broke training on Saturday night. He wouldn't go beyond that, maybe the man had a pint or a half pint instead of a bottle of milk. He never played for Kerry afterwards. I always hold that chance plays a huge part in the careers of players. Dan O'Keeffe might never have played for Kerry if Johnny Riordan hadn't broken training. He was still a young enough man. Goalkeepers have long careers. He would have been there in 1932, he possibly would have been there in 1937. He might be thinking of retiring at the end of the thirties and if he would the logical successor might have been a player called Brendan Reidy, who won three minor all-Irelands as a goalkeeper for Kerry. He never got a game for the seniors because Dan O'Keeffe was established.

The *Irish Press* wondered whether Kerry's early season sojourn to America would catch up with them.

> A fear haunts the minds of some that the strain of these feats may tell at length upon the ardour and freshness of the champions. There was a feeling that they showed weariness against Mayo in the semi-final.

Martin Bracker Regan has disclosed how he had to borrow a boot from Denis Rory O'Connell for the decider. 'I played with two odd boots. I had one of Rory's boots. We had no-one giving us boots that time—no sponsors.'

The *Irish Press* listed Kerry's all-Ireland weekend itinerary, including a post-match céilí mór, at which the team's success on the American tour was to be recognised. The paper stated that 'Mrs. Austin Stack' (Austin Stack's widow, Úna) would present each member of the team with a copy of the book *Story of the GAA*.

In scoring terms, where it matters most, the first half of the final belonged to the Leinster champions. Kerry somewhat fortuitously only trailed by seven points to four at the break. Playing second fiddle for the first thirty minutes prompted the Kingdom selectors to make changes. The *Irish Times* recorded that

> wise councils at half time revolutionised Kerry's display. New forceful tactics were adopted and their pivotal positions in attack were reversed. Whitty's youth and speed had been lost on the seven yards mark—he should never have been placed there. When he came out on Kerry's left wing his art was seen to full advantage. He gave Ryan many chances and they were well used so the game dramatically swung round in Kerry's favour.

Kerry didn't just dominate the second half, they were awesome. They brought the gap down to the minimum, before Whitty made it seven points all after eighteen minutes' play. Kildare went a point ahead. Again, Whitty levelled for Kerry. Two Jackie Ryan points put Kerry ahead. The same player had a hand in the decisive goal, as described by the *Kerryman*.

Play came to the Kildare end in a flash. Walsh saved from Ryan. Russell got on the clearance, and a long punt was mis-fielded by Walsh, who dropped the leather over the line. To make doubly sure Ryan rushed in and kicked into the net.

Ryan put over the final score of the day, with Kerry recording a 1-11 to 0-8 victory.

Martin Bracker Regan felt that a number of Kerry players excelled against Kildare.

The stars that day were Joe Barrett, Jack Walsh, Dee O' Connor, Paul Russell—outstanding. They all played brilliant, and the Landers were great. It was a very clean game. We had a hard job to beat them, but they were very good footballers. I think Jackie Ryan was the greatest of them. He used to catch the ball—go up in the air, and he'd turn in the air. I often tried it but I used to fall!

Some years later Martin Bracker Regan recalled the homecoming of '31.

Wonderful! There were bonfires from Rathmore. The lads in Tralee had a great reception. We brought the cup up the street. Con Brosnan was captain that year; Con had the cup. But if we lost the game the headline would be 'The fall of the mighty—How did Kerry lose?'

———

In 1932 Kerry set out to equal Wexford's winning feat of 1915–18. There was no greater incentive for the three-in-a-row champions from the Kingdom than to emulate the side seen as the greatest of the GAA.

Kerry's quest for the four-timer began against Limerick in late May. The team on that occasion included ten of the 1931 all-Ireland winning side.

This star-studded Kerry team didn't have it all their own way early on against the Treaty County. Kerry led by one point after seventeen minutes, two to one. The green flag was soon raised as Jack Flavin netted for Kerry. That gave them breathing space, and they built on

Flavin's goal. Kerry's half-time advantage stood at 1-6 to 0-2.

Limerick pulled a goal back early in the second period. Rather than being the inspiration for Limerick to drive on, it actually brought Kerry back to life. Limerick added a solitary point between then and the finish, while Kerry tagged on five more of their own, recording a 1-11 to 1-3 victory.

The win over Limerick set up a Munster final against Tipperary in early August. However, events that summer were overshadowed by the efforts of a Kerryman on a sporting field elsewhere. In 1932 Éamonn Fitzgerald declined his place in the Kerry squad, as he was in training to represent Ireland at that year's Olympic Games in Los Angeles. Fitzgerald competed in the hop, step and jump, more commonly known as the triple jump these days, but he had to be content with a very creditable fourth place. An ankle injury prevented him performing at full tilt; it's felt that a medal of some colour would have been his otherwise.

One week before the provincial decider against Tipperary, Kerry had played a touring American selection in Tralee. Subsequently, rumours surfaced, and it was reported in the *Kerryman*, that 'four Tipperary members of the American team would assist their home county. These speculations proved groundless.' *Years of Glory* later revealed that one of the members of that American team was Bill Landers, brother of the Kerry stars John Joe and Tim.

Paul Russell, Miko Doyle and Jackie Ryan all returned against Tipp. Bill Kinnerk of Mitchels also started. With the captain, Joe Barrett, an absentee, Paddy Whitty went to full-back. Mike Doyle had the honour of skippering the team. Doyle partnered Stack at midfield. Con Brosnan was moved to corner-forward. Dropped were Frank O'Neill, Mick Healy and Tim Hayes.

The Munster final against Tipp was a one-sided affair. Victory was assured by half time, thanks to a double strike from Bracker Regan. The *Kerryman* described how

> a free to Kerry put Brosnan in possession. He crossed over to Regan who found the net with a hard low shot. Kerry came away in a grand bout of passing which left their opponents standing. Regan finished with a goal.

Those Regan goals put Kerry's lead at half time at 2-5 to 0-3. They cantered home, a Tim Landers goal helping to take Kerry's tally to 3-10. Tipp finished with 1-4. The *Kerryman's* report on the Munster final and its coverage of Fitzgerald's heroic display in the Olympics ran side by side in the edition of 13 August 1932.

Dublin were to be Kerry's all-Ireland semi-final opponents, following their victory over a fancied Wexford in the Leinster final replay. Dublin's stock had declined in recent years; that was because the players could now play for their county of birth, as opposed to their county of residence.

A low-scoring semi-final may not have been unsurprising, given the wet and slippery conditions faced by the players. However, this encounter remained scoreless after the first half. The second period more than made up for those opening thirty minutes. A dominant Kerry went in front by two points to one. Dublin withstood a barrage of Kerry pressure, then went up the pitch and goaled. The game was nearing a finish when the decisive score came, as described by the *Kerryman*.

> Kerry had a free. Whitty took this and Russell got possession. He punted towards the goal. McDonnell appeared to misjudge the ball which found the net and Kerry were now leading by a point with four minutes to go.

Kerry doubled their advantage before the end, winning by 1-3 to 1-1. The final score may have suggested otherwise, but the *Irish Independent* called the match 'one of the greatest displays of football ever witnessed at Croke Park or anywhere. It was a wonderful struggle.' Yet the *Irish Press* stated that 'not since Kerry first gained All-Ireland honours was their hold on the title more precarious than during a dour hour's play. Kerry's fielding was unaccountably amiss and their catching often faulty.'

The week after Kerry defeated Dublin they took on the touring Amricans once more, winning 4-6 to 1-4.

Mayo were to provide the opposition for Kerry in the 1932 all-Ireland final. It looked for a long time as if the Kingdom would be facing Cavan; however, the northerners threw away a three-point lead going into the last ten minutes of their semi-final. Mayo earned the right to face Kerry, on a 2-4 to 0-8 scoreline. The consensus was that anything other than a Kerry victory would be a surprise.

Only in Mayo itself was there a belief that the westerners could stop the Kingdom gaining the four in a row. That, combined with poor weather conditions, resulted in an attendance of less than twenty-nine thousand. Those present were treated to a game of two halves, with Mayo in the ascendancy from the off. The westerners registered three points in the first five minutes. But in one swift move Kerry undid all Mayo's hard work with an equaliser described by the *Kerryman*: 'Whitty's kick landed in the goalmouth and Doyle in a cluster, with a great left drive sent under the bar, setting the scores level after eleven minutes play.' Kerry managed one further score between then and half time. At the break they trailed 1-4 to 1-1. They weren't behind for much longer, however, as the *Kerryman* report continues:

> Kerry swept through from the throw-in and Gannon cleared to touch to stop the rush. Russell got the touch throw. He drove in front of the sticks. Tim Landers got possession and crashed into the net the equalising score after a few seconds play.
>
> Moments later Kerry repeated the feat, but this goal was disallowed. This setback failed to break the Kingdom's stride. Points from Tim Landers, Con Brosnan and Jackie Ryan put Kerry three points in front, 2-4 to 1-4. Ryan added another point, then Miko Doyle put over and Kerry had a five-point lead after sixteen minutes. Kerry seemed to be home, leading by five points as the clock counted down to that four in a row. Then Mayo goaled, reducing Kerry's lead to two points with four minutes to go. Jackie Ryan's fourth point of the afternoon proved to be the closing score, as Kerry prevailed, 2-7 to 2-4. The four in a row was finally theirs.

The national dailies were loud in their praise of the four-time champions. The *Irish Press* wrote:

> We saw the real Kerry for 20 minutes after the change in ends, a Kerry bewildering in their combination, perplexing in their anticipation and dynamic in bursting through the gaps. This revival from the coma of the first 30 minutes must have been to their supporters something just as sweet as rippling water to parched lips;

but to Mayo it must have seemed something akin to a tornado. When we got something of the real Kerry it wrote finis to Mayo's hopes and aspirations.

The *Cork Examiner*:

In the second half Landers Ltd started the ballyhoo. The tall slim boy gave the ball to Tim and then this 10 and a half stone boy opened out. Elusive as an eel, hopping like a rubber ball, quick to strike as a serpent in attack, he made bohereens through the Mayo defence. Kerry remain the peerless group of Gaelic footballers.

The *Irish Press* saluted members of that peerless group of footballers: Dan O'Keeffe ('a native of Tralee, that nursery of Kerry football. Kerry supporters need have no fears with him between the posts'); Dee O'Connor ('a native of Lawlor's Cross, Killarney, a centre which so long dominated football in Kerry. Has been very much in the picture these last 5 years'); Joe Barrett ('the man who has broken up more attacks than any other back. A determined defender who refuses to be beaten. Learned most of his football in Hare Park Camp, where he was interned in 1922 and 1923'); Jack Walsh ('one of Kerry's most popular footballers. His great height stands him in good stead'); Paul Russell ('his prowess both as a defender and attacker is well known wherever Gaelic Games are played. He invariably manages to get a score, and many a time when the Kingdom was hard pressed, Paul saved the day as witnessed by his sensational goal against Dublin in this year's semi-final'); Paddy Whitty ('a typical Kerry footballer with a long accurate delivery'); Bob Stack ('hails from Ballybunion, where the Irish Olympic team trained. With Brosnan as partner has made the best midfield combination of recent years. Is a hard worker though somewhat erratic in delivery'); Johnny Walsh ('a young footballer of promise'); Miko Doyle ('a comparative newcomer, but no novice. He can hold his own with the best. Has been operating at centre field this year, where his height and strength have enabled him to shine'); Tim Landers ('as versatile a footballer as there is playing today. Is rather a wee lad but can fill any position in the field'); John Joe Landers ('one of the brainiest footballers Kerry has ever produced. Is a constant menace to any backline'); Con Brosnan ('his period at centre field for Kerry was a brilliant one, now found among the forwards. A clean footballer, his play has been the admiration of friend and foe'); Jackie Ryan ('the most prolific scorer in Kerry football. Another product of the Internment Camp. The best winger the County has produced').

That success of 1932 saw six Kerry players pick up their sixth all-Ireland winners' medal. Joe Barrett, Con Brosnan, Jackie Ryan, Paul Russell, Bob Stack and Jack Walsh were all members of the victorious sides of 1924, 1926 and the four in a row of 1929–32. Three of those six—Con Brosnan, Bob Stack and Jack Walsh—played in all fourteen games of the 1929–32 run.

As we wallow in the glory of Kerry's first four in a row, spare a thought for Kerry's Olympian of 1932, Éamonn Fitzgerald, an all-Ireland winner in the previous two years, who narrowly failed to collect a medal in the Olympic Games. Like the Kerry captain of 1924, Phil O'Sullivan, Fitzgerald was something of a forgotten figure. Weeshie Fogarty set out to right that wrong.

> He too, unfortunately, like Phil Sullivan, had a fairly sad end in his own way. He came back and became a teacher, and when he retired he was living in Dublin, and the great Dan Keating, who died at 105 years of age, told me the story. He knew Éamonn Fitzgerald well, and when Éamonn died there were only four or five at his funeral. He was buried in an unmarked grave in Dublin. I was down in Castlecove [in South Kerry] with my wife and family one day and we were touring around, and I went into the Black shop to Brendan Galvin. We were talking about football, and he said, 'You should go into the church next door, and there's a beautiful stained-glass window erected to a great Kerry footballer.' I was amazed with this . . . I went into the church and there in the window it says, 'Erected to the great footballer and Olympian Éamonn Fitzgerald.' I got completely taken up by the story. I followed it up and I discovered he was buried in Dublin, in Dean's Grange Cemetery. I contacted Eugene O'Sullivan, who is a garda in Dublin, and he found the grave with the help of others up there . . . We got the Kerrymen's Association in Dublin to erect a new headstone to his memory . . . Ronnie Delaney, the great Olympian, unveiled it. There were nearly five hundred people present.

1933 afforded Kerry the opportunity of winning an unprecedented fifth successive all-Ireland championship. Their quest failed at the penultimate hurdle. The eventual winners, Cavan, ended Kerry's reign on a 1-5 to 0-5 scoreline.

The legendary Dr Éamonn O'Sullivan trained eight all-Ireland winning Kerry teams. But work and family commitments meant he was not always available, and, unbelievably, he played no part in the four-in-a-row triumph.

Chapter 6 ❧

| GEGA THE GIANT

Following a four-season hiatus for Kerry football, 1937 was to be the dawn of a new golden era. Provincial proceedings got under way with a first-round tie against Cork. In 1936 Kerry had reached the all-Ireland semi-final, losing to the eventual championship winners, Mayo.

The side to face Cork in the '37 opener was much changed from that of the previous campaign. Joe Keohane of Mitchels was brought in at full-back. There was a new midfield partnership of Paddy Kennedy from Rahillys and Johnny Walsh of North Kerry. Walsh had featured in the success of 1932. Charlie O'Sullivan of Camp came into the side on the forty. Experienced players, such as Tim O'Donnell, Miko Doyle and Con Geaney, were also called upon.

When Cork and Kerry meet in the modern era the form book is thrown out the window and the cliché of 'On the day, anything can happen' is applied. This was not so back then. The *Kerryman* claimed that 'Cork stand about the same chance of defeating Kerry in football as Kerry would have against the rebel county in hurling.' There was more drama before the match than during the game itself. Kerry failed to field as selected, and very nearly failed to field a side at all. The *Kerryman* reported the dramatic pre-match events.

A search had to be made to fill the gaps. At one stage it was thought there would be a difficulty in finding the 15. Players had to be requisitioned who were not even selected as subs.

And a third of the selected fifteen failed to take the field. Not surprisingly, Kerry started slowly against Cork. The sides swapped ends, with Kerry 1-2 to 0-2 to the good. The Kingdom bamboozled the Rebels

on the resumption. As the *Kerryman* recounted, Seán McCarthy was the
main benefactor.

> Play swung round in a flash and a centre by Geaney was punched to
> the net by McCarthy. This was the beginning of the end. The Kerry
> forwards surged into the goalmouth and McCarthy shook the net
> with a rasper. After the goalie had saved well McCarthy completed a
> hat trick with a great goal.
>   It finished Kerry 6-7, Cork 0-4, a margin of twenty-one points
> between the teams.

The Munster semi-final against Tipperary, scheduled for 27 June, was
put back to 11 July, as the original date clashed with the congress of the
Catholic Truth Society of Ireland in Killarney. In the meantime Kerry
hosted the New York Kerry team in Tralee, the match ending honours
even.

For any Kerry supporters imagining the Munster semi-final against
Tipperary to be a foregone conclusion there was a timely reminder.
Kerry had been second-best against Tipp the previous season, and only
a late goal saw them win.

A Kerry goal, courtesy of Mick Ferriter, after only five minutes set the
tone for this encounter with Tipp. It was 1-4 to 0-1 to Kerry at half time,
and there was no let-up in the second period. Charlie O'Sullivan goaled
as the Kingdom ran out comprehensive winners. 2-11 to 0-4 was the
final result.

Kerry were expected to cruise past Clare in the Munster final, played
one week after Tipperary had been despatched. The *Kerryman* declared
that it would be a sensation if Clare beat Kerry. That possibility never
arose: the match was in the bag by half time, as the paper reported.

> A free to Kerry, Doyle's kick reached a cluster but O'Leary drew on
> the leather and a grounder reached the net. A ruck in the Clare
> goalmouth soon after was finished by McCarthy punching through
> for a further major.

Come the interval, Kerry led 2-7 to nil. The *Kerryman* continued:

> McCarthy had a goal after hand passing between O'Leary and

Geaney, who left him in possession. Kerry went off to secure a major per Ferriter.

The match ended 4-9 to 1-1 in Kerry's favour.

Over the course of their three Munster championship games Kerry scored 12 goals and 27 points, conceding only 1-9 in the process. That worked out at a game average of scored, 21, and conceded, 4.

It was feared that such a lack of competition in Munster could have severe implications when the Kingdom went outside the province. The *Kerryman* commented:

> If we are to have many more Munster Championships on the lines of the senior competition just concluded then the title will shortly become 'an empty formula.' Kerry followers will conclude from the victories so easily secured that this year's Kerry team is on a par with other great sides of the past. That would be a very mistaken view. There may be outstanding weaknesses on the Kerry side not disclosed by soft Munster games.

Laois were the obstacle between Kerry and an all-Ireland final appearance. The *Kerryman* was anticipating victory over Laois, citing the general belief that they wouldn't be as formidable as Mayo, who knocked Kerry out the previous season. However, that assessment of Kerry's prospects had to be reviewed in the wake of revelations regarding the availability of players. Jim O'Gorman, Paddy Kennedy and Tim Landers were all absentees. A lack of belief in an ever-changing Kerry line-up appeared justified as the encounter with Laois wore on, despite Kerry's first-half lead. The half saw only two scores. Laois pointed almost from the off. Then, as described by the *Kerryman*, 'Fitzgerald drove into the goalmouth where there was a tussle. McCarthy drew on the ball, which found the net.'

Laois certainly had the better chances in the opening period, but they failed to convert their possession and opportunities into scores. Come half time, Kerry led by one goal to one point.

The second half surpassed the first thirty minutes in every aspect. Laois turned the game on its head, scoring a goal on their way to opening up a three-point lead. Kerry soon cancelled that advantage, as recounted by the *Kerryman*.

Ferriter and Kelly assisted in a Kerry breakaway and the best score of the match was seen. O'Leary beat his man near the wing and dribbled towards goal. He gave to McCarthy who passed to Geaney. Geaney dribbled to the square and a hard low shot found the net.

A few more twists in the tail lay in store. Time was almost up when Bill Dillon pointed Kerry into the lead. Laois then wided a free from about twenty yards out. The Laoismen were afforded one last opportunity to equalise, a free from twice the previous distance. It was sent over the bar, and 2-3 to 1-6 was the final score. A second outing was necessary.

When it came to the replay, victory was Kerry's, but they had to dig very deep to come away with the honours. As in the drawn game, they led the way at the short whistle. Laois had the opening score of the replay, a point after twenty minutes. Tim Landers then showed why he had been restored to the Kerry team for this replay. The *Kerryman* reported that 'Dillon's free went to Tim Landers who dribbled in. He sent in a hard low shot, which hit Tom Delaney and cannoned into the net just inside the post, giving Kerry the lead.'

Tim Landers was also responsible for Kerry's second score of the half, a point. That's how it stood at half time, 1-1 to 0-1. The Kerry lead didn't last long, however, as Laois goaled almost from the throw-in. The Leinster champions then went two points in front. An injury to a Laois player gave Kerry a chance to regroup, with numerous positional switches made in a bid to stem the Laois tide. The *Kerryman* described how 'O'Donnell went in full forward, Dillon taking his place. McCarthy came to midfield, Healy going to left half.'

Laois pointed on the resumption to go three in front, 1-4 to 1-1. Kerry's changes then reaped rewards, as described by the *Kerryman.*

Dillon sent in a long ball which O'Donnell fielded. He passed to Tim Landers who dribbled in. A hard low shot went wide of a cluster of Laois defenders to the net and the scores were level. Kerry returned a kickout in determined fashion and a long ball from Healy reached Lyne. There were terrific Kerry cheers when the Killarney boy gave his side a point lead.

After what the paper proclaimed a 'titanic struggle, abounding in thrills,' Kerry had won through to the all-Ireland final on a score of 2-2 to 1-4.

One startling statistic from the two games against Laois is that the Leinster champions had fourteen wides the first day, then sixteen on the second. Kerry registered five and six, respectively. Altogether, that's thirty to Laois and only eleven for Kerry.

The result may have delighted Kerry—not so the travel arrangements for the replay, which was played in Waterford. *Years of Glory* later recalled that Kerry's complaints were made at a Central Council meeting. 'When the train on which the Kerry players were travelling arrived at Mallow, the mail train had gone and the players had to travel from Tralee without as much as a cup of tea!'

Cavan, by virtue of their surprise win over the reigning champions, Mayo, were to be Kerry's opponents in the final. The *Kerryman* recounted how the Kingdom were pulling out all the stops for the decider.

> The prospective players were mobilised, taken from their occupations and put up at a Tralee hotel. Each such period of training resulted in a heavy financial loss to the County Board. It has now been decided that the players [should] train in their own houses. They will train under the supervision of a County Board member, appointed for the purpose. On 2 days each week they assemble in Tralee for practice matches.

A building strike was threatening the GAA showpiece, to be played at Croke Park on 26 September, and there were concerns about whether an alternative venue would have to be found. The *Kerryman* was happy to note that the potential crisis was averted.

> It was announced at a meeting of the central council that the national stadium, improvements to which have been held up by the Dublin building dispute, will be put in order for the match, both parties to the strike having agreed to allow the work to be carried out.

Both counties could now concentrate on the coming clash. Kerry were boosted by the return of Paddy Kennedy at midfield. But there was frustration in store for many supporters, as documented in *Kerry's Football Story*. 'So dense was the throng that many people who had travelled from the outlying parts of Kerry and could not reach Croke Park early, were unable to gain admission.' The *Kerryman* reported that 'a record crowd, 52,325 watched the match—the gates were closed but later thrown open and thousands admitted free.' The match was described in the *Irish Times* as 'the most thrilling of our Championship finals, not that the game in itself was productive of first-rate football.'

Kerry began like the proverbial house on fire, as reported by the *Kerryman*.

Johnny Walsh sent Kerry to the attack and O'Sullivan gave to O'Donnell who transferred to Tim Landers. He passed to JJ, who lobbed past Young into the net after six minutes play. Dillon sent a free back and there was a delightful movement between the Kerry forwards before JJ Landers was left in possession. A low left foot drive went wide of Young to the net.

Kerry were two goals in front after twelve minutes but, amazingly, failed to score again in that half. Kerry led by 2-0 to 0-4 at half time, an advantage that was very quickly halved. They recovered to go four to the good. Cavan reduced the gap to that most dangerous advantage, two points. Cavan then goaled to go in front. Kerry equalised, then went ahead by the minimum with five minutes remaining. A Cavan free tied the proceedings; the score at the end read Kerry 2-5, Cavan 1-8.

However, fans both inside the ground and listening at home were led to believe that Kerry had lost. The *Kerryman* reported:

The white flag went up to signal a Cavan point in the last minute, but the whistle had gone—Boylan was adjudged to have thrown the ball over the bar. An announcer in the field gave Cavan victory by a point. A crowd gathered on top of the new structure under the scoreboard made it impossible for the scores to be recorded on the board. A big crowd swept in over the pitch and the Cavan players were hoisted on the shoulders of their admirers. A few minutes later there was a corrected announcement, giving the official scores as a draw.

Drama at the end of the drawn game and drama early in the replay, with fears that the match would be abandoned! The *Kerryman* informed its readers that 'the opening stages provided some dirty football. At the first stoppage it appeared the game would not be finished.'

Cavan's tactics in the drawn encounter left a lot to be desired as far as Kerry were concerned. The Kingdom believed that their opponents had been too physical, and they wanted to ensure that there would be no repeat of this. It was Kerry's intention to lay down a marker early in the replay. T. J. Flynn, joint author of *Princes of Pigskin: A Century of Kerry Footballers*, describes how, during the drawn game,

> a couple of the Kerry players, and selectors, felt a number of the Kerry forwards would have got rough and harsh treatment from the Cavan defence . . . They hatched this plan to ensure that the Kerry forward line would get fair treatment. The main enforcer on the Cavan team would have been the fullback, Jim Smith. The plan was that the first high ball to drop between Smith and Miko Doyle, Doyle was going to give him a belt across the face. The first ball that came in, true to their word, Doyle turned around, didn't even see where the ball was going, and gave Smith a belt. A scuffle broke out. Kerry went on to win, one of the reasons being that they laid down the law early on in the game.

There was an early blow to Kerry's hopes. Tim O'Donnell went off injured, to be replaced by Tom Gega O'Connor. Canon Jackie McKenna was fortunate to line out alongside a host of Dingle's Kerry stars in the 1930s. McKenna wasn't sure that Gega was the man the selectors had intended to replace O'Donnell.

> Tim O'Donnell had to go off injured. Gega was put on as a sub. It was against all the thinking. While the selectors were trying to make up their mind on the field who would they put on as a sub, Jerry Leary, I think 'twas he, said to Gega, Throw off your coat and go in. He was one of the selectors and made up their minds for them. Gega was an unknown at the time. The man broadcasting the match was called Fr Hamilton. He was the chairman of Clare County Board and very prominent in the Munster Council, he was doing the commentary on the match from Croke Park. When Tim O'Donnell got injured and went off and the sub came in, the commentator didn't even know who this man was. His name wasn't even on the

programme. The commentator decided he was one of the other subs and decided on a name, the wrong name. We didn't know until the day after that Gega was the sub.

Losing O'Donnell at such an early stage didn't seem to upset Kerry. They responded in the best fashion possible, as the *Kerryman* noted: 'After eleven minutes Brosnan got the ball over White's head and drove into the goalmouth. JJ Landers crossed in front of the square and O'Leary touched a low ball past Young to the net.'

It was honours even at the break, Kerry 1-0, Cavan 0-3. Cavan had the better of the early second-half exchanges, going two points in front, before Kerry swung into top gear. The *Kerryman* wrote:

> Kerryman Flavin got Healy's free and gave to Tim Landers. He dribbled in and shot a low ball to the net, Doyle putting the finishing touches, to raise the green flag after seven minutes had gone.

Kerry now led by a single point. They doubled that advantage and then completely took over. As the *Kerryman* report continued, the Cavan goal fell twice more before the end.

> The leather went into touch. JJ Landers got this. He eluded a tackle and passed to Tim. Tim dribbled in and gave to O'Leary at the edge of the square. A low grounder shook the net to the accompaniment of wild Kerry cheers.

When Landers followed with a point it was 3-2 to 0-5 after seventeen minutes. After Cavan halved the gap, Kerry hit back once more.

> Brosnan left Tim Landers in possession. He was fouled and Brosnan's free went into the square. A low left drive by JJ Landers went through a cluster of players to the net.
>
> That goal put the game beyond Cavan. A six-point victory was Kerry's, 4-4 to 1-7.

In the wake of that defeat of Cavan, the *Kerryman* had a warning for the watching world. 'Kerry's success has caused alarm in certain circles. It is well known that the team has not yet reached its best.'

The *Irish Times* was also approving of this Kerry side and the replay.

> In many respects it was more satisfying than the drawn game. It was more severe as a test of men, and it introduced us to a young team of footballers who would do credit to any nation.

———

Kerry went into the 1939 championship season after defeat to Galway in an all-Ireland final replay. An under-strength Kingdom side had succumbed to the Tribesman on the second day. In the drawn game, as a last-minute point by John Joe Landers made its way over the bar the referee blew his whistle for full time. The score was disallowed, and Kerry were denied the win. Towards the end of the replay the referee blew his whistle for a foul. Galway were leading, and many mistakenly believed it to be the full-time whistle. The crowd invaded the field. The spectators were eventually cleared and the final minutes played out. Some of the Kerry players were missing, however, as they too believed the replay to be over, and substitutes had to fill their positions for those closing three minutes. Kerry lost, 2-4 to 0-7, surrendering the title they had won the previous year. So, in 1939, Kerry were aiming to reach their third successive all-Ireland final.

That season began with the Munster decider. Because of their tour in America, Kerry had received a bye to the provincial final. There they would take on Tipperary, in Clonmel.

It would be considered a shock if Kerry didn't win against Tipp and in the process qualify for the semi-final. Connacht opposition lay in store for the Munster winners. However, the issue of just who would represent the western province in the last four was unclear. This followed the previous week's abrupt conclusion to the Connacht final, which the *Kerryman* recalled as having

> ended in a fiasco. Mayo were all over winners two minutes from the end when thousands encroached on the pitch. Stewards were swept aside like flies. All efforts to restart the game were in vain. It is really

hard luck on Mayo because Galway were a well-beaten team. Mayo are well set for All-Ireland honours. Mayo can be licked and Kerry is probably the one team capable of doing it.

Before Kerry minds could turn to Mayo, or Galway, Tipperary had to be taken on. For that 1939 opener against Tipperary, the Kingdom was able to call on eight of the men who had played in the 1937 all-Ireland triumph: Dan O'Keeffe, Bill Myers, Joe Keohane, Bill Dillon, Tom Gega O'Connor, Johnny Walsh, Charlie O'Sullivan and Miko Doyle.

The light had by now gone out for the inter-county career of one of the Kingdom's finest forwards, another member of that victorious team of '37: John Joe Landers. Thankfully, his brother Tim was back in the fold for the 1939 campaign.

The Kingdom had built up a game-winning 1-5 to 0-2 lead at the break, the goal scored by Tony McAuliffe. The opening minutes of the second period saw Kerry seal the victory, a goal by Murt Kelly putting the tie out of reach. Kerry won, 2-11 to 0-4, a victory every bit as comprehensive as that score indicates.

Kerry played only one match in progressing out of Munster, which can't have helped their cause, nor can it have been of benefit for a semi-final with Mayo. The westerners, earlier that year, had won an incredible sixth National League title in a row. But they secured only one all-Ireland in that same period. In 1936 Mayo defeated Laois in the decider, after seeing off Kerry in the last four.

Mayo's inability to turn League glory into all-Ireland success was the main talking-point before their showdown with Kerry on 13 August. The *Kerryman* pondered:

Why Mayo have not repeated in the championship proper, what they accomplished in the league is the most baffling problem in Gaelic sport. Does Mayo lack the fighting qualities of which champions are made or do its footballers lack the big game temperament? That the venue is Croke Park must cause uneasiness in the Mayo camp. The team has too often failed in that arena, without any satisfactory explanation of their collapse.

Unbelievable as it may sound, Kerry failed to put up a single score in the first half against the westerners. Mayo fared slightly better, registering two points. Lady Luck was not on Kerry's side, as the *Kerryman* reported.

> Walsh sent Kerry on the attack. Lyne came out and flashed the ball to Spring, who gave to Kelly. He crashed a grounder towards the net. Burke dropped the ball on the line as the Kerry forwards rushed in. There was a fierce tussle under the Mayo crossbar and excitement was intense. Burke was hurt, but soon resumed, and an apparent goal was disallowed, Mayo being awarded a free out from the square.

The following week's edition of the *Kerryman* declared its belief that the goal should have stood, claiming that the Mayo goalkeeper hadn't in fact prevented the ball from going over the line.

Improvement was needed by Kerry, and it duly arrived in the second period. O'Sullivan and Kelly pointed to draw Kerry level after three minutes. Four minutes later Mayo went back in front. Again Kerry responded, Seán Brosnan doing the necessary this time. Brosnan had Kerry a point in front after twenty minutes. Mayo put over the equaliser after twenty-three minutes, ending the scoring. Four points apiece is how it ended, with the *Kerryman* declaring that Kerry's forwards had frittered away winning chances.

Nowadays, travel to Croke Park is taken for granted—not so in 1939. The *Kerryman* described how

> two young fellows cycled 16 miles from the Castlegregory district and travelled by the ghost train ex Tralee midnight Saturday. When the train reached Tralee on Monday morning at one o'clock they had to jump once more on their bikes and cycle the sixteen miles home. A Kerryman travelled to the match and sensing Dublin opinion on the result he thought it was a favourable opportunity of turning an honest penny. So he backed Kerry to win, he got odds of 4 to 1 against!!!

The punter in question failed to collect; and you can be sure that such generous odds were not available for the replay.

For a while, however, it seemed as if there might not be a replay. The *Kerryman's* description of the Kerry v. Mayo draw was that it was 'not a rough game but spiritedly contested.' The view from the west was different, with claims that the referee was prevented from doing his duty 'by the terrorism of Kerry.'

The Mayo captain, Paddy Moclair, declared that he wouldn't participate in any replay against Kerry.

> I am not going to risk my life in Croke Park. With our goalkeeper unconscious between the posts, Tommy Hoban beaten into insensibility and myself struck and floored three times, and when not near the ball, but 20 and 60 yards away, do you ask me again to risk my life. Don't think that I have any misgivings as to the result of a replay. We have the capacity to beat any team in the world and even with the violence on Sunday we would have defeated Kerry had the referee remained impartial. Deliberate assaults on us by the players, deliberate dragooning of the referee by Kerry officials was allowed go on openly.

Meanwhile the Kerry squad was busy preparing itself for the replay—if there was to be one. As the *Kerryman* noted, the panel was under the watchful eye of one of the county's greatest midfielders.

> The Kerry players are undergoing special training. They are in charge of Con Brosnan, and in capable hands. Some of the players have been unable to leave their positions, but these are expected to train privately and fit themselves for the stern task ahead.

Leading up to the replay, Mayo's allegations against Kerry, following the drawn game, were exposed at the Central Council. The *Kerryman* reported:

> 'Twasn't me said it at all, sir, 'twas the other fellow. This was the small boy excuse put forward by Mayo at the last meeting of the Central Council when asked to substantiate their charges of roughness against the Kerry players; intimidation and partiality of the referee, and intriguing by the governing body, to bring about a replay of the now famous semi-final. These charges had been deliberately made with malice aforethought, at a special meeting of the Mayo County Board. No Gaelic event in Mayo had ever received such widespread publicity.

A county had been offended, and the call was made by the *Kerryman* for its representatives to exact revenge.

> The Kerry players and their county have been grossly insulted by Mayo. There could be no greater incentive to win. Our lads carry a heavy responsibility. The honour of their County, as well as themselves, has been called into question. Our boys must avenge that insult; vindicate their own men and their County's honour. Kerry teams of the past always licked Mayo. A trouncing is now due the western men more than ever before. We never harmed Mayo, they insulted Kerry grossly.

Sure enough, victory was Kerry's, and it was emphatic. The *Kerryman* headline declared: 'Blackout of Mayo's football stars—Kingdom trounce Westerners'—all this despite the fact that Kerry conceded a goal in the first minute! That goal kept Mayo out of Kerry's reach early on. The sides shared six points, and Mayo's advantage was now 1-3 to 0-3. However, as the *Kerryman* reported, two quick Kerry goals turned the encounter on its head.

> Brosnan secured the goal kick. He was fouled. He took the free beyond the 50 and sent into the goalmouth. Spring touched the ball and helped it to the net, leaving the scores level after 23 minutes. Dillon fielded a high ball and left Walsh in possession. He was fouled. Landers sent the free to the corner of the square. Sullivan rushed in and crashed into the net. There was a short consultation between the umpires and referee and thunderous Kerry cheers rent the air when the green flag went up, putting the kingdom a major in the lead.

Kerry added two further scores before the break. A five-point advantage was theirs at the turnaround, 2-5 to 1-3. Mayo had opened the game with a first-minute goal. When the second half began it was a similar tale. This time, however, it was the Kingdom celebrating, with the *Kerryman* describing how, immediately the ball was thrown in,

> there was a hop. Kerry had a free then, and O'Connor's kick far out

was saved by Burke. Kerry had another free at the corner. Tim Landers drove across the square and Spring punched into the net.

3-5 to 1-3 in Kerry's favour; the result was never in doubt thereafter. Come the final whistle the score stood at 3-8 to 1-4, and a third successive all-Ireland final appearance was the Kingdom's.

After the replay the *Kerryman* reproduced an article from the *Western People* that delivered a harsh verdict on the Mayo team: 'Mayo's fifteen senior footballers presented a pitiful spectacle in Croke Park.'

In his column, Paddy Foley revealed the relaxed manner of the Kerry team leading up to the games with Mayo.

On the night prior to the drawn game I called to the Dublin hotel where the team was staying. It was pretty late and the players had not returned. They were out at a show, which featured Gene Autry, the cowboy star.

It was noted that, for the replay, 'Kerry reached Dublin on Saturday night—most of them went to the dogs at Shelbourne Park.'

A success of 1-9 to 1-1 against Cavan earned Meath their place in that year's final. The issue was then of the colours Kerry were to wear. With Kerry and Meath both sporting green and gold, something had to give. Canon Jackie McKenna explains:

The custom that time was that they just tossed for it. Who'd have to change? Naturally the two of them couldn't wear green and gold, even though it wasn't the same pattern. Kerry lost the toss, and they had to change. Dingle were county champions. The Dingle representative going to the county board meeting discussed the situation . . . It was strange for the Kerry fans but once they knew in advance that's the way it was going to be they were prepared for it. We're proud of it ever since that Kerry won the all-Ireland wearing the Dingle colours.

In the build-up to the final an article in the *Drogheda Independent* was reproduced in the *Kerryman*. It was disclosed that the Leinstermen were in confident form.

Kerry's first class exhibition against the Westerners has not lessened Meath's optimistic outlook. On the contrary, there are many Meath men who would rather that Kerry were the opposition than Mayo.

A correspondent calling himself 'Boyne Valley', writing in the *Kerryman*, claimed that

> there is great confidence that the last line will hold the Kerry attack. I believe Meath's display will surprise the critics. For the first time in their career they have gone through a special course of training. They will make a bold bid for victory.

There was late drama for Kerry leading up to the final. The selectors were forced to alter their plans, with the captain, Seán Brosnan, unwell and unable to play. This meant that the captaincy passed to Tom Gega O'Connor.

It was a hard-fought first half between Kerry and Meath, even though the Kingdom had the much better start. The *Kerryman* reported that

> Kerry had a free, Casey got this and his long drop was secured by Landers, who passed to Kelly, the white flag going up for the kingdom inside a minute. Gorman sent back the goal kick, and Spring got possession. He shot a hard ball to the net. McEnroe got his hand to the leather, and punched out, but the green flag went up, indicating that the ball had crossed the line.

Kerry were now four points up, with the clock showing the same number of minutes. Kerry were pegged back. It was 1-2 apiece at half time, yet the Kingdom wouldn't have to spend too long on level terms. A Murt Kelly point nudged the Kingdom back in front. A second Kerry goal twelve minutes into the second half, as described by the *Kerryman*, put them in the driving seat.

> Gorman got a kickout and crossed in front of the posts. Spring got possession and took steady aim. He sent in a terrific shot. McEnroe got his boot to the ball but the leather screwed off his foot into the net.

A further Kerry point had the Kingdom leading by five and seemingly destined for glory. As in the first half, however, their opponents hit back. Meath netted, leaving them only two points behind. Goal chances came and went in the closing ten minutes. The issue was in doubt up to the very end, and, as the *Kerryman* reported, the Kingdom survived one last major scare.

> Meath came back in one last great effort. They had a free; Cummins and Keohane went for the ball, which fell near the Kerry posts. They both went to the ground and the leather went just wide of the Kerry net.

A relieved Kerry held on. Aided in no small part by those two Dan Spring goals, the Kingdom won, 2-5 to 2-3.

Kerry's victory over Meath meant that Con Brosnan achieved what was then a unique feat, described by Joe Ó Muircheartaigh, joint author of *Princes of Pigskin*.

> He became the first player to go on and train an all-Ireland winning team. That was the 1939 all-Ireland winning team, they won in 1937 with Dr Éamonn involved in the team. But in 1939 Con Brosnan trained the team. That was a great day for Kerry. They won the all-Ireland, war had just broken out but all that mattered down in Kerry was that they were all-Ireland champions.

The *Kerryman* noted that fifty-eight frees were awarded in the final, twenty-three in the first half and thirty-five in the second. Thirty-two of that total were awarded against Kerry and twenty-six for.

Murt Kelly, the late replacement for Seán Brosnan on the team, put over two points against Meath. Murt's son Colm says that his father spoke very little of his all-Ireland triumph.

> We found it very hard to break into those conversations. He would always say, 'Yerra, I just played okay.' He was a particularly good free-taker. There was one, against Meath, where he pointed a long-range free that turned the game. He spent most of his time praising the other players. He would say, Only for them he'd never have made it.

Kerry's win over Meath meant that, should the green and gold win the Sam Maguire in 1940, they would join Dublin at the top of the roll of honour, with fourteen all-Ireland senior football titles. It's natural for the title-holders to be thought of as contenders for the following season's championship. However, according to the *Kerryman*, such ambitions looked unattainable before the Munster opener.

> Amongst the possibles and probables, all jumbled together, there is not a man who has not previously played in some capacity for the county. The student of form will ask himself the question on reading the names 'I wonder is there another all-Ireland in them'. The answer is no in regard to some of them; while there are others listed not up to Senior County standard. It would be better to face up to these facts at the very start before the championship begins and thus save ourselves from any hallucinations later on.

The ultimate honour of wining the Sam Maguire Cup may have been thought a long way off. However, there were no such doubts when it came to Provincial honours—well, up until the Munster final, anyway!

Limerick provided the opening obstacle, and Kerry could call on two-thirds of the previous season's all-Ireland final winning side. There were two J. O'Gormans on the team against Limerick, Jimmy of Mitchels and James from Stacks. The James of Stacks is the man better known as Gawksie.

The Kingdom, led by stalwarts, including Bill Myers, Joe Keohane, Tom Gega O'Connor and Johnny Walsh, despatched Limerick on a scoreline of 4-9 to 1-2. Gawksie Gorman was among the first-half goal-scorers for the Kingdom. Kerry's advantage was 3-6 to 0-2 at the short whistle. The only noteworthy moment of the second half was Kerry's final goal of the afternoon. This saw the other Jimmy Gorman hit the net. 4-9 to 1-2 was the result, that comprehensive victory securing a Munster semi-final with Tipperary. As was the case against Limerick, the game against Tipp was in the bag by half time. The *Kerryman* reported that

> about ten minutes passed with poor kick about football when Seán Brosnan placed Gawksie Gorman for a goal. Johnny Walsh quickly followed with a point. Tipp had a point from a free and Kerry had a goal by Dan Spring. He soon had another.

At the turnaround the Kingdom led 3-5 to 0-1. The *Kerryman* reporter was apathetic about the second half.

> Kerry had brought their tally to 17 points before Tipp had another flag. The end of a one sided poor game, which does not call for description, came with the scores 4-8 to 1-5. A cynic would probably describe the game as a farce. He would not be very far wrong. It was not Kerry's football brilliance which made the semi-final a veritable farce. It was the sheer incompetence of the 15 which did duty for the Premier County.

Waterford were all that stood between Kerry and Munster honours. It was a barrier that was expected to be easily overcome. However, Kerry actually trailed by three points at half time against Waterford. Despite this, the *Kerryman* headline read: 'Champions were never extended.' Waterford led by five points to two at the break. However, they added only one further score. Kerry were Munster champions once more, on this occasion thanks to a scoreline of 1-10 to 0-6.

Cavan were to be their opponents in the all-Ireland semi-final, and a different proposition entirely, following another smooth run through Munster for the Kingdom.

1940 saw the introduction of the rotational system for all-Ireland semi-finals. Before that there was a set system, which was somewhat lopsided. For the fifteen seasons before 1940 the number of times the Munster champions had played against each of the provinces in the all-Ireland semi-final were Connacht, six times; Leinster, six times; and Ulster, three times.

The game against Cavan was goalless at half time, despite a number of chances at each end. Cavan led by three points to two at the break; they went further ahead in the opening minutes of the second period. Kerry trailed by five points to two, but, as the *Kerryman* reported, the Kingdom were gifted the equaliser.

> Dan Spring was in possession close in. He was pulled down, unobserved by the referee, but the leather never left the square and Gawksie Gorman got his foot to it. The ball was fielded by the hitherto unbeatable Cavan keeper Kelly, but he allowed the leather

slip out of his hands, over his shoulders into the net. He waved his hands in a gesture of disgust.

Worse was to come for the netminder.

> A long free by Healy was secured by Johnny Walsh. Off he went along the wing. He sent a clever pass to Gawksie Gorman close up. Gorman shot diagonally along the ground from the corner and the slippery ball again went off the Cavan goalman to the net.

Kerry were now two points in front, and Johnny Walsh put the seal on the victory. The *Kerryman* reported that 'Walsh got on the ball and went off in a characteristic solo run. Clean through the defence he went and finished with a scorcher.' That put the score at 3-3 to 0-6. Cavan, architects of their own downfall, were out. Kerry progressed to their fourth all-Ireland final in a row, doing so on a scoreline of 3-4 to 0-8.

Now they were to meet Galway, who, on the same day and at the same venue, had defeated the Meath side beaten by Kerry in the final the previous season. Galway's victory afforded Kerry the opportunity of avenging their 1938 final replay.

Assessing the Galway team in the *Kerryman*, Paddy Foley enlightened his readers about the emergence of the Maroon-and-Whites.

> One wonders if Galway's football resurgence does not date from governmental changes in this county. For the Tricolour now replaces the Union Jack over Renmore barracks, in the Galway suburbs, headquarters of the Irish-speaking battalion. It may be noted that Renmore are army champions in hurling and football, defeating other barracks of vastly bigger size. University College are now a force in Galway football. Galway's Gaelicised university and Renmore are now prolific sources of material for the Galway county team. Prominent footballers have taken up residence, like Flavin of Kerry and Beggs, Dublin. It used be said of former Dublin selections that they included 'a man from here, a man from there, and a man from god knows where!' One could say the same of the Galway team of today, not meaning to be disparaging.

Foley felt that Galway were underestimated when the counties met in 1938. He proclaimed that such excessive confidence wouldn't be in evidence in this 1940 decider. A bullish Galway supporter had a letter printed in that same week's *Kerryman*.

> I read your comments about our Galway team with much interest. It seems to me that you are aware Kerry is facing another licking and that you are kind of preparing your readers for it. You hint that Kerry were beaten the last time because they underestimated Galway. Perhaps they did, but surely that is no excuse . . . Up Galway, even though our team is drawn from several Counties.

Kerry supporters had to contend with a scare before the final. Bill Casey sustained an ankle injury, and word spread that he would be missing for the decider. He did manage to take his place, however. Kerry had the better of the play in the first half against Galway but did not make their domination count on the scoreboard. They led by three points to two as half time approached. A Galway goal put them in arrears. The Kingdom were unlucky to be losing, having had the better of the play, but they were far from out of the proceedings.

Having failed to convert their first-half opportunities, Kerry set about wronging that right in the second period. Paddy Bawn Brosnan, a sub, pointed to halve the deficit. A Murt Kelly free at the three-quarter stage had the sides level, 0-5 to 1-2. Galway went in front once more, but another Murt Kelly free put the Kingdom on par. The *Kerryman* described a tense finish.

> With time almost up and the scores level, Kerry went off in one last do or die rally. Kennedy sent in a long ball. [Charlie] O'Sullivan rushed out and secured it. Excitement knew no bounds as the Kerry sharpshooter steadied himself about 40 yards out. A grand left punt sent the white ball just above the bar, giving Kerry a point lead.

It was a lead that wouldn't be relinquished, and Kerry had retained the Sam Maguire. The *Kerryman* lavished praise on the consecutive all-Ireland champions. 'More glamorous teams have represented Kerry but the present 15 are as gallant a band as ever wore the green and gold. They have grit and determination to spare.'

The 0-7 to 1-3 victory gave Kerry its fourteenth title, equalling Dublin's tally at the top of the standings. It also afforded Kerry revenge for their 1938 final defeat against Galway.

The champions, captained by Dan Spring, returned home the following day. The *Kerryman* correspondent was among the waiting masses.

> A large crowd gathered at the Tralee Railway Station on Monday night, loud cheers were raised as the train steamed in and there were individual ovations for the different players as they emerged from their carriage. An escort of torchbearers fell in after the Cup and to the strains of the Strand Street Fife and Drum Band the cheering crowd marched to Strand Street, the home of the O'Rahillys, whose club had the honour for the first time in its history of nominating the captain of a champion Kerry team. A huge bonfire blazed at the railway gates in Upper Strand Street, and there was much rejoicing.

———

Kerry remained the team to beat come 1941. In addition to chasing three all-Ireland titles in a row the Kingdom was aiming for a fifth consecutive final appearance. Kerry had won three of the four previous deciders, going down only to Galway in 1938, and that after a replay. The *Kerryman*, however, felt that doubts persisted about the Kingdom team.

> Last year's All Ireland team is practically intact but this is not to imagine that everything is rosy in the garden. It is not and we had better face up to the fact at once. Kerry's problem lies in attack.

The 1941 championship for Kerry began with a Munster final against Clare. Clare had caused a surprise by beating Cork in the first round. They then received a bye in the semi-final, Tipp giving a walkover because of foot-and-mouth disease. Fourteen of the fifteen who had started in the 1940 final victory over Galway were named in the team to take on Clare.

Kerry eased past Clare in a game that the *Kerryman* described as

so one sided as to be practically farcical. It was no true test of our
men. We could have fielded players, off colour or below inter county
standard, and the opposition was so poor that such weaknesses in
the champion's ranks would not be disclosed. Munster football
outside Kerry has fallen on evil days.

Kerry led by 1-4 to 0-3 at the short whistle, Charlie O'Sullivan the
goal-scorer. 2-9 to 0-6 was the final result against Clare, Murt Kelly
netting in the second half.

Kerry's win against Clare meant that they had won the Munster title
for the seventeenth time in nineteen seasons. The only years in which
they failed to do so were 1928, when they suffered a surprise one-point
defeat to Tipperary in the semi-final, and 1935, when Kerry failed to field
in the Munster championship, because of the difficult political
circumstances.

Kerry's victory, and Dublin's progression from Leinster, meant that
the pair were to meet in the all-Ireland semi-final on 10 August. The
stakes were higher than usual: not only would the victor earn the right
to contest for the Sam Maguire but they would also move one step
closer to the top of the all-Ireland roll of honour. Dublin had last tasted
success in 1923, when they beat Kerry in the final. All this meant that the
counties went into the season tied on fourteen championship successes.

The *Kerryman* believed the Dublin fraternity to be uneasy.

It is an open secret that Dublin do not relish Kerry's serious
challenge. For more than 50 years Dublin headed the list—they will
not lightly relinquish that honour. With the capital complex they do
not like being relegated to second place by the country fellows. Half
the present metropolitan selection are Kerrymen. Best known here
are J. Counihan, Annascaul, who used play with Tralee O'Rahillys;
M. Falvey and P. Kennedy, who played for Dingle Christian Brothers'
Schools.

While some Kerrymen in the capital lined out for the Blues, others
continued to wear the green and gold. Accordingly, they were reminded
of their duty by the *Kerryman*.

The players resident in Dublin should be in trim. Wherever a player resides he should realise, without any reminder, how incumbent on him it is to put in some training on his own.

In April that year Munster, made up of thirteen Kerry players and two Corkmen, had won the Railway Cup, beating Ulster by 2-6 to 1-6 in a replay. When the merits of the semi-finalists were weighed up it was a worry that Kerry had not played very much since that match; Dublin, meanwhile, had defeated Kerry in the National League semi-final. They had also accounted for a fancied Kildare.

The semi-final with Dublin was more about the chances squandered than the points scored. A low-scoring encounter was in store: after only three scores in thirty minutes Kerry had an advantage of two points to one at half time.

The second-half scoring was only slightly better. Kerry were 3-2 to the good. Dublin then edged ahead and seemed set for a place in the all-Ireland final, leading four to three inside the last minute. The *Kerryman* described the drama that followed.

Kerry had a free about 20 yards out, in front of the canal goal. Could Kerry equalise? They had missed half a dozen similar frees during the course of the match. Murt Kelly took the kick amid terrific tension. The ball hit the right upright high up and bounced up in the air. Did the ball pass through or outside? Up went the white flag!!! The scores were level.

The game, not dirty by any means, ended at four points apiece. Exciting football does not always mean good football, however.

Kerry faced the prospect of returning to Croke Park one week later, but on the toss of a coin the home advantage was granted to the Kingdom: Dublin were to come to Tralee.

Kerry held the edge from early on, leading three points to one after nineteen minutes. They then pulled away from their opponents. The *Kerryman* reported that

a good centre by Paddy Bawn Brosnan was caught at the edge of the square by Murt Kelly. He was bottled and kicked over his head, the ball landing in the goalmouth among a cluster of players. Tom

O'Connor charged in and boxed past the post to the net.

The sides turned around with Kerry ahead, 1-3 to 0-3. The killer blow arrived soon after the break.

> Paddy Kennedy was fouled near the centre and his free set Kerry attacking. Tom O'Connor passed to Charlie O'Sullivan and a long low grounder beat Kelly all ends up for a goal.

That made it 2-3 to 0-3. Thereafter it was a question of 'by how many?' A twelve-point win was Kerry's. While they kept Dublin scoreless in that second half, they tagged on one goal and six of their own, to emerge victorious, 2-9 to 0-3.

To ensure that people weren't getting carried away with this result, the *Kerryman* provided a timely reminder for Kerry supporters.

> Kerry are facing formidable opposition in the final, a much different proposition from Dublin. For Galway, like Dublin, are drawn from many Counties, including Kerry, and the team has had the advantage already of a period of special training. Dan Kavanagh of the Kerry Gaeltacht starred in the Galway midfield last Sunday.

The Sunday match referred to is Galway's surprisingly one-sided defeat of Cavan in their own semi-final, in which Galway won by 1-12 to 1-4.

The *Kerryman* quoted the *Connacht Tribune,* which believed that in the final the previous year, which was also between Kerry and Galway,

> Galway's failure occurred in attack where there were a couple of weak points. These have been remedied this year. Kerry will face a much faster team and their excellent speed and fielding should cause a lot of worry to the Kerry defence. Galway followers are confident.

The acquisition by Galway of Dan Kavanagh was hailed as a master stroke but a missed opportunity by the Kingdom. According to the *Kerryman,*

> the Galway line out could aptly be termed the team of the tribes for

it is representative of several Counties . . . Galway's greatest discovery was Kavanagh, a young Kerryman, at the university. He played for the West Kerry Gaeltacht last year in the Kerry County Championship. Played for the county in some matches, but was not impressive, Kerry judged him rashly. Then only a gorsoon, he has been naturally on the upgrade since. By all accounts he saved Galway at Roscommon. A tireless worker and great fielder, he will do duty at centre field.

The 1941 final was fixed for the first Sunday of September, the 7th. For the fourth game in succession Kerry lined out with the same fifteen players. This was to be the third all-Ireland meeting between the counties in four seasons, with Kerry having won in 1940 and Galway in 1938.

As a result of the Second World War a petrol shortage restricted travel. Trains and buses were heavily affected. The *Kerryman* reported that many Kingdom supporters were left without means of getting to the decider.

> Lack of travelling facilities prevented the customary huge Kerry following travelling to the metropolis. The cancellation of Sunday services doubtless deterred the big majority from making the trip. There was no ghost train and the auxiliary on Saturday evening was not availed of to the extent expected. Nevertheless all available motors in Kerry were called into running.

For those who were able to venture to the capital the journey would prove more than worth while: history was about to be made.

With less than a quarter of an hour gone the Kingdom were down three points to one. Tom O'Connor reduced the gap before Paddy Bawn Brosnan levelled. Galway edged ahead again, but Tom O'Connor pointed once more. The score was level, at four points each, at the break. The *Kerryman* felt that the first half belonged to the opposition.

> Galway sparked in the first half hour. The Kerry defenders showed their old time brilliance, but still the Galway men got possession often enough to raise more flags. On the general run of the first half, Galway should have been about 3 points in the lead. That they did

not enjoy this comfort was due to a more sterling Kerry defence, but largely to erratic Galway shooting.

Kerry fell two points behind at the start of the second half. There was a one-point deficit after seven minutes. In a low-scoring decider, a goal would prove to be decisive, and so it was, as the *Kerryman* reported.

> Tom O'Connor got possession from a short kickout. He was bowled over at once. Seán Brosnan took the free inside the 50. The ball reached Tom O'Connor. He worked free from a cluster and banged for the goal. The ball was got away from the goalkeeper and eluded his outstretched hands, to find a safe resting place in the corner of the net.

That score put Kerry ahead, 1-5 to 0-6, half way through the second half. Jimmy Gorman put three points between the sides after twenty-one minutes. The sides then swapped points. Murt Kelly put over a free, and the Kingdom were four points in front.

Time was against Galway, and the westerners went in search of the goal necessary to bring them back into the encounter. The *Kerryman* describes a hectic conclusion to the game.

> Galway came away in a loose rush. Dunne started a round of short passing. Up they came to the Kerry square, where a Kerry back fouled. Was it a penalty? The referee consulted with the umpires. He signalled a 14 yards free, and Kerry packed the goal. Dunne tipped the ball ahead in a do or die effort to find the net. The Galway forwards hurled themselves on the human Kerry barrier and a terrific tussle took place within the square. Men went down like ninepins. Healy emerged with the leather clutched to his bosom. The ref's whistle went. Kerry had a free out.

The Green-and-Golds had won, with a score of 1-8 to 0-7, their second-half performance decisive. Tom Gega O'Connor played a leading role in ensuring that Bill Dillon got his hands on the Sam Maguire, being responsible for 1-2 of the Kingdom's match-winning total. For that campaign Kerry had the same starting fifteen for all four matches.

Despite travel restrictions, the attendance still reached more than forty-five thousand. However, the *Kerryman's* Killarney correspondent later recalled how that town's contribution to the attendance was

> probably the smallest on record. The queer times in which we are living was responsible. The feverish excitement that rocked the town in previous all-Irelands was absent. Not even a poster advertising the game was to be seen, and as for the usual spate of Railway posters, well it was just as if there was nothing happening in Dublin on Sunday.

T. P. O'Rourke, the *Kerryman* correspondent, did make the trip, recalling his day in the capital.

> There are no trams. Optimists try desperately to board buses that are chock full of pessimists; optimists charter cabs and taxis at a bob [a shilling] a head. Through the groaning turnstiles passes the crowd. The Hogan and Cusack stands are packed with people that look like pigmies so vast is the background. Hill 16 is a riot of colour with the pink of faces prevailing. People in the sideline look apprehensively at new arrivals. There is no use describing the match—the world knows all about it. Five minutes after the Kerry goal the crowd begins to go away. After the first libation subdued congratulations are exchanged. After the second the consensus of opinion is that it was a good match. After the third it is enthusiastically revealed that it was the greatest match ever. The team goes off to the Mansion House ceilidhe, where they are to receive their medals, and any still thirsty adherents seek out certain establishments where they are assured that the proprietor or manager is prepared, at the risk of his licence and reputation, to provide a temporary home from home.

All-Ireland number 15 had been secured by Kerry, putting them proudly at the top of the roll of honour. They have never been surpassed, and it's unlikely that they will be for many a year. No wonder Paddy Foley enjoyed the journey home.

> On Monday evening we motored from Dublin, a more picturesque journey than following the iron trail. Under the settling Indian sun

the Irish countryside looked its best with fields of waving corn . . . Motors went by; the green and gold flags waving proudly from the bonnet. Cyclists too were on their way to the south west, carrying the Kerry colours.

Chapter 7 ∿

| A RICH HARVEST

In 1946 the Sam Maguire Cup was resting in Cork. Five years had passed since Kerry's last all-Ireland victory. In 1944 the Kingdom had lost the decider to Roscommon. The reigning champions, Cork, were the first hurdle for Kerry in 1946, and they had defeated Kerry in the 1945 Munster final, 1-11 to 1-6.

A fortnight before the Kerry v. Cork encounter in 1946 Kerry had taken on Tipperary in a challenge match in the hope of fine-tuning the side. Paddy Foley, in his column in the *Kerryman*, stated his belief that the meeting with Tipp had taught Kerry nothing. He also reflected sorrowfully how the previous year

> Cork went on to win all-Ireland honours and will now be represented by practically the same side. It was unfortunate for the Kerrymen, passing through a lean period, that they should be drawn against the champions in the first round. This year the Kingdom are confronted with an unprecedented situation; they face their most serious test at the start.

In the wake of the previous season's setback against Cork, changes were made for the 1946 campaign, as noted by the *Kerryman*.

> With the object of getting the players into shape Kerry started the county championship this year much earlier than usual. A changed Kerry team was expected. It may be criticised but the selectors had a tough job and they picked the players on current form rather than past reputation—rightly so. Many familiar faces are missing. It is an experimental team but one capable of rising to great heights.

Of the side that lost to Cork in 1945 only Dan O'Keeffe, Paddy Kennedy, Denny Lyne, Jackie Lyne, Batt Garvey, Tom Gega O'Connor and Eddie Walsh started this time. O'Keeffe, Kennedy, O'Connor and Walsh were all members of the three-in-a-row winning side of 1939–41. Another man involved in that three-in-a-row success, Bill Casey, returned against Cork, having missed the 1945 campaign.

Fifteen thousand people turned up at Fitzgerald Stadium in Killarney for Kerry v. Cork, a match that the *Kerryman* proclaimed as

> an exhilarating game of football, played at a sizzling pace that grew hotter as the minutes fled. This game will go into the annals as an encounter never to be forgotten . . . The champions were taken from their throne but had to be dragged every inch of the way, and it was not until the last second of a titanic battle that the monarchs had fallen.

The laurels were to be Kerry's; but what a battle they had! Kerry led only by two at the break, five points to three. The early minutes of the second half saw them explode into action. A slice of good luck aided the Kingdom's cause: a fortuitous goal, as described in the Kerryman.

> Cork will long remember and goalkeeper O'Driscoll will never forget the nasty trick fickle fortune played on them in the first minute of the second period. A centre by Tom O'Connor was badly muddled by three Cork defenders and the ball bounced slowly off one of them to roll slowly into the down stretched hands of O'Driscoll. Into his hands it rolled but to the consternation of everyone present he failed to hold it and it trickled between his legs for one of the softest goals ever scored against a team.

Jackie Lyne then hit the crossbar, before Tom O'Connor pointed. Kerry were now six points up. There was a sting in the tail, however, a Cork goal, then a point, making it a two-point game. A point apiece from Batt Garvey and Paddy Burke stretched Kerry's lead to four, and that's how it finished. A 1-8 to 1-4 victory had dethroned the Munster and all-Ireland champions. Plaudits came from the *Kerryman*.

Kerry's display came as a revelation to their followers. Apart from

their aerial superiority Kerry were better in field craft. Special
mention of Bill Casey, Teddy Connor, Gega Connor, Batt Garvey
and Dan O'Keeffe . . . The crowd was easily the largest ever for a
Munster football championship game. Had trains and buses run the
attendance would have been enormous.

As outstanding as this victory was, Kerry had only progressed to the
Munster semi-final with the win. However, with Cork out of the way the
remainder of the provincial campaign was viewed as a formality.

Following the display against Cork it wouldn't be easy to keep
people's feet on the ground. The old saying 'After the Lord Mayor's show
comes the dung-cart' was very much in evidence in Ennis on the day
Clare entertained Kerry. The Kingdom, with confidence sky-high after
the defeat of Cork, were most fortunate to emerge intact.

Kerry trailed by seven points to two at half time and, despite keeping
Clare scoreless in the second period, stole the winning scores only in the
dying minutes. A five-point deficit faced Kerry heading into the second
half. Still, the supporters were only waiting for the Kingdom to kick into
gear. It was a long wait, as the *Kerryman* reported.

> Eventually after sixteen minutes and after Kerry had been disallowed
> a goal, Paddy Burke opened with a point. Still there was a 4 point
> deficit and less than ten minutes of play. Then came the long
> awaited long goal. A Clare rush was cleared. The ball travelled down
> into the Clare square. It was well fielded but Gerald Teahan, who had
> moved into the forward lines, bottled up the back. Paddy Burke
> gripped the break and parted to Jackie Lyne who crashed under the
> bar.

Jack Falvey then pointed the equaliser. Paddy Burke put Kerry in
front, and Jackie Lyne added another point to finish the scoring. The
narrowest of escapes for Kerry: 1-6 to 0-7 the final score in favour of the
Kingdom. The *Kerryman's* relief was evident.

> With time ebbing past and defeat an all too ugly possibility, each of
> the few Kerry followers at Cusack Park looked around for some hole
> to creep quietly into and forget. Believe me, that is no exaggeration.
> At the end of the game we were a weak, pallid and nerve shaken lot.

We won on the post but once more our ego was badly shattered.

Two weeks after downing Clare came the Munster final. When the team to face Waterford was revealed, the *Kerryman* focused on the conundrum that was the Kerry full-back position.

> One sweet gorgeous headache! Yes, that is how the Kerry full back problem has developed. This latest experiment by the selectors is the third since we started the ball rolling in 1946. Ever since the selectors began to entertain doubts about Joe Keohane's ability, the full back crux has loomed big in county football talk. Tom McElligott is facing a stiff task. They have tried Paddy Brosnan and Billy Myers. Each has been found wanting. In any case it's getting a little too late for any more experiments.

Victory was expected—and delivered—against Waterford in Tralee. Kerry went two points up, then a mix-up in the Kingdom defence gifted Waterford a goal. Kerry registered four more points before half time. The break came with Kerry ahead, 0-6 to 1-1. Tom Gega O'Connor was responsible for all the Kingdom's scores, all of them coming from frees. The second half belonged to the Kingdom, Waterford's only score being a goal in the closing minutes. The final score was 2-15 to 2-1 in Kerry's favour.

The victory didn't answer too many questions about Kerry's prospects for the remainder of the season. The *Kerryman's* focus was instead on two particular areas of the pitch.

> Tom McElligott on trial as centre full was confronted with a big occasion. His weakness was roaming, leaving Dan O'Keeffe often unguarded. Our two midfield men, Eddie Dowling and Teddy O'Connor, good players as they are, do not play as a pair. In the early part of the year the general opinion was that we had backs galore and no forwards. Now, our problems are in defence and not attack.

Antrim, still in search of their first all-Ireland title, had come through Ulster. This was to be only the second semi-final meeting of Kerry and Antrim. In 1912 Antrim had defeated Kerry by 3-5 to 0-2, but its progression to this stage of the competition came as a shock. They had defeated a hotly favoured Cavan in their provincial decider.

Kerry reverted to Joe Keohane in an attempt to solve the full-back quandary that persisted in 1946. Johnny Foley, the future Kerry goalkeeper, remembers it as a smart move.

> Keohane was outstanding that year when he made his comeback against Antrim. Kerry had tried three full-backs up to the semi-final. Keohane was the best of the lot of them.

Keohane, coming in for Tom McElligott, was one of four Kerry changes for the semi-final with Antrim. Gus Cremin was to partner Eddie Dowling at midfield, and his inclusion made this his first appearance of the season. Cremin also recalls getting special dispensation from the county board for the semi-final.

> I played in the juniors in 1946, and they drafted me into the seniors for the all-Ireland semi-final against Antrim. Kerry went into training for that semi-final. I was the only member of that team that didn't go into training. I had a letter from D. J. Baily [of the County Board] saying to me take it easy for the rest of the week. You may be on [the team] Sunday.

The game against Antrim had to be won twice by Kerry. After they defeated them on the field of play the county's honour then had to be defended. The first half failed to separate Kerry and Antrim. Kerry had the only goal, described by the *Kerryman*.

> Bill Casey held an Antrim free and Jackie Lyne was left in possession. He made ground before passing cleverly to Bill Bruddy O'Donnell and a hard low punt beat Vernon all ends up for the opening goal inside two minutes.

Antrim had the next four scores, all points. Kerry managed to add only two points before half time. It was honours even at the break: Kerry 1-2, Antrim 0-5. The second half was a similar story. The teams swapped points before Kennedy and Kavanagh put Kerry in front, 1-5 to 0-6. When O'Donnell added to that, the Kingdom were three ahead after seventeen minutes. Bill Bruddy O'Donnell's free increased the gap to four. Then, as the *Kerryman* reported, both sides were reduced to fourteen men.

> Antrim were hand passing up the middle. Bill Casey pulled down an opponent. O'Neill ran in and hit Casey. Other players then joined in but their comrades quickly pulled them apart. Casey and O'Neill were sent to the sideline.

Antrim managed to reduce the deficit to a minimum. Kerry responded to finally see off their Northern opponents. The *Kerryman* described how

> Burke got possession and bullocked his way goalwards; the Northern backs packed the goal, but Dan Kavanagh and Batt Garvey came up in support. Kerry cheers burst forth as Garvey punched past Vernon into the net in a goalmouth tussle.

Kerry won by three points, 2-7 to 0-10. Antrim then objected to Kerry's display, displeased at what they saw as the Kingdom's excessively robust tactics. *Years of Glory* records that

> after more than two hours of debate the objection was defeated by 19 votes to 10. Bill Casey and Harry O'Neill were each suspended for two months.

Roscommon, victors over Kerry at the final stage two years previously, once again stood in the way of Kerry and their sixteenth all-Ireland title. Roscommon had reached the decider in a 3-5 to 2-6 victory over Laois.

Sometimes even Kerry football has to play second fiddle. This was so in 1946, when Kerry v. Roscommon was fixed to take place on 22 September, but the decider was put back to 6 October so that the harvest could be gathered. This unexpected turn of events led to Bill Casey, suspended following the semi-final, being available in fact for the decider. Tom Gega O'Connor was back in the Kerry team for the final. It was hoped that the inclusion of Dan Kavanagh alongside Gus Cremin at midfield would have the desired effect for the Kingdom.

The *Kerryman* described how interest in the game had led to many being unable to gain access to Croke Park.

Half an hour before the match was due to commence the gates were closed. Thousands were locked out. Loudspeakers enabled these to follow the broadcast.

Few all-Irelands have produced such dramatic conclusions as the 1946 final. Roscommon were once more set to inflict defeat on Kerry in the decider; even at half time it looked like curtains for the Kingdom. Kerry registered a solitary point in the first half to Roscommon's 1-5. The Kingdom did better in the early stages of the second, but the game still appeared to be beyond them. At the three-quarter stage Kerry trailed by five points, 1-6 to 0-4. Roscommon then made it a six-point game. That advantage looked like an unassailable one. The game seemed beyond Kerry.

But in sport, as in life, a moment is all it takes to change everything. The Kerryman explained how,

> following a hop, Kerry charged down on the Roscommon posts in a desperate onslaught. Paddy Kennedy headed the rush and passed to Paddy Burke close in. Burke was tackled at once but he swerved past him and sent a low punt past Dolan into the net. For the first time in the hour the game turned in Kerry's favour. A sideline kick by Teddy O'Connor about 30 yards from the Roscommon goal was short tipped to Tom Gega O'Connor. The latter eluded a tackle and steadied himself. His diagonal ball went just above the heads of a cluster of players in the Roscommon square and passed under the bar, leaving the scores level with a few minutes to go.

Following a most unlikely conclusion, Kerry had snatched the draw, 2-4 to Roscommon's 1-7.

Canon Jackie McKenna had drama of his own that afternoon.

> Our radio broke down, which was not an uncommon thing in those days. It cut out altogether. What were we to do but go into one of the neighbours' houses. Before we went down Kerry got one of those goals and our reaction was of course, it wasn't so bad now, it was only three points they were been beaten by. They wouldn't be disgraced altogether. So we hit off down the stairs to go into one of the neighbours' houses. While we were going down the stairs we

heard a big cheer coming from the house next door. We got into the second house then and it was that Kerry had scored the second goal.

Tom Long, the future Kerry player, also recalls the draw against Roscommon.

> The radio was our only link with the Kerry team at the time. Transport was only for adults—the little bit of transport that existed. The 1946 drawn match would appear to be my first memory, and I think it was because the atmosphere was like that in a morgue. Entering the final stages, Kerry were down by six points. Suddenly there was a goal. Before the applause had died down the second goal was scored.

Leading up to the replay, the *Kerryman* wrote of a clear-air training camp, adding that from the moment the players came under the wing of Dr Éamonn O'Sullivan, rules and regulations were adhered to with ritualistic attentiveness.

These days, inter-county players are wrapped up in cotton wool before big games. However, a most unfortunate incident before the 1946 replay shows that injury can just as easily be sustained on the training pitch. The *Kerryman* correspondent was among those watching.

> Trial games were held on Sunday and Monday. The weather on the first day was just vile, but on Monday the selectors witnessed a good test, which left quite a few headaches. One of these was an injury to Eddie Dowling who had a bone broken in his right leg in Monday's trial. Eddie was showing up well in practice and was freely being tipped for a place on the team.

Dowling had been one of those dropped for the drawn game, a most unfortunate end to his season. Gus Cremin and Bill Bruddy O'Donnell would also experience heartbreak over the all-Ireland final. Dr Éamonn O'Sullivan was in charge of the team for the replay, and both Cremin and O'Donnell were omitted. Cremin had skippered Kerry in the drawn encounter, and he feels he was shafted when it came to the side being selected for the replay.

I was captain for that game. For the replay I was dropped. I blame Dr Éamonn O'Sullivan for it. He wanted Paddy Kennedy captain of the team.

The replay took a much different path from the drawn encounter, and the Kerry performance was vastly improved. The teams were level after twenty minutes. Two late points gave Roscommon a lead at the interval of six points to four.

Kerry were the dominant force in the second period. They were on terms by the eighth minute. Roscommon went two in front once again; then an injury to Jack Falvey necessitated a change for Kerry. Gus Cremin it was who replaced him, eventually, with a little help from one of the selectors.

Joe Barrett RIP couldn't understand how I was off the team. He was shoving me on, at least six times, before I went on. Dr Éamonn didn't want me on the team.

Trailing eight points to six when Cremin came on, Kerry turned things around. The *Kerryman* reported that

Batt Garvey sprinted along the wing and passed to Tom Gega O'Connor. He short passed to Paddy Burke. Burke rounded Casserley and crashed past Dolan to the net.

Kerry now led, 1-6 to 0-8, after seventeen minutes. Roscommon drew level, with nine minutes remaining. Batt Garvey restored Kerry's slender advantage, but again Roscommon equalised. Five minutes to go now. The game-turning score was soon to arrive. Gus Cremin, the scorer, remembers it well.

A free outside in the middle of the field, and I dropped it in between the fourteen and twenty-one. And Carlos went up for it and brought it down and kicked it out the field. I got the return. I could see Gega O'Connor waving at me to kick it to him. I could see the goals opening out. I went for my point and scored it.

Canon Jackie McKenna also has clear and fond memories of Cremin's point.

> He got a wonderful point from the middle of the field. I can see him yet in my mind, steadying himself in the middle of the field and kicking it into the railway goal. It travelled the whole way over the bar. It was the turning-point in the match. It spurred on the rest of the team.

Cremin's point was all that separated the teams entering the closing seconds. The *Kerryman* describes how there was time for one final drama.

> Lost time was being played as Kerry drove home their advantage. Tom Gega O'Connor sent the ball just under the bar. Dolan, the Roscommon goalman sprang high and clutched the leather firmly. Even as he did the Kerry forwards rushed him and sent ball and goalman to the back of the net. There was a brief consultation between umpires and referee, and when the green flag was hoisted there was a wild Kerry roar.

That goal sealed the victory, 2-8 to 0-10. The *Kerryman* argued that Bill Casey's was the match-winning performance.

The Kerry mascot that day was the son of the Kerry goalkeeper, Dan O'Keeffe—how appropriate, given that O'Keeffe Senior was winning an unprecedented seventh all-Ireland medal. Winning his first that afternoon was Frank O'Keeffe, whose son Johnno would bring many more medals to the family in the 1970s and 80s. That 1946 victory once more pushed Kerry out in front in all-Ireland championship victories, sixteen to Dublin's fifteen.

Two men feeling aggrieved after the success, however, were Gus Cremin and Mick Finucane. Following his omission from the starting fifteen, which robbed him of the captaincy, Cremin skipped the homecoming.

> I came home on my own. I was disappointed in losing the captaincy. My sister died that year. I was in no form for celebrations.

Finucane felt he was done out of a medal in the wake of the victory.

> I could only take part in a couple of them trial matches. Eddie
> Dowling broke his leg in one of those trials. Eddie was above sitting
> in the sidelines with his leg in a cast. He wasn't able to walk, only
> with crutches. Eddie deserved a medal, because he had played with
> them all along. I think I deserved it too, because I was in the panel
> too. The man that got the medal there, who shall remain nameless,
> wasn't on the programme. I received a letter to tell me that I had lost
> an all-Ireland medal in the toss of a penny with this player. I wrote
> back saying I was very disappointed. I lost a medal at a gamble
> where I wasn't present. That hurt some people at headquarters
> because they never invited me after to any of the functions that
> Kerry had for a while.

Following the success of 1946, Kerry were to spend the next six seasons
in all-Ireland wilderness. The closest they came to winning the Sam
Maguire was a defeat to Cavan in the famous 1947 Polo Grounds final
in New York. Kerry lost all-Ireland semi-finals in 1948, 1950 and 1951,
while they failed to progress from Munster in 1949 and 1952. It was felt
that the team had something of a soft centre, that they were lacking a
cutting edge. Changes were necessary. Changes were made.

Luke Keane, a long-time Kerry supporter, was a schoolboy as the
beginning of the 1953 season approached.

> In January 1953 a fellow-pupil of ours brought a cutting from the
> previous day's *Independent* . . . a cutting which declared that Ned
> Roche, John Cronin and Tom Moriarty were declaring for Kerry. We
> were after a barren spell of years from 1946 to 1953—no all-Irelands.
> That was music to our ears.

Roche and Cronin would both take to the field in 1953. Not so Moriarty,
who was banned at the time. (Members of the GAA were not permitted
to participate in certain other sports, including soccer and rugby. If
caught, players were suspended.)

1953 began with a provincial semi-final against Clare. Given Kerry's
failure to come out of Munster the previous year, nothing was being
taken for granted. Jackie Lyne was the sole member of the 1946 all-

Ireland winning side to do duty against Clare.

Clare were swept aside with little effort on a scoreline of 6-10 to 0-2. Little sympathy was forthcoming from the *Kerryman*.

> Somebody asked me who scored all the Kerry goals and I replied the Clare goalman. The answer may be unjust as it is uncharitable but it seemed to me when he let a few soft shots beat him the Clare team gave up the ghost.

The fact that the *Kerryman* offered less than usual for a match report told it all.

So Kerry, helped by a Paudie Sheehy hat trick, were through to the Munster final against Cork a fortnight later. The previous season, Cork brushed Kerry aside, eleven points to two. A four-point victory for Kerry was the outcome against Cork this time. The result was never in doubt: a whirlwind start by the Kingdom, described in the *Kerryman*.

> Brendan O'Shea parted to Jackie Lyne, who drove high above the bar after five minutes. Kerry returned the kickout and Seán Kelly was fouled at an angle about 25 yards range. Tadhgie Lyne sent a beauty between the uprights from the resulting free. Clever work by Jackie Lyne left his namesake in possession to raise another white flag. Jim Brosnan sent back the goal kick. He gave to Seán Kelly who was fouled going in and Tadhgie Lyne pointed from the free, 4-0. Paudie Sheehy raised the white flag from a free. Sheehy was fouled in the next minute. He drove the kick into the goalmouth and there was exultant Kerry cheering when Seán Kelly punched past Roche into the net.

Just before the break Cork grabbed their sole score of the period: a goal. Kerry were five points to the good, 1-5 to 1-0. The Kingdom kept up the pressure when the game resumed, going six points clear after ten minutes. Cork brought the gap down to four.

Tom Ashe had a surreal few minutes, as the *Kerryman* recounted.

> Seán Murphy kicked to the corner, where Gerald O'Sullivan secured. He crossed into the square and sub Tom Ashe dashed in to punch into the net. Then, Tom Ashe and a Corkman got into handgrips. The Kerryman was ordered off but he was not the aggressor.

A late Cork goal only served to give the scoreline an air of respectability. The gap at the end may have been only four points, but Kerry were more convincing than the score of 2-7 to 2-3 conveyed.

That win over Cork meant that Kerry were back in Croke Park, and Louth awaited. The Kingdom had the chance to avenge a semi-final defeat against the same opposition three years previously.

Kerry were forced into changes for the semi-final. Jerome O'Shea was absent through illness. Micksie Palmer was out injured. The injury was a most unusual one.

> I had a pitchfork stuck in the back of my leg, and I got tetanus. I spent a few weeks in hospital. I came on, but I wasn't fit.

These changes weren't the only ones made by Kerry. In a surprising move, Johnny Foley replaced the goalkeeper, Dónal Marcus O'Neill. O'Neill was bemused by his being dropped for the semi-final.

> We were training in Killarney for the semi-final. There was another goalkeeper brought in. We were playing backs and forwards, and I was told to leave my position for the time being. Johnny Foley got the goals. I didn't travel to the final. Why should I be dropped? I did nothing wrong. I played in the Munster games.

Three first-half goals laid the foundations for the Kingdom's eventual victory. This trio of strikes was described by the *Kerryman*.

> John Cronin, a commanding figure, put his side attacking and Tom Ashe grabbed a high one, rounded Tuft and a pile driver shook the next after six minutes. John Cronin's long kick was snapped up by Tadhgie Lyne. He sent a grounder across the posts and Tom Ashe dashed in to crash to the net for Kerry's second goal. Kerry pressed to the attack, they had a free in a nice position. Seán Kelly got this and Kerry cheers rang out when the green flag went up once more.

It was double-scores in favour of Kerry at half time, 3-1 to 0-5.

The second half saw the sides share ten points. Louth brought the gap down to two. Points by Paudie Sheehy and Seán Kelly put Kerry ahead by 3-4 to 0-9. The Kingdom held on, and it was into the all-

Ireland final. Louth had been defeated, 3-6 to 0-10, following a game that was thrilling, according to the *Kerryman*.

> There were fierce clashes, stoppages for injuries and replacements. The suspense of the closing stages when Louth strove gallantly to pull the match out of the fire will long be remembered. The main difference between the teams was that Kerry were able to score goals. Louth had what is generally described as the better of the exchanges. Heroes of Kerry's victory were their backs. Star of the line was Jas Murphy whose display was reminiscent of his Cahersiveen namesake in the memorable drawn game with Kildare back in 1926.

Seán Murphy is in agreement with that assessment of his namesake and team-mate.

> Jas always played well, and that day in particular he shone. I would think he was instrumental in winning that game. He was marvellous.

Jas himself admits that that display against Louth was his finest ever.

> The best game I ever had in my life with Kerry was playing against Louth in 1953 in the semi-final. I got Man of the Match that day, I played so well . . . Everywhere I went the ball was around me. I was that lucky—one of those days. Every fellow has one good day. I thought myself I played great . . . I cleared every ball up the field, and Ashe was there above.

Armagh were now all that could stop Kerry from bringing Sam Maguire back to the Kingdom for the first time in seven seasons. Armagh had seen off Roscommon in their semi-final, by eight points to seven.

Éamonn O'Sullivan would be seeking a fifth all-Ireland victory as Kerry trainer. Tom Ashe, the Kingdom's corner-forward, recalls the routine of the man whose first title had arrived twenty-nine years earlier.

> When we were training that time, for a semi-final you would only train a week, and a fortnight for a final. The food we used get wasn't

all that good. You wouldn't see a steak only now and again, even though it was cheap. Dr Éamonn knew all about nutrition. You got plenty to eat, but it was all vegetables, tomatoes, ham. After your lunch every day everyone had to go to bed for an hour and a half or two hours. Lie down in the bed: that was the rule. Dr Éamonn set that rule. You had to do what you were told. You couldn't go out. We used stay in the Park Hotel in Killarney.

You didn't really have to go to bed: you could play cards. You could do anything, but you couldn't go out.

Dr Éamonn had his own idea of training. He instilled into you what it meant to play for Kerry. You went out then with that feeling. Not alone had you to do justice to yourself, you had to do justice to the crowd and the people in general of Kerry. When you went out you had to honour his trust in you.

Paddy Foley was keeping an eye on proceedings as the big day approached. He reported to the *Kerryman* from a trial match before the final that

> it was pleasing to see Micksie Palmer and Jerome O'Shea back in harness again. Hannafin was impressive but the one to catch the eye was Dowling, O'Rahillys. I have not seen him play for over a year and he has come on terms in the interim.

John Dowling's time hadn't yet come, but it wasn't too far away. John Joe Sheehy, father of the Kerry forward Paudie, was a selector in 1953. Paudie had captained the side throughout the season and was expected to continue in that role for the final. However, Sheehy's below-par display in Kerry's semi-final defeat of Louth was to cost him dearly, as Johnny Foley, the Kerry goalkeeper of 1953, remembers.

> Stephen White was on that Louth team. He was a great footballer. He happened to beat Paudie Sheehy, and Paudie lost his place over his display.

What exactly happened when John Joe Sheehy and the other four selectors sat down to pick the team for the 1953 all-Ireland has never been fully disclosed. T. J. Flynn, who jointly wrote *Princes of Pigskin*, puts forward one version of events.

> The most widely accepted story is that when it came to choosing the six forwards, John Joe excused himself from the meeting. He told the other selectors that they knew what to do in relation to Paudie. The other four selectors interpreted that as John Joe stating that Paudie maybe wasn't worth his place on the team for this particular game. When the team was named, Paudie wasn't on it. His captaincy was lost and his place on the team was lost. The great opportunity to have a father-son combination win an all-Ireland final was lost. Paudie of course had been very disappointed by this . . . What it goes to show is that John Joe Sheehy was extremely loyal to Kerry football and as a result of that the players who would have really respected him to start off with would have respected him even more.

John Joe had the power to ensure that Paudie was on the team but hadn't used it. Paudie's disappointment was intense, and it's reported that at the banquet after the final he was apparently in tears. This, however, was not to be the last of Paudie Sheehy.

His omission for the final meant that a new captain had to be appointed for the decider. The person chosen, Jas Murphy, discovered in very strange circumstances how he had received the accolade.

> We were over in Killarney training for the all-Ireland final, and we were walking down the town of Killarney. Some one of the lads came up to me and said, You're captain for the next day. It was a big ordeal to be captain of an all-Ireland team! I felt for Paudie Sheehy, because we were close to each other. We were from the same town and everything. There were a lot of fellows there dying to be captain. I didn't go forward at all. I was very lucky to be captain. That was a great joy.

In scenes reminiscent of Joe Barrett handing the captaincy to Con Brosnan in 1931, Murphy's promotion to leader of the team was groundbreaking. According to T. Ryle Dwyer,

> John Mitchels had no other player on the team, so they had to invite somebody else to be captain. They invited Jas Murphy. He was from

Kerins O'Rahilly. Jas Murphy would seem to have a lot of strikes against him in John Joe's eyes, in that he was a garda. He was based in Cork, and the son of an RIC man—not only an ordinary RIC man, but James Murphy, the father, was one of the two men who brought Roger Casement in from Ardfert on Good Friday, 1916. If I knew that, I know John Joe Sheehy had to know it. It was part of this 'hands across the division,' so to speak.

The *Kerryman* described the Kingdom's training regime for the two weeks leading up to the 1953 decider.

> 7.30 a.m.—Rise
> 8 a.m.—Mass
> After Mass, a walk until 9.30, when breakfast is served.
> At 11 o'clock the whole lot assemble in the Fitzgerald Stadium, where they will take part in sprinting, running and football tactics under the eyes of both Paul Russell and Dr. O'Sullivan.
> At 1.30 they return for lunch, after which there is relaxation in their rooms until 4 o'clock, when they return to the Stadium for more exercise and massage.
> Tea is at 6 p.m., after which they go for a walk, return for supper and then to bed at 10.30 p.m.

Tom Ashe had his homework done on the opposition for the final, Armagh, not that it helped him.

> I was on John McKnight. Dr Jim [Brosnan] and Paudie Sheehy, they were playing for the Sigerson Cup that time. I asked them what this John McKnight was like, because he used be playing for the Sigerson Cup. They told me, No problem to you at all. They forgot to tell me he was a hundred-yards champion runner for Ulster. The first ball that came, he would have gone before I would have thought about it. I knuckled him down a bit. To give Armagh their due, they were the nicest team I ever played against. They were the fairest. It cost them an all-Ireland to be so fair. There was no spoiling tactic.

Kerry went into a lead of two points to one, before the game took a sensational turn, and one that was fortunate also in the eyes of Donie

Murphy, Kerry's corner-back.

> They got what I consider a lucky goal. It's just one of those things.
> Our full-back and their full-forward went out for a ball, and the ball
> looked as if it was coming over their heads and they wouldn't get it.
> Our goalie moved out to get the ball into his chest. Our full-back
> was Ned Roche at the time, and his hands were a bit longer than the
> goalie thought. He gave that little tip to the ball, which drove it over
> the goalie's head and sent it into the net.

Two Tadhgie Lyne scores drew Kerry level, 0-4 to 1-1. Armagh had the
next two points, before Jim Brosnan sent over for the Kingdom. That
was how the half ended, 1-3 to 0-5 in favour of Armagh. Jim Brosnan put
over the equaliser two minutes into the second period. Again, Armagh
pulled away and went two points in front, 1-5 to 0-6.

Tadhgie Lyne halved the deficit, before Jim Brosnan once more had
the teams level after fourteen minutes. Lyne pointed Kerry in front from
a free, and John Joe Sheehan doubled the advantage. Kerry's lead stood
at 0-10 to 1-5. The Kingdom men seemed to be well on their way to the
title, but they were suddenly stopped in their tracks. Armagh were
awarded a penalty. Johnny Foley, Kerry's keeper, now had to concentrate
on this potentially game-turning spot kick.

> I didn't have time to think about anything but I just saw the way the
> Kerry fellows outside were standing. I remember Colm Kennelly RIP
> crossed Billy McCorry when he was taking the penalty kick and
> jumped across him. McCorry took a longer run, as far as I
> remember. It went harmlessly wide. You'd never dive for a penalty,
> because nine times out of ten they'd kick it straight at you. I can't
> believe fellows today diving for penalty kicks and they going in the
> other side. I don't believe in that at all. You dive when he kicks it.
> You'd stand on your line. You might even stand behind the line a bit
> and dive forward. A lot of the goalkeepers now are influenced by
> soccer players.

Micksie Palmer's role in that penalty miss was pivotal.

> Actually I touched the ball. At that time you could run with the fellow

taking the penalty. I was on this side, Jas Murphy was on the other side. As he was kicking the ball I had my finger on it, and we shouting at him, the two of us . . . You couldn't shoulder him or anything. At least you could put him off if you could. Just as well it went wide, they were going well at the time.

At the mention of the all-Ireland penalty miss of 1953 it's not Johnny Foley or Bill McCorry who come to mind. No, it's the famous horseshoe and its legendary role that day. Johnny Foley may have been making his first all-Ireland appearance—but not so the horseshoe he was given!

It was sent up to me one night, wrapped in green and gold paper, to wish me good luck. I took it. The same horseshoe was taken by O'Keeffe in the 1946 final. I hung it up in the back of the net. It brought me luck all right. I think the horseshoe is below in O'Keeffe's now.

The missed penalty happened six minutes from time. Two further scores, points by Sheehan and Lyne, doubled Kerry's lead. Kerry were now ahead by 0-12 to 1-5. With the Kingdom four to the good and with time almost up, the game was well and truly beyond Armagh. John Joe Sheehan put over point number thirteen for the Kingdom, who won by four, with Armagh tallying 1-6. The *Kerryman* claimed that

the game will surely rank among the greatest finals ever. Kerry's half forwards were the chief architects of the victory. Tadhg Lyne returned to form, and his deft touches between the posts from all angles were a delight to watch. Sheehan was a pronounced success on the 40 and his mastery of O'Neill had a big influence on the result.

Johnny Foley attributes the triumph to the Kingdom winning in all positions on the field. 'Kerry won in all positions, 55 to 45. Tadhgie Lyne was outstanding, got immaculate points.' Lyne may have been outstanding, but Joe Ó Muircheartaigh explains that he suffered from his nerves before the big game.

Before the final he went up to Dr Éamonn O'Sullivan, looking for a sleeping tablet. There was Dr Éamonn, and he had some pills on the table. He cut them up and gave them to Tadhgie Lyne and said, There you go. But it turned out they were aspirin, and it was all psychological from Dr Éamonn. The following day Tadhg was still suffering from nerves and he couldn't get into the game. He went over to the sideline and asked Dr Éamonn to take him off. Dr Éamonn said, No, go out to your position, it's going to happen. Dr Éamonn then shouted instructions out to Seán Murphy: he said, Next ball, in to Tadhgie Lyne. A few minutes later Seán got the ball and gave it to Tadhgie. Lyne kicked it over the bar, and he was away.

Kerry's cause against Armagh was aided by the introduction of Paul Russell to the coaching set-up, with Dr Éamonn drafting in a player he trained to win all-Irelands three decades previously. The official attendance for the final between Kerry and Armagh was a little over 85,000. However, approximately 92,000 people are believed to have witnessed the game. The *Irish Times* estimated that 7,000 people got in without paying.

> Shortly after the finish of the Minor Final, over half an hour before the Senior game, two large exit gates were opened by the crowd. The locks were broken by the pressure of several thousands, and some people withdrew the bolts. Another breach was made at the canal end entrance where the crowds burst open a large metal gate . . . Even with the unprecedented crowds inside Croke Park thousands of people who had tried to see the game were unable to get in.

Micksie Palmer used his ball-handling skills to good effect in that win over Armagh. He took a huge risk in doing the same thing in a soccer match three weeks before the all-Ireland, playing in goal, and in so doing endangered his Kerry prospects. T. J. Flynn explains:

> Micksie Palmer maintains that maybe in some ways Kerry should never have been allowed collect the cup. He tells it, of course, with tongue in cheek. Micksie would have been a great character and one of the characters that helped endear Kerry football to the Kerry public. In 1953 he would have played in an innocuous enough soccer

game in Dublin, the Dublin Soccer Hospitals Cup Final. It was played in Dalymount Park.

The one thing that might have exposed him was a photograph from the soccer game, including Micksie, published in the following day's *Irish Times.*

Micksie said he wasn't too worried, because back then supporters of Gaelic football would never have bought the *Irish Times.* He was a little bit worried for a couple of days. Micksie, being Micksie, forgot about it soon enough. He went out and played a fantastic all-Ireland final, and helped Kerry overcome Armagh in that final.

A number of players failed to board the homecoming train, including Jas Murphy.

I'll tell you about the homecoming. You adjourned into a pub in the evening after the match. We went to a pub, a crowd of us. Didn't we miss the train that was coming down! The cup and all was gone down. I was left behind. We had Paddy Bawn with us, Micksie Palmer, and a few like that. Lucky enough we got a very fast train down after the original one. They had just arrived a short time before us. We got off in Killarney. I was delighted, because I was anxious that Jackie Lyne would hold the cup going into his home town.

Micksie Palmer says:

We were treated like kings, because Kerry hadn't won an all-Ireland in about seven years. We were put on the back of a truck in Killarney and Tralee, and crowds gathered.

Seán Murphy was also taken aback by the homecoming.

I would call it overwhelming, from the moment we got on that train in Dublin. All along the line you could see the presence of Kerry people—in Port Laoise, Limerick Junction, until you came to Banteer, I think. From then on the crowds that were assembled at the railway stations were so great the train stopped. Dr Éamonn

O'Sullivan got out at every platform between Banteer and Tralee. He said a few words to the congregation, generally chose some one of the players to thank them, back on the train. Same thing in Killarney and Tralee, except the crowds were getting bigger and bigger as we got closer to home. It meant your efforts were appreciated. It meant you had an input to a Kerry legend. You were part of the Kerry football story.

The homecoming celebrations were cut short, however, as Johnny Foley recalls.

The best part of it was when we got to Jas Murphy's mother's pub. It was 2 a.m. We thought we were going to have a good old couple of drinks together. She let us in and gave us all a drink; and gave us a second drink; and she said, That's the lot, now, because I'll want my stock for the morning for the fellows that will be in going to work!

The late Donie Murphy was not a fan of the elaborate homecomings that have taken place over the years, and he did his own thing in 1953.

In every county they take the cup to every school and nook and cranny in the county now, which is a bit ridiculous in a way. At that time you just had the one night. You got off the train in Killarney, you went up to the Park Place Hotel, then you went on to Tralee. I remember that. It was an aspect of the game I wasn't really interested in.

We arrived in Killarney on the train anyway. There was a great rush to get off. I wasn't in any rush to get off. By the time I got off the train I think the team had left for the parade through the town. I met a friend of mine and we walked home. The way it happened for me it worked out grand. I had no problem with it, and I was quite satisfied that was the way to celebrate.

| KERRY 3 DUBLIN 0

Kerry went into the 1955 season aiming to reach a third consecutive all-Ireland final but, more importantly, to atone for their defeat to Meath in the previous year's decider. There had been collective training when Kerry won in 1953, but it was banned for 1954.

Donie Murphy was a member of the losing Kerry side of 1954, and he's in no doubt that that year was one that got away.

> I was working down in Newcastle West, Limerick, at that stage. I went up to the Gaelic field a few times—to an empty field, and I going up to play in an all-Ireland final, with no training! There'd be some people better off than me, maybe a few of them together, and things like that. Hopefully none of my Meath friends will hear this! That was a Meath team long past their best. At least I lasted for the two-and-a-half years of the three years that should have been a three-in-a-row.

Gary O'Mahony was also on the side that lost to Meath in 1954. He recalls training at the local dog track in Tralee, and the abolition of collective training.

> We didn't know each other, because some of us trained in Tralee, some in Killarney. We actually trained above in the dog track, with the great Rory O'Connell up there. He was giving the boys a rub-down. We were just running around the track—like greyhounds, I suppose! It was a pity really. There wasn't much atmosphere in the dressing-rooms before the game.

Waterford were the barrier to a Munster final appearance in 1955. Kerry were able to call on ten of the side that had lost to Meath in 1954: Gary O'Mahony, Ned Roche, Donie Murphy, Colm Kennelly, John Cronin, John Dowling, Tom Moriarty, Paudie Sheehy, Bobby Buckley and Tadhgie Lyne. Five of those—Roche, Murphy, Kennelly, Cronin and Lyne—were seeking a second all-Ireland medal in three years.

Kerry met with little resistance when they faced Waterford—in the second half, anyway. Kerry's half-time advantage was two points: five to three. At that stage there was little indication of the one-sided second half that lay in store. Tom Costello goaled three minutes into the second period, and Bobby Buckley did likewise in the twelfth minute. The competitive edge had now gone from the contest, the teams merely going through the formalities after that. Almost on full time, Tom Costello goaled again. Waterford were despatched, 3-7 to 0-4.

Cork lay in the long grass for the Munster final. The *Kerryman* reporter was concerned about the Kingdom's chances.

To a Corkman a Munster title is something important, something big. Kerry lack this Munster urge. Then there is the physical aspect. Cork are thoroughly prepared and coached by Éamonn Young who knows all that can be known about the code and can size up Kerry's strong and weak points to a fraction. Our men are not facing up seriously to Sunday's task. The players are too widely scattered to bring them together in the evenings for training, unlike Cork. The Kerry selectors have been in a quandary as to whether men who failed to turn up to two trial games should be picked, or whether they are to be judged on past form compared with last year. Kerry will be represented by a weaker team and will be minus Jackie Lyne and Jim Brosnan, just the type of forwards to tackle the robust Cork backs.

Lyne had by now retired, while Brosnan was in America, concentrating on his studies.

Kerry v. Cork proved to be a classic, the *Kerryman* correspondent declaring it 'the best football match I have seen in the south in years.' Kerry had slightly the better of the exchanges in the first half. After they pointed, Cork goaled. Kerry were level by the tenth minute, 0-3 to 1-0. The Kingdom then led 0-6 to 1-1. The teams swapped ends, with Kerry ahead, 0-8 to 1-2.

There was an early turnaround on the scoreboard when the game resumed. Cork grabbed their second goal of the day, then pointed to go in front. Paudie Sheehy levelled proceedings after nine minutes. Two Tadhgie Lyne points edged Kerry ahead. Late in the match, when Paudie Sheehy put over, Kerry were three to the good. The Kingdom then had a lucky escape, with Cork hitting the post. Kerry were through to the all-Ireland semi-final, thanks to a win of 0-14 to 2-6 over Cork.

The *Kerryman* felt that the accuracy of Paudie Sheehy and Tadhgie Lyne was vital to the result.

> Main difference between the sides was Sheehy's play for Kerry. He gave a scintillating exhibition and raised five flags from all angles. Sheehy rose to great heights and he, along with Tadhg Lyne, were mainly responsible for victory. Because Cork had not a forward of the calibre of either they lost.

Seán Murphy feels that beating Cork can always be the launching-pad for success.

> When you mention Cork, I've always maintained, right back to the first day I played for Kerry, if you beat Cork you can win an all-Ireland. They were a team that taxed you. They were always top-class footballers. When you come to think of Neily Duggan, Con McGrath and Niall Fitzgerald—just to mention a few of them—they were top-rate footballers. They played Kerry football. Whether they were well managed is something I always queried.

Cavan were to be Kerry's opponents in the all-Ireland semi-final. Paddy Foley, writing in the *Kerryman*, had doubts about the Kingdom side and their build-up to the match.

> Following the Munster Final I heard all kinds of criticism of the Kerry team—some held our men were lucky to win and that on the form shown against Cork would go no further. Others thought the players had possibilities if properly trained. Each man of our front six was an individualist; each went for his own ball and kicked it; there was no understanding between them. One thing stood out in the match and that was that our attackers and defenders need match

practice in company. The players are not to be faulted for this. Our men are too often moved about, there are so many vital changes in different matches that the team had no opportunity of settling down. Without exception all the provincial finalists in hurling and football had collective training, except Kerry.

The *Kerryman* was happy to report that the Kingdom had found a way of bending, not breaking, the rule.

A method of training the Kerry team without infringing the rule operating against what is known as collective training has been devised by the selection committee and endorsed at a meeting of the County Board. The meeting had agreed that cars would leave North Kerry, Tralee and Cahersiveen, each collecting players and bringing them to Killarney for a series of exercises.

Ned Roche, the full-back, returned against Cavan. Micksie Palmer moved to the corner, and Donie Murphy was omitted. Johnny Culloty at corner-forward was making his championship debut, replacing Gerald O'Sullivan.

Donie Murphy's absence was an enforced one. His season was over.

Between playing the Munster final [in July] and the all-Ireland semi-final in August I was in a sanatorium. In 1951 I'd got pleurisy, and there was a shadow left on my lung. I picked up the TB bug, it developed, and I was in a sanatorium for seventeen months. That was almost the end of my football career. I had two operations, lost some ribs and so on. What they used do, they'd take away a couple of ribs, and the top part of the lung would collapse: that part wouldn't be functional. I did play junior football, Leinster championship, with Kilkenny afterwards.

Fears about Cavan were well founded. The Kingdom started brightly. When Tadhgie Lyne pointed, the score was four points to two in Kerry's favour after ten minutes. Later in the half it stood at six points to four to Kerry. Not long before half time the Cavan defence was breached. Johnny Culloty was tackled in possession but managed to lay off the ball for Mick Murphy to send home.

Gary O'Mahony, the Kerry netminder, still remembers that goal.

> The one that Mick Murphy got, it was a blaster, you know. I
> remember seeing the dust rising in the goal.

That strike had Kerry four ahead at the break, 1-7 to 0-6. Cavan hit
back and were on level terms with only seven minutes gone in the
second half. It was hard to separate the sides for some time after this.
However, as noted by the *Kerryman*, Cavan had gained the upper hand
entering those closing minutes.

> Kerry, 2 points behind with a minute left, were fighting with their
> backs to the wall against a rampant Cavan side; fitter, faster, almost
> everywhere in control.

As the closing moments of the semi-final approached it appeared that
the Kingdom's bid for all-Ireland glory was coming to an end. Yet again,
however, Kerry pulled a rabbit from the hat. The *Kerryman* described
that great escape.

> John Cronin cleared near the Kerry upright. Seán Murphy got
> possession and a long low kick reached Johnny Culloty at an angle.
> He sent a dropping ball into the Cavan square. Morris, the goalman,
> with Brady, the full back, were under it. Tadhgie Lyne rushed in and
> outstretched hands of all men reached for the leather. Lyne's hands
> got there first and the ball was punched past Morris into the net.
> The silent Kerry crowd let out a mighty roar as the green flag went
> up with the kingdom in front.

Tadhgie Lyne admits to this goal being the most important score of his
inter-county career.

> The one against Cavan in '55, the punched goal, the one that Johnny
> sent in from the corner—that was the most vital score I ever got for
> Kerry.

An almost certain defeat had turned into a seemingly famous victory.
But there was more drama to come, as Cavan went straight up the field

and equalised. Result: Kerry 2-10, Cavan,1-13.

Kerry recorded a fourteen-point win in the replay—hard to imagine, given the nature of the drawn encounter. Johnny Culloty has revealed that Cavan themselves provided Kerry with all the motivation they needed for the replay.

> I always remember reading the headline in the paper before the replay. One of the Cavan fellows said there'd be no goals the next day. But Kerry got four goals. So you should never say anything like that.

Not one of those Kerry goals arrived in the first half. The score at half time was only four points to three in Kerry's favour. But two early goals in the second half, described by the *Kerryman*, decided the issue.

> After a minute's play Johnny Culloty got possession on the right wing. He dropped a high diagonal ball on to the corner of the Cavan net. John Joe Sheehan, who had changed to the corner, rushed in and punched it home. Five minutes later further disaster befell the Breffni men. Tadhgie Lyne went for a low ball across the Cavan posts and Johnny Culloty rushed in to punch past Morris.

Those goals made it 2-4 to 0-3, in Kerry's favour, after only eight minutes. Cavan were restricted to two points in the second thirty minutes. Kerry continued to threaten the Cavan net. They had a goal disallowed before John Joe Sheehan placed Mick Murphy for a goal. The game had now become a rout, and, though Donohue pointed a free, Kerry were back to goal by Mick Murphy. An amazing second-half display had guided Kerry to yet another all-Ireland final. Cavan had gone down, 4-7 to 0-5.

Johnny Culloty, a goal-scorer, was looking at the bigger picture.

> I can remember getting a hand to a cross. I think it was from Tadhgie Lyne . . . It went into the net—oh, great thrill really. The overall performance was the main thing anyway. After the first day we weren't very optimistic. We improved generally as a team . . . It was a good all-round performance. We were into an all-Ireland final against Dublin, and they were the crowd we wanted to beat.

Cavan's second-half collapse had everyone scratching their heads, including the *Kerryman* correspondent.

> Kerry held their own at midfield during the opening half and had complete mastery in the second. I have no hesitation in saying that John Cronin was Kerry's man of the match. Johnny Culloty again had a great game; he made the first goal, and scored the second. That Kerry showed a big improvement all round there is no room for doubt; but the question remains—what happened to Cavan? To this I can find no satisfactory answer. The second half collapse was amazing.

The same day, 11 September, and also at Croke Park, Dublin accounted for Mayo in what was also a semi-final replay, 1-8 to 1-7. Gary O'Mahony, the Kerry goalkeeper, feels that that Dublin display led to their being fancied for the final.

> They were red-hot favourites. I think they beat a great Mayo side in the semi-final. I think that's what made them favourites, because Mayo were highly fancied as well. They were a great side on that day as well. A very close game. Dublin just squeezed by them. It suited us, being the outsiders going in.

Kerry, it seems, would be travelling to Croke Park only to make up the numbers.

The Kerry half-back for that final was Seán Murphy. He says that facing this Dublin 'machine', as it was called, was a new experience for the Kingdom.

> There was a word introduced in the language of Gaelic football. It was called the Dublin 'machine'. Machine—it's a very impersonal thing. But that was the way Dublin played. They performed as a unit, very difficult to contain. They had a mixture of catch and kick and the new hand-passing, running off the ball, constant motion, which was something new for Kerry to come up against in an all-Ireland final. You had the traditional approach versus the new machine.

Micksie Palmer recalls that Dublin were full of confidence before the final.

> They were cocky. They thought it was only a matter of turning out. They got a surprise, no doubt. We played them in a Whit tournament in Killarney that year. For the first three-quarters of an hour we held them easily. The last quarter we weren't fit. They were obviously fit enough. They walked through us; they beat us by six or seven points. They thought we were the kiddies. All the papers were about Dublin. On radio, Mícheál O'Hehir or anybody interviewed—it was a case of 'by how much will they win?' It would get you worked up. If they think you're a dud, you're bound to react.

The *Kerryman* called on the green-and-gold brigade to stand firm against the expected onslaught.

> It can be expected that Dublin will start like a whirlwind with the object of sweeping the Kerrymen off their feet and setting up a winning score in the opening quarter. To deliver some knockout blows before Kerry have properly found their feet will be Dublin's trump card. If the Kerrymen can withstand their early shock the exchanges should run in their favour from that till the end. The match should be a dour struggle and should end with the Kerrymen proud winners.

Nonetheless, a Dublin victory was widely anticipated. However, the Kingdom would be strengthened by the return from America of the attacker Jim Brosnan.

> I was missing for all the games until the last one. I went to New York. I got the results, and my sister sent on the papers to me. I knew nothing until John Kerry O'Donnell handed me a ticket for home. I can remember flying in and joining the team in Killarney. I wasn't able to train. It was a little bit hard physically, all right.

Johnny Culloty was named as corner-forward for the final. According to him, Dr Éamonn O'Sullivan was focused purely on having Kerry ready for the decider.

He never concentrated on the opposition. He just prepared his team to play the best they could . . . He just concentrated on getting every fellow to play to the best of his ability in the place he was playing. He said, If every fellow did that there'd be no fear of us.

Seán Murphy has a different view from Johnny Culloty of the tactics for that 1955 final.

In my time playing with Kerry we had the same plan, as far as I could see. We never had any special tactics, apart from I can recall one—one tactical manoeuvre. That was playing against Dublin in 1955, when Dr Éamonn told Ned Roche what he thought he should do [to mark Dublin's best player, Kevin Heffernan]. I think Ned Roche carried out his instructions. History shows that it was a good tactic. In general there wasn't any tactics. Play your sector, play the ball. That was it.

The dietary routine for the match baffled Jerome O'Shea.

I never really understood this myself, but one of the things which, looking back on now, was unusual, part of the training scene was that you'd drink a raw egg and milk in the morning before your breakfast. Whoever came up with this I don't know.

Nowadays, Croke Park is all ticket for such occasions. Not so in 1955. One Kerry supporter, Jerry Savage, travelled from England for the final.

We queued on Sunday morning. No tickets. We queued at eleven o'clock Sunday morning to get into Croke Park. It was first come, first served. We met a lot of friends that we hadn't seen for years.

So, could Dublin live up to the hype when it came to throw-in time for the 1955 final? The resounding answer was no, as the Kingdom swept to victory, despite a late scare.

Kerry went in front in the opening seconds, through Tadhgie Lyne. They trailed two to one after a quarter of an hour. Lyne had two points in a row, then a fifty by John Dowling made it 4-2 to Kerry. Kerry were ahead by five points to three at half time.

Within three minutes of the second half Kerry had doubled their advantage. Two Jim Brosnan scores meant that the Kingdom now led, seven points to three. Dublin pulled the game back to eight points to six. Four Kerry points in a row gave the Kingdom what seemed to be an unassailable lead, and the game was now Kerry's to lose. They were six points to the good four minutes from time. A nervy finish ensued, when Dublin, somewhat fortuitously, goaled.

Gary O'Mahony admits that the ball should never have reached the net.

> They got a fourteen-yard free . . . Maybe it was nerves or something like that, but it went along the left-hand side. I was on the right-hand side. It just happened. There was fierce pressure on . . . A high ball came across from the Hill side. Jerome O'Shea got it. Anything could have happened that day, if he didn't catch it and keep it, if he broke it down, because Dublin were all over us . . . The first one to come out to congratulate me was my own brother. I didn't know until during the week when he told me.

Jerome O'Shea, who famously broke up that Dublin attack, regards those closing minutes as legendary.

> Kerry's backs were to the wall in the last five minutes of the game, defending furiously against Dublin. That you'd remember, because every single kick in that particular time counted. It stands out not just in my mind but in other people's and in journalists' at the time as being one of the great periods, that five minutes of an all-Ireland. It would be said that the traditional game of catch and kick would have been under threat. In other words, the tradition of Kerry was under threat, which was probably what helped Kerry to win this.

Kerry did hold on and won by 0-12 to 1-6. The Dublin machine was defeated, and another all-Ireland was in the bag for Kerry. The *Kerryman* was rejoicing.

> It was a thrilling encounter, fought at a fast and furious pace from start to finish. The brutal fact of the matter is that Dublin were very much over rated. Foundation of Dublin's defeat was the beating of

their front row forwards by O'Shea, Roche and Palmer. It was a cause of much surprise in city football circles that Kerry did not make defensive changes with a view to countering the Heffernan menace. One point from an hour's play is a poor return from the most talked of footballer of our generation. Ned Roche saw to that and hats off to the man from Knocknagoshel. Seán Murphy played his best game of the year, catching cleanly and kicking at great length. At midfield Kerry held sway. John Dowling was in sparkling form and little behind him was Denny Shea. The most polished footballer on the field was Tadhg Lyne.

Seán Murphy agrees with that assessment of his team-mate.

Tadhgie had a great day. I can still see him collecting the ball in full flight. He was fast, long strides, then just turning a whole semi-circle facing the goal, and that ball left his boot, unerringly right between the post.

Six Tadhgie Lyne points had led Kerry to victory. Jerry Brosnan lists Lyne's display as one of the best he's witnessed. Jerry was also relieved that his brother performed admirably.

After the first ten minutes he fielded balls. That was the best all-Ireland I ever saw, because Jim was involved after coming home. We were afraid that Jim would let them down that day. He scored two points right after half time. We won that, and we weren't expected to win that at all.

Luke Keane, a Kerry supporter, includes the victory against Dublin among his favourites.

That was possibly Kerry's greatest ever win. Dublin were unbeatable in every paper—the Dublin machine. Ned Roche had a wonderful game that day on Kevin Heffernan. He had the upper hand on Heffernan, and it was in all the papers before the game that Heffernan would destroy Ned Roche. Ned did his duty that day, and we were proud of him.

The honour of collecting the Sam Maguire Cup fell to John Dowling. Gary O'Mahony, however, says that Dowling asked him to do the necessary.

> Going up to get Sam, John Dowling—he was very shy—he pushed me in front of him at one stage. He said, You take the cup. I said, I can't take the cup: you're the captain.

Séamus Mac Gearailt, the future Kerry great, recalls listening to that final.

> There was only maybe one radio in every village. All the villagers would gather around in that house. The window would be open. We'd all be listening. There'd be a huge crowd in every house that time, listening to the matches, listening to Mícheál O'Hehir. What stuck out in all our memories are the names like Tadhgie Lyne, and the local names that time were Mick Murphy and Tom Moriarty. We had Paudie Sheehy, John Dowling—they were the names that were mentioned, but of course before that in national school the name that everyone had, because he was a local guy and local legend, was Paddy Bawn Brosnan. Everyone wanted to be a Paddy Bawn Brosnan. Once the radio in 1955 came then the names changed to the modern era . . . Mícheál O'Hehir's voice always stands out in my memory.

The return of collective training had played its part in the success of 1955. Its importance has never been lost on Johnny Culloty, Kerry's forward at the time.

> The thing that people probably forget about is that in 1953 and 1955 there was collective training. Collective training meant that the team were brought together for the full day for a couple of weeks before an all-Ireland final. They stayed in the Park Place Hotel, High Street, Killarney. They trained twice a day for seven days of the week. In 1954 I think there was a motion brought in that there was no collective training allowed. Kerry won in 1953; beaten in 1954 by Meath. The collective training came back again in 1955. Dr Éamonn was there in 1953 and 1955. Kerry won again in 1955. If the collective training had been there in 1954 they'd probably have won three in a row.

Weeshie Fogarty, now a match analyst for Radio Kerry, believes that the win over Dublin was a landmark.

> It was the so-called unbeatable Dublin machine. Kevin Heffernan, Ollie Freaney and all those fellows were playing with it. Kerry were being trained by Dr Éamonn O'Sullivan . . . Kerry went out that day and, with Tadhgie Lyne playing in the forwards, they gave one of the greatest exhibitions ever seen. It was a defining moment in Kerry football. It only showed what Kerry can do when it's put up to them . . . If Dublin had beaten Kerry, which was expected, it would mean that they really would be on the downslide. We don't know when they'd have recovered.

There's a famous story of Micksie Palmer putting down £80 on Kerry beating Dublin in the final, receiving odds of 6-4 from a pair of Dublin men. He subsequently collected his winnings. He considers that year's victory as special.

> The 1955 all-Ireland is always regarded as one of the best. It was tight. Then again Dublin were so cocky. To beat them was something.

———

Kerry headed into the 1959 season following three big seasons of disappointment. In 1956 they surrendered their Munster crown in a replay to Cork. In 1957 there was the infamous one-point semi-final loss to Waterford; and 1958 saw Kerry suffer an all-Ireland semi-final defeat to Derry.

Some silverware found its way to Co. Kerry early in 1959 as the county captured the National League title for the first time since 1932. Seán Murphy says that the attitude to the League that season was different from others.

> [Usually] the National League didn't figure on any Kerry plans through the year. They'd almost forgotten about it . . . Playing against various teams, some didn't bother turning up . . . For some reason we were revitalised in 1959. We did win the National League. I was thrilled to win it; a National League Medal was unusual.

Kerry, captained by John Dowling, beat Derry 2-8 to 1-8 in the League final. Then, as League champions, Kerry were to tour America later that year. The pressure was now increased on the Kingdom to go on to win the all-Ireland and to make the American tour a success.

The Munster campaign began against Tipperary. In the previous season the Kingdom robbed the Premier County of a famous victory. The *Kerryman* reminded its readers that 'Tipp were leading till the closing stages when a sideline kick by Mick O'Dwyer went through for a goal.'

Only four of the all-Ireland winning team of 1955 were to line out against Tipp in 1959. Jerome O'Shea, corner-back, and Paudie Sheehy, half-forward, were two. One of the others was John Dowling, who had now moved from midfield to full-forward. The fourth was Johnny Culloty, whose career change was even more remarkable.

In 1955 I was a corner-forward. Then I got on the Munster team. We played in the Railway Cup. I got injured on St Patrick's Day in 1956 . . . I had to have an operation for my knee—cartilage. An operation on your knee at that stage was very serious, compared with now: if you have a cartilage operation they have microsurgery, it's only a small thing . . . It took a long time to recover. For a while I wasn't able to play at all, for about twelve months nearly. The next thing then I started to come back . . . I was playing with the Kerry hurlers in goal. When I came back with Kerry then I was playing with the Kerry juniors. I went up with the Kerry seniors, I was a sub again for the forwards. We were playing Galway, I think it was a *Gaelic Weekly* tournament. At the time I think Marcus O'Neill was busy. He was playing in goals with Kerry at the time. He wasn't available for that game, so they were short a goalie. I was put into goal for that game because I was playing with the hurlers.

   The same thing happened in a couple of League games. I was put into goal for another couple of games, and I stayed there after that. I played in goal with Kerry in the football, and when I was playing with East Kerry I was playing corner-forward. We won four county championships. It suited me fine: I was fit enough to play out the field at county championship level. I slotted into goal with the county, and I stuck there with them.

The Tipperary match was a stroll for the Kingdom. It took some time, however, for Kerry to demonstrate their superiority on the scoreboard. The match was seven minutes old before Jim Brosnan gave Kerry the opening score. Dan McAuliffe then goaled, and Kerry opened up a six-point advantage by the quarter-hour mark. Even an early second-half goal for Tipp couldn't upset Kerry's rhythm. Kerry outscored Tipp by nine points to a goal in that second half, going through to the Munster final on a score of 1-15 to 1-2.

Cork were the Kingdom's opponents in the Munster decider on 2 August. Kerry made a dream start. The *Irish Press* noted that 'even with the strong wind in the first half, Cork took nine fatal minutes to settle down and by that time Kerry had rammed home two vital goals and a point.'

With a free, Dan McAuliffe registered Kerry's opening score. That was the first point of seven for McAuliffe that afternoon. Kerry's opening goal arrived only seven minutes in, with the second coming two minutes later. Kerry now led by 2-1 to nil. Perhaps it was too early to say the game was over, but even at that stage the Kingdom were in a match-winning position. Cork, though, had other ideas: a goal and a point later the Rebels had brought the deficit back to three points. Dan McAuliffe then pointed three frees for Kerry, each one being cancelled out at the other end. Cork tagged on two more scores before the break, after which Kerry led by the minimum, 2-4 to 1-6.

Kerry blitzed Cork in the first ten minutes of the second half. Two points by Dan McAuliffe, then further ones from Dave Geaney and Jim Brosnan, had Kerry five in front: Kerry 2-8, Cork 1-6. Cork responded to bring the gap down to three points. But six unanswered points by Kerry put the tie beyond Cork, who goaled late, but too late, as Kerry progressed by 2-15 to 2-8.

The *Irish Press* felt that Kerry had only shown their real power when the need had arisen, adding that the midfielders—the brilliant Mick O'Connell and the stylish Séamus Murphy—had laid the foundations of victory.

After beating their old rivals, Cork, next up were the Kingdom's arch-rivals, Dublin, bringing with them a chance for Kerry to knock out the reigning champions.

The Kerry selector Jackie Lyne told the *Kerryman* that he wanted the defence to shore up in the wake of their display in the win over Cork.

> Our backs were shaky on that occasion, and it was really the centre field and forwards who carried the day. But with an improvement in our back sector we should whip Dublin

John Barrett reported in the *Kerryman* that Dublin were in a frenzy to avenge their defeat of 1955.

> To every Dublin player, next Sunday is *the* game of his career. This will not be the cocky over confident bunch who fell into the trap in 55. They are sure they can do the trick this time but know they are in for one heck of a struggle.

Nowadays, football is seen as a professional game in everything but name. Players are training in some shape or form for more or less the whole year—be it actual football training or work in the gym. But In 1959 it was a different story, as Mick O'Connell remembers.

> We trained at home and practised at home. Two weeks after that [win over Cork], the following Sunday week, we played Dublin. We had some practice sessions. It puts in perspective the amount of travelling now and preparation which players are awarded. In those times the facilities weren't there. It would be a scandal now if the county team didn't have any training session until the month of August . . . We didn't complain, we just got on with it.

Kerry were not to be denied against Dublin. The champions would be dethroned after a titanic struggle between two great rivals.

From first whistle to last it was in the balance. Dublin led by three points to two after ten minutes. Mick O'Connell had Kerry on terms before the fifteenth minute. It was all square after Dan McAuliffe raised the white flag on twenty-four minutes. Then Paudie Sheehy nudged Kerry in front. The Kingdom went further ahead still, as described by the Kerryman: 'In one fierce tussle between backs and forwards, the ball broke loose and Dan McAuliffe got his boot to it and the leather was in the net.' The half ended with Kerry four points up, 1-5 to 0-4.

Four unanswered points in the first thirteen minutes of the second half seemingly put Kerry out of sight, leading as they were by 1-9 to 0-4. Dublin kept Kerry scoreless after that, adding a goal and a point of their own, which meant that with nine minutes to go the gap had been reduced to four. Dublin goaled again, with five minutes on the clock. Suddenly there was only the minimum between the sides. Kerry had not scored since the thirteenth minute of the half. Then Tom Long pointed, and the Kerry lead stood at two points as they entered the closing minutes. It was an advantage they maintained to the end. The result: 1-10 to 2-5.

The *Kerryman* lauded the boys in green and gold.

> After as thrilling and pulsating a football match as I have ever seen, Kerry defeated Dublin, the reigning champions. Kerry's experimental defence rose to the occasion. Dublin lost because they had no answer to high firm fielding. Mick O'Connell gave a scintillating display.

Liam Shanahan, a Kerry supporter, regards O'Connell's display in that semi-final as his finest hour.

> His greatest individual performance ever was in 1959, against Dublin in the semi-final. That day he took over the whole field. He played so well that it's said the Dublin fans clapped him off the field.

Paul Russell, six times a member of a Kerry all-Ireland winning team, was now a columnist with the *Kerryman*. He believed that the win 'demonstrated again the effectiveness of pure Gaelic Football as played mainly in the air and emphasized the value of the long, flowing pass.'

Galway would be Kerry's all-Ireland opponents, after the Tribesmen had qualified for the decider with a 1-11 to 1-4 defeat of Down.

Seán Murphy knew Kerry were in for a tough encounter.

> Galway were and still are a team very skilful, very well trained, well motivated. I thought that was a superb team, with Purcell and Mahon. The personalities on that Galway team meant that they were a very, very difficult proposition to play.

A fortnight before the final, Kerry's prospects received a blow, as noted in the *Kerryman*. 'Jim Brosnan, who dislocated a shoulder in the semi final, will not be fit. He was examined by a surgeon last weekend and afterwards made the decision not to play.'

Nonetheless, that semi-final display against Dublin meant that confidence among the Kingdomites was high. The *Kerryman* remarked that

the belief is widely and strongly held in this County that Kerry will beat Galway; some go so far as to maintain [that] the team will win with ease. This great confidence has been conditioned by the display of the team in the recent semi-final against Dublin and the resounding victory, which the most competent critics had regarded as an impossibility. Next to Dublin no team in Ireland receives better coaching, indulges in such intensive preparation as Galway ... I am not going so far as to say that Galway will beat Kerry. But the danger signals have been hoisted.

Dr Éamonn O'Sullivan was in agreement.

A number of Kerrymen who were at the Galway-Down semi-final seem to think that this Galway team is a shadow of its former self and a Kerry victory is a foregone conclusion. I am definitely inclined to take the opposite view.

In 1959 Tom Long was playing in his first senior all-Ireland final. Before the match he found himself beside Tadhgie Lyne in the dressing-room. He was about to discover the effect that pressure has on certain people.

I happened to be togging out beside him. For some strange reason I thought he looked excited, and I thought I saw a tremor in his hands. I said something like What's wrong with you? ... He said something like this: When you're around for a long time too, you'll be like this. It was true for him, I suppose: the longer you go the greater the expectations and the more nervous you feel about it.

A tight first half against Galway gave no indication of what was to follow. Kerry were two points to the good within three minutes. But less than two minutes later they found themselves trailing, with a Galway goal putting the Kingdom in arrears. Dan McAuliffe levelled the score in the tenth minute. Galway forged ahead again mid-way through the half, then doubled that advantage. It was two minutes from half time before Kerry moved level, Tadhgie Lyne pointing a free. The sides were tied at half time, Kerry 0-5, Galway 1-2.

Kerry ran amok late in the second half, holding Galway to two points in the process. Both teams added a solitary point in the first fifteen minutes of the period. Kerry then blitzed the Galway net, as reported in the *Kerryman*.

> Tom Long punched into the Galway goalmouth and Dan McAuliffe shot to the net. In the next minute O'Dwyer added a point. A shot by John Dowling was caught by Farrell the Galway goalman, but before he could get rid of the ball, Dan McAuliffe punched it into the net after eighteen minutes. Garry McMahon came on instead of Dave Geaney and he was not long in action when he got the ball and an angle shot reached the net with five minutes remaining.

Sam Maguire was coming back to the Kingdom, thanks to a 3-7 to 1-4 victory. It was a win made all the more remarkable in that an early knee injury to Mick O'Connell curtailed his influence on the game, leading to his eventual withdrawal.

Seán Murphy was concerned that O'Connell's departure would lead to Kerry's demise.

> That was a worry. When I saw Mick O'Connell going I was dumbfounded . . . I found it very difficult to see a Kerry team at that stage winning without Mick O'Connell; but they did. It shows that very often it's a team rather than a personality that wins these games.

A knee injury was not the only ailment O'Connell had to contend with.

> For another reason I shouldn't have been playing at all that day. I had a sore throat. Dr Éamonn O'Sullivan, trainer, gave me some tablets that morning. I could hardly swallow a spit. But you cannot pull out at the last minute. That's another thing that often happens.

People don't take into account that one may be very off form from a medical point of view on the day. I had tonsillitis that day. My throat was closed, but I had to go on the field. I tried, but the twisting of the knee was what put me off.

Gary O'Mahony was in goal when Kerry won the 1955 final. He ranks Seán Murphy's display in the 1959 decider as one of the greatest. 'I thought he took on the whole Galway team himself. Nothing passed him.'

For Johnny Foley, netminder in 1953, Seán Murphy's performance in 1959 also stands out. 'He wasn't beaten for any ball. He was great in 1953. He was great in 1955. 1959 was the best that I saw him.'

The 1959 decider has since been dubbed the 'Seán Murphy final'; but his was not the only stand-out performance in a Kerry jersey that day. The *Kerryman* also wrote that

> Paud Sheehy had a distinguished hour, so had Tom Long and Johnny Culloty. Culloty brought off some wonderful close range saves which would have beaten a less reliable goalman. Surprise packet of the Kerry team was John Dowling; he was much too good for Meade, and I believe this was the first nail in the western coffin.

Luke Keane, a Kerry supporter, believes that Tom Long's name can be added to the list of those who excelled in the final of 1959.

> Tom Long's display that day also was wonderful. He was switched out on Frank Evers, and Evers was dominating a little bit. Tom Long put the shackles on Evers. I would rate Tom Long as one of the greatest ever.

The year 1959 provided title number 7 for the famed Dr Éamonn O'Sullivan. Joe Ó Muircheartaigh believes that Dr Éamonn was a class apart in his approach to the game.

> The book that Dr Éamonn O'Sullivan wrote in the late fifties after he had trained so many all-Ireland winning teams from the twenties onward, it was called *The Art and Science of Gaelic Football*. In many ways the title of the book sums up the man . . . [He] was immersed

in the whole psychological process and the science of football. He tried to break down each individual area on the field ... He was rigid in his enforcement, his view of how Kerry teams should play once they went out on the field.

There was another famous story, with regard to the relaxation of 'curfews.'

> If Paddy Bawn Brosnan liked to go for two or three pints every few nights, Dr Éamonn wasn't one for having a total blanket ban on drinking and knocking it out altogether. For the two weeks before the all-Ireland he would allow them but would ration back what they would be allowed drink over those two weeks. He felt that it would do more harm than good if you suddenly told a man who likes his few pints, You can't do that, it's my way or the highway. He didn't do that. He worked with players in that sense. He worked with each individual player on an individual basis rather than making rules and guidelines that would cover the whole team. Everyone was treated differently and maybe that was the secret of his success.

Mick O'Dwyer offers this assessment:

> The game has changed and has evolved over the years. In my time it was more a catch-and-kick game. Dr Éamonn O'Sullivan, I played under him actually. He marked out fifteen sectors on the pitch, and no matter what sector you got the ball in you had to play it first time. Catch it, kick it as high in the air, and make it travel. The fellow, where it was landing, in that sector should be able to catch it as well. It was a great system when you had players able to win the ball high in the air. Maybe there wasn't a place for too many small players.

O'Dwyer says that the victory in 1959 is his favourite.

> We beat Galway in the final, and they had two players, Stockwell and Purcell—the 'terrible twins' they were known as. They had wrecked all the teams in Connacht on the way through to the all-Ireland

final. God rest Kevin Coffey and Niall Sheehy: they took care of both of them, and we went on to win.

Kerry homecomings held fond memories for Mick O'Dwyer.

> The one memory I would always have, when we'd arrive in Rathmore there was a famous priest by the name of Father O'Doherty. He used meet us there regularly. He was the man that got all the teams here in South Kerry together when he was a priest in Cahersiveen. He was a great follower of Kerry and a great friend of mine. I always expected him to be in Rathmore . . . He was a wonderful man. He was the man that made it possible for quite a lot of South Kerry players to go on and play for Kerry. There weren't too many players from South Kerry on Kerry teams until Father O'Doherty and Ned Mahony and a few of those fellows got together here and got all of South Kerry together. We managed to win our first county championship and then went on to play for Kerry.

1959 is also the year in which the Kerry captain, Mick O'Connell, famously forgot the Sam Maguire Cup, leaving it in the dressing-room!

Kerry's season was still far from over, however. In October they went on to defeat Down, 1-11 to 0-9, in the final of the *Gaelic Weekly* Tournament at Croke Park. That match was felt to be important, as it came before the American tour. It was feared that a Kerry loss to Down would diminish the appeal of the Kerrymen in America. In America, Kerry defeated New York to win the St Brendan's Cup final, winning by 2-11 to 1-8 at Gaelic Park in front of a crowd of nearly fifteen thousand.

The talents of certain members of that 1959 all-Ireland side extended beyond the playing-fields of the GAA. Also, players of that generation— as of this one—are merely continuing a time-honoured trend of, as they say, giving it all for the jersey. Weeshie Fogarty remarks that

> what amazes me today is when I hear Kerry players say all the time they are putting in and all the sacrifices they are making—that has always been the way. That has been going on for generations. Kerry players have been cycling miles and miles, they have been out on the fields working, they have been labouring, and they go out training in the evening. They'd leave their farms and homes and they'd go

running on their own. It mightn't have been organised like it is now, but it was certainly going on then. You even hear today about Kieran Donaghy and Michael Quirke, the basketballers, playing football for Kerry. Back in the fifties half the Kerry team were playing basketball. Jerome O'Shea, Maurice Fitzgerald's father, Ned, Johnny Culloty played basketball with Kerry. Niall Sheehy played basketball with Kerry. Jerome O'Shea played basketball with Kerry. All the great players played basketball that particular time [in the fifties and sixties.]

Come 1962, the men of the Kingdom were hoping to put two years of frustration behind them. Down had put paid to Kerry's all-Ireland hopes in the two previous seasons, in 1960 in the final and in 1961 in the semi-final. However, it wasn't only 1960 and 61 that Kerry were hoping to atone for. They had played and beaten Offaly at Wembley in 1962 but twenty-four-hours later got a severe wake-up call when they lost to Roscommon in Killarney. Roscommon pulverised Kerry, leading 2-6 to 0-2 at half time, then by 2-13 to 0-5 at the final whistle. The performance sowed seeds of serious doubt in Kerry minds for the campaign ahead.

The road to redemption began with a Munster semi-final against Waterford. Kerry could call on ten of the 1959 championship-winning side: Johnny Culloty, Niall Sheehy, Tim Lyons, Mick O'Dwyer, Mick O'Connell, Séamus Murphy, Dave Geaney, Paudie Sheehy, Dan McAuliffe and Tom Long.

Kerry had five championship newcomers when they met Waterford. Alan Conway of John Mitchels was at corner-back. His clubmate Seán Sheehy came in at half-back, and another Mitchels man, Séamus Roche, at half-forward. Noel and Jimmy Lucey lined out at centre-back and midfield, respectively.

The *Kerryman* felt there were major surprises when the selectors named their team to take on Waterford.

The big five certainly dropped a bombshell when they made the audacious move of placing Tom Long at full-forward. In the past they had wrestled with the idea of converting the Ventry-born teacher into a centre-back and apparently have now despaired of the idea. Into the vital centre half forward berth steps Séamus Murphy and many are the arguments which can be heard in support of the contention that Murphy is best suited to midfield or alternatively to a wing forward position. Personally, I prefer the Camp man on the halfway line where he has shown a perfect understanding with O'Connell in the past.

A twelve-point victory over Waterford was Kerry's, but the score hides the real story. Kerry were made to fight all the way, grinding their opponents down only in the last third of the encounter.

Waterford put it up to Kerry from the off. The sides swapped points before Tom Long goaled for the Kingdom. Kerry moved five in front, but a Waterford goal brought them back into contention. They drew level and then went in front five minutes before the break. Kerry responded, as described by the *Kerryman*.

> Left half forward Roche certainly showed his opportunism when he shot a grand goal. He took a loose ball, raced right through on his own and drove low and hard to the left corner of the net.

Kerry's half-time lead stood at the minimum: 2-4 to 1-6. Points by Dan McAuliffe, Mick O'Dwyer and Dave Geaney put the Kingdom in control, but Waterford goaled in the eighth minute of the half, and Kerry were back to square one. Amazingly, given the fight they had put up so far, that goal was Waterford's final score of the game. Kerry, meanwhile, pointed eleven more times in the closing twenty-two minutes, chief among the scorers being Paudie Sheehy, with four, and Mick O'Connell, with three. The result was Kerry 2-18, Waterford 2-6.

The *Kerryman* jury was out on O'Connell's partner and on the other new boys.

> Jimmy Lucey, one of the four newcomers on the team, certainly had a successful championship debut but I wonder is he the ideal partner for O'Connell. No doubt about it but the Carragh Lake man is a great trier and a hard hitter but he wastes a lot of energy unnecessarily in trying to play too much of the field. What of the other three newcomers—left half forward goal-scorer Roche had a reasonably good game. Seán Sheehy had a disappointing hour although a fine run by him down the right wing in the first half led to Kerry's first goal by Tom Long. Noel Lucey will almost certainly

be retained on the strength of his display at centre half back.

Cork were to provide the Munster final opposition. The introduction of Donie O'Sullivan was one of two changes to the Kerry team for the decider. O'Sullivan feels that the Kerry squad at that time had a nice blend of youth and experience.

> For all of us who were young that time playing—you had the nucleus. A very strong, experienced nucleus, from Johnny Culloty in goals, Niall Sheehy, Tim Lyons, Séamus Murphy, Mick O'Dwyer, Tom Long, Mick O'Connell—half a team in themselves. Dan McAuliffe was playing also that year. That was a strong nucleus of good, very experienced players.

The Munster final turned into a rout for the Kingdom. They were eleven to the good at half time, and sixteen clear come full time. The early exchanges were decisive, as reported by the *Kerryman*.

> Though McCarthy opened Cork's scoring with a point, within two minutes, McAuliffe goaled for Kerry three minutes later. A misunderstanding between Breen and Twomey let McAuliffe, from Long's pass, through for Kerry's opening goal. When Long, seconds after, again raised the green flag the game looked as good as over. Points by P. Sheehy, Driscoll, Long and McAuliffe gave the Kerrymen a commanding lead. When Driscoll punched a Paud Sheehy free to the net the game became one sided.

Kerry's half-time lead was 3-4 to 0-2. Mick O'Connell goaled late in the second half as Kerry ran out easy winners. A final score of Kerry 4-8, Cork 0-4, meant that the Kingdom had secured their fifth Munster crown in a row.

With Cork brushed aside, the Kingdom were concentrating on facing Dublin for a place in the all-Ireland final. The Kerry captain of 1955, John Dowling, who also played when the Kingdom had beaten Dublin in 1959, was asked by the *Kerryman* for his views on the Dublin encounter. He felt that, following the surprise defeat of Down, any of the four semi-finalists would fancy their chances. Dowling tipped Kerry to win but believed the absence of Noel Lucey, suspended after his sending off in the Munster final, could harm Kerry's chances.

Fortunately, Lucey's absence didn't much affect the Kingdom, for it was at the other end of the pitch that the damage was done. This match was done and dusted by half time, as reported by the *Kerryman.*

> Kerry had a free, Paud Sheehy grabbed the ball and passed to Long who crashed into the Dublin net in the fifth minute. Kerry had a free near the corner. Long secured, and passed to Sheehy who gave to McMahon. A lightning shot passed Flynn to the net and Kerry were a dozen points up after 25 minutes' play.

The game was over as a contest by half time. The score was Kerry 2-9, Dublin 0-3. The second period was merely a matter of going through the motions. Dublin made a fight of it, bringing the gap down to seven points, then hitting the crossbar. Kerry went more than twenty minutes without a score but then registered three points in a minute. It ended Kerry 2-12, Dublin 0-10.

Despite Dublin's second-half attempts, Kerry were never in danger, and the *Kerryman* proudly proclaimed that the

> greatly overrated Dublin were crushed. The wining margin at the finish is a true index of the superiority of the men from the Kingdom. The game came as a big disappointment to neutral spectators. As in 1955 and 1959 the ballyhoo which preceded the game, lauding Dublin's greatness to the high heavens was completely misleading.

1962 saw the first live television coverage of games by RTE. Kerry's win over Dublin drew an estimated audience of a hundred thousand. Among the viewers was Charlie Nelligan, the future Kerry goalkeeper.

> Back in 1962, when I was five years of age, we didn't have any television in the house. My father got an invite from a sales rep in Newcastle West, if we'd like to go see the all-Ireland semi-final between Kerry and Dublin. I remember sitting down in a room upstairs over a pub somewhere and watching the match. That was my first recollection of seeing Kerry play.

Roscommon, who had earlier in the year beaten Kerry by fourteen points in Killarney, were to be the all-Ireland opponents. Roscommon had accounted for Cavan in the last four, by 1-8 to 1-6. Their big problem would be holding the Kerry midfield, according to Paddy Foley in the *Kerryman*. He added that Roscommon caused one of the greatest surprises of the season by beating Galway in the western decider.

A man who went under the name 'Green and Gold', writing from Castlerea, Co. Roscommon, wrote in the *Kerryman* that Roscommon felt that Kerry were overrated. Roscommon, he said, believed that Kerry had been made the Goliath by the pen-prophets and that Roscommon themselves were the David who would lay them low.

The sole change in personnel by Kerry for the final saw Noel Lucey return and Donie O'Sullivan miss out. Séamus Murphy took O'Sullivan's number 2 jersey, with Lucey coming in at centre-back. The reason for O'Sullivan's absence would today be considered remarkable.

> I was in Maynooth that time, in the seminary, and we just didn't get out to play games. We were allowed play during the holiday time, and that was it. It was a big game, but the rules were there. We had known beforehand. It had happened to John Kennedy with Galway in 1959. He was a marvellous player, and he wasn't allowed out. Galway lost—at least Kerry won in 1962. That was it, but of course it was disappointing to watch it, being young and seeing all the rest in Croke Park playing and winning and just being there.

While Donie O'Sullivan was an enforced absentee for that final, Séamus Mac Gearailt was a surprise addition. The minor final took place as a curtain-raiser to the senior decider. After starring in goal for the minors in their victory, Mac Gearailt was then asked to hang around, just in case.

> The first all-Ireland I ever went to was 1962. I was playing myself in the minor. I was playing in goal. Dr Jim Brosnan was our trainer. He had a word with me. He knew I had never been to Croke Park. He said, 'Whatever you do, don't look around until the match is over.' I suppose he was afraid I would spill a goal in the meantime. I can always say I played in Croke Park before I saw it!
>
> I was also a sub goalie with the senior team. Johnny Culloty was

'The moment that made Gaelic football a part of the national identity.' Action shots from the legendary Kerry v. Kildare trilogy of the 1903 season.

'To the men of the past is our reputation due.' The consecutive all-Ireland champions of 1903 and 1904. (*GAA Archive*)

'The first superstar of the GAA.' Kerry's 1913 and 1914 all-Ireland winning captain, Dick Fitzgerald (in the middle of the second row from top), is flanked by his team-mates. (*GAA Archive*)

'One down, three to go.' Kerry's 1929 all-Ireland winning squad, many of whom would go on to feature as the Kingdom won the next three championships also. (*GAA Archive*)

In the olden days, clergymen often started the all-Ireland final by throwing the ball in, as above in 1931. Meanwhile numerous members of each side lined up at centrefield for the throw-in. (*Irish Examiner*)

Terrorists according to Mayo: the Kerry footballers of 1939! (*GAA Archive*)

The Kerry sharpshooter of the 1920s and 30s, John Joe Sheehy (fourth from left), attends the 1955 all-Ireland senior football final. Sheehy, winning captain in 1926 and 1930, was inducted into the hall of fame in 1963. (*Kennelly Archive*)

Victorious Kerry captain Mick O'Connell gets his hands on the most prestigious trophy in Irish sport. (*Kennelly Archive*)

For the love of the game. The Kerry legend Mick O'Connell getting off the boat from Valentia in the late 1960s. Many people forget the sacrifices and journeys undertaken by players in order to fulfil their inter-county duties. (*Fionnbarr Callanan*)

'My first all-Ireland final, and I ended up getting the ultimate accolade.' Pat Spillane deputises for the absent Kerry captain, Mickey Ned O'Sullivan, and Years of Glory begin . . . (*Sportsfile*)

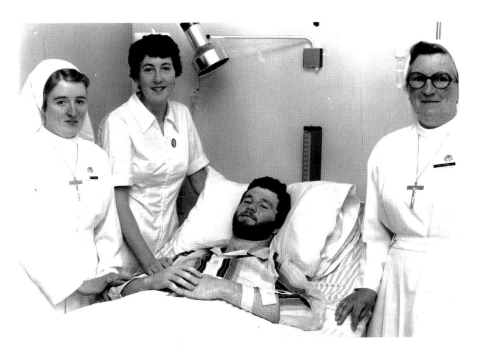

In safe hands. The Bomber missed the 1980 all-Ireland final because of acute appendicitis. He was taken to hospital for an operation on the Wednesday before the match. (*Kerryman*)

'It was the one final that Kerry shouldn't have won.' There almost seems to be a sense of relief on the face of the 1980 Kerry captain, Ger Power, as he raises the Sam Maguire Cup towards the heavens. (*Sportsfile*)

A thoroughbred. Tim Kennelly in action in the 1981 all-Ireland semi-final victory over Mayo. (*Sportsfile*)

We've done it! The heartbreak of '82 and '83 is forgotten as the Kerry captain, Ambrose O'Donovan, prepares to lift the Sam Maguire Cup following victory over Dublin in 1984. (*Sportsfile*)

The only man to win eight all-Irelands in one position, Denis Ogie Moran, shoots towards the Dublin goal in the 1985 all-Ireland final. (*Sportsfile*)

A footballing dynasty. The Spillane brothers with their uncle, Con Lyne. The late Con—'a very proud uncle,' according to Tom Spillane—was a brother of the Spillanes' mother. Con's brother Jackie trained Kerry to their all-Ireland successes of 1969 and 1970, while another brother, Denny, was Kerry captain when they lost the 1947 all-Ireland decider. (*Kerryman*)

'It meant your efforts were appreciated, it meant you had an input to a Kerry legend. You were part of the Kerry football story.' Kerry's captain of 1986, Tommy Doyle, with Sam in tow, speaks to an engrossed crowd at the Annascaul leg of the homecoming. (*Kerryman*)

'We won our first all-Ireland in eleven years, and the place went hopping mad.' Kerry players celebrate their return to the top table of Gaelic football after the 1997 all-Ireland final win against Mayo. (*Sportsfile*)

The Kerry captain, Séamus Moynihan, leads the celebrations after the Kingdom win the Millennium all-Ireland football final replay, played on a Saturday. (*INPHO/Billy Stickland*)

Goal by the Gooch! 'I thought for a split second, to just keep it down and not to lash it and let it just roll away into the corner.' Colm Cooper goals for Kerry in the 2004 all-Ireland final. (*INPHO*/*Morgan Treacy*)

There are two sides to every story. The full-time whistle sounds in the 2006 all-Ireland final, and as Ger Brady of Mayo slumps to the ground, on each side of him victorious Kerry players celebrate. (*INPHO*/*Cathal Noonan*)

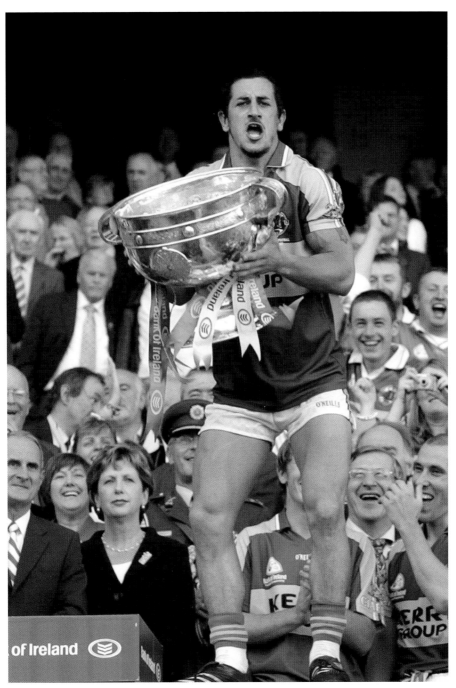

'Everything we had achieved and everything that Kerry football stood for was on the line, a hundred years of being the greatest county.' Paul Galvin gets his hands on Sam following success over Cork in 2007. (*INPHO/Donall Farmer*)

'My father inspired me. Everything I ever did or still do is for my father.' It's 2009, and Tadhg Kennelly emulates his brother and late father by playing in an all-Ireland winning Kerry team. (*INPHO/Morgan Treacy*)

in goal, but there was no fear he got injured. There was no medal for sub goalie that time. If I got one I would have a record that would be very hard to beat, because I would have won the two medals on the one day. I won a minor medal again the following year, in 1963 ... Minors and seniors trained together an odd night. That time you had only twenty on the panel in the senior team. They didn't carry a sub goalie. But the fact that I was with the minors, they kept me as a sub goalie with the seniors.

Within one minute of the final, Garry McMahon of Kerry goaled, and they never looked back. It was the quickest goal ever in an all-Ireland final. Kerry fans everywhere may have been celebrating this striker. However, Eoghan Corry noted that Dr Éamonn O'Sullivan wouldn't have been so appreciative of that McMahon goal.

> His book says, 'A man stays in his position; you don't move.' He gave out to Garry McMahon when he scored the goal against Roscommon in the 1962 all-Ireland. Everybody in Kerry celebrated except Éamonn, because he said that wasn't your corner.

Tom Herlihy, a Kerry supporter, believes that McMahon's goal was planned.

> Before the game one of the Kerry selectors said to Garry McMahon that the Roscommon corner-back had a tendency to go for everything. In the first second of the game the high ball came in and the corner-back went out full-blooded for it, and Garry waited behind him. In thirty seconds the ball was in the net.

Kerry added a point, and then two more scores by Mick O'Connell had Kerry in the driving seat. Timmy O'Sullivan and O'Connell tagged on further points. It left Kerry leading by 1-5 to no score only eighteen minutes in. Roscommon then finally got on the scoreboard, converting a penalty. Kerry responded immediately, Mick O'Connell doing the necessary after a foul on Dan McAuliffe. Two more Kerry scores followed before the short whistle. Roscommon had the final say of the half: a point. There was a seven-point margin in Kerry's favour as the half ended, 1-8 to 1-1.

Roscommon outscored Kerry in the second period, but the Kingdom always maintained superiority. Kerry's advantage stood at eight points, 1-10 to 1-2, four minutes into the half. The next point, arguably the score of the match, belonged to Mick O'Connell. The *Kerryman* reported how

> O'Connell snatched a high ball at midfield and was grassed at once. He took the free out beyond the 50. The ball cleared the cross bar amid exultant Kerry cheers.

Two Roscommon points brought a little more respectability to the score, before Paud Sheehy provided Kerry's final point. Kerry put over only four points in that second period, but it was more than enough, as they finished on 1-12 to 1-6. The *Kerryman* commented that Roscommon were 'outclassed form start to finish.'

Donie O'Sullivan has a degree of sympathy for Roscommon.

> You don't blame Roscommon. They were trying to slow it down a bit. They didn't have all the luck either, because apart from conceding the early goal Gerry O'Malley got injured. He had to go off, centre-half-back. Fabulous player—footballer and hurler. He never won an all-Ireland medal . . . He played for years and years. That was his final. He was captain. They lost and he got injured.

The *Kerryman* recalled a strange happening early in the match.

> In the first minute . . . Jim Lucey made an extraordinary mistake. He fielded a loose ball and gave an almighty kick in the direction of his own posts, which nearly led to trouble but danger was averted.

Mike O'Dwyer pulls no punches when asked about the victory over Roscommon.

> That was one of the worst all-Irelands I have played or seen in my time. We beat Roscommon that day in a bad final, to be honest.

While Kerry fans and the majority of the players were planning for a triumphant homecoming, Séamus Mac Gearailt, the substitute keeper of 1962, had to return west to resume his studies.

I was boarding in St Mary's in Galway. I remember Dr Jim, he gave me two pounds, which was a lot of money that time: I think I had fifteen shillings to myself for the school term.

But the *Kerryman* summed up the feelings of the fans.

Few gave Kerry a chance of winning at the start of the season. It was a proud occasion for old followers to see Seán Óg, John Joe's son, holding up the Sam Maguire in triumph.

Seán Óg's brothers Paudie and Niall were also on the team.

| INDESTRUCTIBLE

Kerry went into 1969 following a defeat in the previous year's all-Ireland, in which the Kingdom lost to Down, 2-12 to 1-13. Kerry had also lost all-Ireland finals in 1964 and 1965, both to Galway, while 1966 and 1967 saw the Kingdom fail to progress from Munster.

It was a frustrating period, but it was felt that Kerry's time was coming. Jackie Lyne's appointment as manager in 1968 was seen as vital to the county's progression. Weeshie Fogarty certainly believes so.

It all started in '68 when Jackie Lyne came in and took over the team. No-one else would train the team, and I remember him stating publicly that there's nothing wrong with Kerry football, even though they had been beaten from '62 on. From '59 up to '69 they won just one all-Ireland, in '62. Football in the county was very bad: fellows had retired—Johnny Culloty, Mick O'Connell, Séamus Murphy and Mick O'Dwyer. What did they do? They came back, and they played, and they were all thirty, thirty-one, thirty-two and thirty-three years of age, and they were the stars of that Kerry team.

The most dramatic comeback of all was in '68. Teddy Bowler was in goals for Kerry. Longford were beaten by Kerry in the all-Ireland semi-final. They picked the team [for the game against Longford] and they left the goalkeeping position open. Three selectors left the selection room and walked up the road, into Johnny Culloty's house, and they said to Culloty, We're picking you. Will you come out of retirement? Culloty made a comeback after being picked in his own house.

Liam Shanahan, a Kerry fan, believes that Mick O'Dwyer's comeback was just as spectacular.

He broke his two legs. They said, Sure he'll never again play. Himself and O'Connell retired for two years, and they had a trial game and they gave an exhibition. They went on into the Kerry team.

Tom Prendergast still remembers the all-Ireland defeat of 1968. He feels that Kerry had the personnel but that the side just needed a bit of tweaking.

> 1968, we were narrowly beaten, and then in 1969, with a few changes, personnel and in particular more positional changes . . . I'd say you had thirteen or fourteen of the team that were there in 1968, only playing in different positions. Even in my own case I had played corner-forward in '68 and I was wing-back in '69. D. J. Crowley had played full-forward in 1968 and he ended up centrefield in '69. There were some good positional changes made, and I think they made the difference.

Donie O'Sullivan believes that the team didn't do itself justice in the 1968 final.

> The most disappointing thing in that is that we knew we were better than we played. We played poorly on the day, and I think it's the worst way of all to walk off in a final, knowing you didn't do well and you could have done better as a team. There was still something left in the tank. It was one of those days, it happens, and we made several mistakes, and tactics mightn't have been great, and we still lost by two points. It was a disappointing day, and then for some of us—well, some were older than I was; it looked like the end of the road.

D. J. Crowley was one of the players who came onto the scene the year before that 1968 defeat. His introduction to life as a Kerry footballer was bizarre.

> When I seriously came on the senior team it was Whit Sunday and I was at the stadium watching a match with my father. There was a local derby on first, and over the Tannoy system it said, Was Den Joe Crowley from Rathmore in the stadium, and would he please go to the Kerry team's dressing-room. I met Jackie Lyne for the first time,

and he asked me, Any chance you have your gear with you? I said it's outside in the back of the Morris Minor. He said, Go out and get it fast. You're playing on the forty.

In 1969 Kerry won the National League final. Liam Higgins, the former Radio Kerry commentator, scored the winning goal against Cork in the divisional final. Kerry defeated Offaly in the home final to go through to the League final proper in New York.

Tom Prendergast feels there were huge benefits to be had from the entire National League campaign.

> The National League at that stage was very beneficial to us. We had been beaten in '68, and then there were a few changes being made, here and there, and players were being pushed about. So the National League helped in many ways to settle the team going into the championship.

But before Kerry could pack their bags for America they had the small matter of their Munster championship opener. The Kingdom, without an all-Ireland title since 1962, was to begin that year's quest for the Sam Maguire against Waterford.

The game provided a worthwhile test. Waterford goaled after nine minutes. Two Mick O'Connell points put Kerry in front by 0-5 to 1-1, but Waterford were on terms by the sixteenth minute. Kerry then took over, adding 1-6 to their total before the break. That left Kerry leading 1-11 to 1-4 at half time. The Kingdom went eight in front, but Waterford then goaled and tagged on a point. The lead was cut to four—but that's as close as Waterford got. Kerry outscored their opponents five points to one in the final quarter, to register a 1-18 to 2-7 victory.

The *Kerryman* singled out two men for their role in the success.

> Mick O'Connell was again a tower of strength at midfield. If for nothing other than his deadly accuracy from long range, in all he notched 5 well-taken points, Pat Moynihan was the big success in the Kerry attack. He was a joy to watch in the opening half as he roved outfield, won possession and grabbed 4 precious points.

That win ensured a Munster final with Cork, a match that was delayed one week at the request of the Kerry County Board because of the trip to America. In America, Kerry were to face New York in a two-legged league final. The matches would see Séamus Mac Gearailt and his teammates come up against some of their fellow-countymen.

New York had a very good team that time. They had a lot of Irish players who had played inter-county and who had emigrated. They had some very good Kerry fellows with them, the Foleys and Mick Moynihan. They really expected to beat us.

John Barry, a *Kerryman* reporter, was among the travelling party.

They were two amazing games. New York had a really great team. Those two matches were absolutely fantastic affairs. In the second leg Kerry looked a beaten team. They were three points down with a few minutes to go. Mick O'Connell, who had been injured in the first game, came on as a sub at half time. In those last three minutes he scored three points to take the game into extra time. New York wanted Kerry to stay over so the game [replay] could be played the following Sunday. Kerry players felt they couldn't take another week off. Extra time was played, and Kerry won handily. The second leg was incredible, played in heat that was in the high 90s. I saw something in those two games that led me to believe Kerry were something special, and they proved that.

Both legs of the final ended in a draw, and extra time had to be played on the second day. Séamus Mac Gearailt remembers the conditions they had to play in.

We were level after the two games. We had to play extra time in 110 degrees of heat. While they were debating what should be done after the second draw we were standing under a railway line in the shade, and we must have drank buckets of water.

That journey to New York, combined with an earlier trip to England, provided the foundations for the remainder of the season, according to Mac Gearailt.

It's always said that you have to lose one to win one, and we lost to Down in '68, and I think that cemented our team together to make a special effort in '69, very capably led by trainer Jackie Lyne. We went to Wembley in June '69, we played in the Wembley tournament, then we went to New York, and played the league final later on in June. Those two trips really cemented the team together.

Once Kerry returned home, attention turned to the Munster final. Brendan Lynch recalls that it was approached with caution.

What I remember is of being very apprehensive of the result beforehand. We had played Cork in the National League, and they really won everywhere but on the scoreboard. They were quite a strong side, and I expected that Munster final to be a very close game.

In the decider, Kerry raced into a lead of four points to one by the thirteenth minute. The next significant moment came two minutes later: Cork were awarded a penalty—two, in fact—as reported by the *Kerryman*.

Denis Coughlan took the first and hit the foot of the left upright. The ball rolled across the square and Kerry corner back Séamus Fitzgerald dived on it to prevent the inrushing Cork forwards from goaling. From the resulting second penalty Dónal Hunt shot low and fairly straight at Johnny Culloty, who quickly covered the ball and cleared. Ironically, just before these penalties happened some of the Cork forwards claimed the ball had gone over the goalline. Johnny Culloty agreed afterwards that the ball may have been just inside the line.

Kerry had just one point from the thirteenth minute to the half-time whistle. Cork put over three in that time, which meant that at the break it was Kerry five points, Cork four.

The second period belonged to the Kingdom, Cork having to wait until the very last minute to get their sole score of the half. Kerry scored five points in the first fifteen minutes of the second half to open up an advantage of ten points to four. Six more Kerry points followed before a last-minute consolation goal for Cork. 0-16 to 1-4 was the result.

Mayo were to be Kerry's opponents in the all-Ireland semi-final. It was a game that Kerry should have won by a bucketload, considering the number of chances they had. However, many of those opportunities were squandered, leaving Kerry hanging on by a thread at the end. Mayo led Kerry by two points after the opening twelve minutes. Two Mick O'Dwyer frees cancelled out the advantage. Approaching the twenty-fifth minute, Kerry had moved into a lead of six points to five. Pat Griffin made it seven to five, but Mayo were level by the break.

Two Mick O'Connell points had Kerry ahead by eleven points to eight after twelve minutes of the second period. On 49 minutes Kerry stretched the lead to five points and appeared to be coasting home. But a Mayo goal nine minutes from the end brought the game back to life. Joe Corcoran of Mayo pointed a free, to leave the minimum between the teams with only four minutes remaining. The *Kerryman* wrote that

> the tension was almost unbearable in the last four minutes—Mick O'Dwyer had two wides from awkward angles, one from a free and the other from play before Mayo were presented with a glorious chance of scoring the equaliser. John Morley took a quick free at midfield and found Willie McGee less than 21 yards out to the right of the posts. McGee made straight for goal and if Séamus Mac Gearailt had not pulled him down the Mayo man might easily have scored a match-wining goal.

Mac Gearailt claims he was merely acting on the advice of his captain.

> It was I committed the foul. Johnny Culloty roared, 'Don't let him in!' so I took Johnny's advice. What I remember about it was Johnny saying to me the most they can get out of this is a point and we'll get another chance, whereas if you had let him in he could have scored the goal. It was a fourteen-yard free, a little bit to the side of the goal.

The *Kerryman* reporter was bemused by what happened next. 'Joe Corcoran placed the ball and a point seemed a formality. But Corcoran did not take the kick. It was left to Séamus O'Dowd.' Corcoran was Mayo's recognised place-kicker, but O'Dowd had scored from a similar position in the first half. Less than two minutes remaining, and the chance was there for Mayo to snatch a most dramatic draw. D. J. Crowley had the best view of all for the kick.

> I have full memory of that incident, because Séamus O'Dowd took the free and I covered the kick, which is something that isn't done as much today. It was nearest man to the ball or, if it was your man taking the kick, you stood fourteen yards way. You'd intimidate him some bit. I remember putting up my hands, and the ball passed just outside my left wrist, and I looked around. I thought it was gone over the bar, and it just went barely outside the left upright.

Kerry—just about—were through to the all-Ireland final, 0-14 to 1-10. In the *Kerryman,* John Barry spoke for a whole county.

> It will be a long time before we forget the fright we got in the last nine minutes. For the previous 51 minutes we had happily watched our men establish mastery over Mayo and although they had a lead of only 5 points to show for their supremacy we were in no way worried. In the finish Kerry pulled through by a point but they can count themselves decidedly lucky to have done so.

That year's all-Ireland final was to be contested by Kerry and Offaly, a repeat of the National League final, which Kerry had won. In the all-Ireland semi-final Offaly accounted for Cavan, 3-8 to 1-10, after a replay. The squad prepared for the Leinster champions, as D. J. Crowley recalls.

> When Jackie Lyne took over in '68 and '69 and '70, we played in those three all-Irelands, we trained seven days a week. I came from Kinsale to Tralee seven days a week. Pat Griffin met me outside Macroom. He was in Clonakilty, and the two of us travelled together. Brendan Lynch, Mick Morris, Mick Fleming and those travelled from Cork. I was 12 stone 7 in the final of '68. I was a year older and bone was a bit stronger. I was 13-4 for the final of '69.

Weeshie Fogarty recalls the training he used to put in with Johnny Culloty.

> He taught me how to play in goal. We used to train together, after

working in St Finian's Hospital. All during the winter we'd tog out, hop in his car and drive somewhere, and we'd go running on the roads. We'd run from O'Sullivan's place up to the church in Kilcummin, and we'd have a little flashing light in our hands to protect us from the traffic, and we'd run back down again. We'd go back to the golf links in Killarney and do the whole course, and other nights we'd go to Killarney Racecourse. We'd literally climb the gates and might run around the racetrack six or seven times, and we'd do a number of sprints.

When it came to the final, Kerry had a great advantage over their opponents, as the Kingdom had been in attendance at Offaly's semi-final. Brendan Lynch explains that

we had been forewarned, in that for their semi-final, Kerry played in a curtain-raiser against Kildare, so we were all present and able to see them up close. They were quite impressive, so that put us on our guard. We had beaten them pretty convincingly in the National League final, so I think having seeing them in the semi-final perhaps eliminated any complacency.

There was an injury scare for the Kingdom, as reported in the *Kerryman*.

Pre match doubts about the fitness of Mick O'Connell had become almost unbearable as match time approached. And then suddenly there he was to take his place in the team picture. At that moment every Kerryman in Croke Park knew that it was birthday time—our 21st.

Séamus Mac Gearailt remembers well the moment O'Connell appeared on the field.

Micko was injured coming up to the game, and we weren't sure ourselves until the last minute whether he'd be playing or not. When it came to running out at Croke Park he sent us all out first and waited himself for maybe thirty seconds. I'd say he was probably saying to himself that the Kerry supporters would be wondering,

Am I coming or am I not, and he came out to rapturous reception. I thought the stands would collapse with the noise when he appeared on the field.

Kerry won the toss and elected to play with the strong wind. The decision reaped immediate dividends, Mick Gleeson putting the Kingdom ahead in the first minute. Offaly were level after five minutes, and Tony McTague pointed a free to give the Leinster champions the lead after thirteen minutes.

Kerry then took over, registering points from Liam Higgins, Brendan Lynch and Mick Gleeson. The score read Kerry 0-4, Offaly 0-2 after sixteen minutes. Chances were at a premium on a day of difficult scoring conditions, and every one counted. Entering the twenty-fourth minute, Offaly spurned a glorious opportunity, as noted in the *Kerryman*. 'Offaly broke away in a sustained attack and only a daring dive by Mick Morris and two fine saves by Johnny Culloty saved Kerry.' Offaly hadn't scored since the thirteenth minute and wouldn't do so again until the second half. Kerry meanwhile increased their advantage before the break. D. J. Crowley pointed from about fifty yards. An advantage of five points to two was Kerry's at the break.

According to Tom Prendergast,

it was an atrocious day. There very high winds. We were playing against a gale-force wind in the second half, and we were only leading at half time by three points. I'd say everybody was of the view that that was another all-Ireland gone, but we stuck it out.

Every match has a defining moment, and the one in this game arrived less than a minute into the second half. Johnny Culloty, the Kerry goalkeeper and captain, produced an outstanding save from Seán Evans. Mícheál Ó Muircheartaigh believes there would have been a different result but for Culloty's intervention.

It was a man from Castlemaine hit it, Evans . . . Offaly would have won that all-Ireland only for that save. Johnny was a very calculating goalkeeper, had a great sense of positioning, and with the forward instinct he was a good man to clear a ball, to put somebody in possession.

Culloty is modest in his own assessment of the save, 'To me anyway it looked like he could only put the ball into my left side of the goal, so I went to my left, and he shot to the left.'

Culloty's save may have been seen as instinctive, but Weeshie Fogarty says there's a story behind the moment.

In the weeks leading up to that we had been training in Tralee. But Johnny'd call for me in the evenings when we wouldn't have Kerry training and we'd go down to the St Brendan's College field and we'd be practising. One particular day he said to me, I want to try out this now. We had another fella with us, some fella kicking in the ball. He said, I want you to get the ball, turn around and kick it all in one movement to my left-hand side. Do that now, he said, a number of times. We'd a fella kicking in the ball to me. I'd jump up, catch the ball, turn around all in one movement and kick the ball to his left. I did that ten times, he says that's the way Seán Evans shoots—I want to be ready for that.

Two unanswered points meant that Offaly had cut the deficit to one within seven minutes of the second period. Scores from Mick O'Dwyer and D. J. Crowley restored Kerry's three-point advantage. After ten minutes it was seven points to four to the Kingdom.

Kerry were hanging on, seven to six, entering the final quarter. The remaining fifteen minutes belonged to the Kingdom, during which time they registered three points to Offaly's one, three points that ensured that Sam was returning to the Kingdom.

The following week's *Kerryman* headline read: 'Indestructible D. J. Crowley was the hero of a historic triumph.' Crowley believes he just had 'one of those days.'

Ten points to seven was a respectable score, given the conditions the teams had to endure. Brendan Lynch, the Kingdom forward, believes that the pressure of the occasion didn't help either.

While we had a very good side in '69, we didn't play well in that final. It was not a good game, and we were grateful to Mick O'Connell's kicking, which won us the game . . . not a great spectacle to watch, but it was important to win.

The following day Johnny Culloty and his team-mates were guests of honour at Guinness's brewery in Dublin and RTE, as Séamus Mac Gearailt recalls.

> The homecoming was very special for the 21st. Monday morning we used to be invited to Montrose. We'd be shown a film of the match and then we'd have a reception there after. Jackie Lyne, our trainer, was working for Guinness and he invited us down to St James's Gate, the Guinness plant. We all had a sample. We came home by train. Our first stop was Rathmore, where I still remember Father Kelly, Seán Kelly's uncle, giving a rapturous speech and speaking of how delighted Kerry were to welcome home the 21st all-Ireland winning team.

That wasn't the only speech to stand out, as D. J. Crowley well remembers.

> The crowd in Rathmore was unbelievable. We all went up on the railway bridge. I was the first person ever to win an all-Ireland from Rathmore. I'd say it must have been the first time that Mick O'Connell ever spoke in public. He said he'd like to congratulate D. J. Crowley, the first player from Rathmore to win an all-Ireland, the best midfielder in Kerry. There was a bit of a pause, and he said, 'After myself.'

As sixth sub for the final against Offaly, Weeshie Fogarty didn't receive an all-Ireland medal. Unfortunately for him, this was not the only time that his contribution to the 1969 cause was disregarded.

> I didn't get a medal . . . Up until 1970 or '71 there was only five substitutes' medals; there was no goalkeepers' medals. Even though I had been up the line for the Munster final and semi-final, when it came to the final and the medals were to be decided I was dropped to sixth. Then (after '69) the rule was that there was a special medal for the goalkeeper, a special medal to cover the full-back line, half-back line, midfield, half-forward line and full-forward. The thought was that you have a sub for each line of the field. I was bitterly disappointed that I didn't get a medal, because I had put in an awful

lot of work and I had trained and played Leagues and put in an awful lot of time. But I was more hurt later because twenty-five years after and it's a tradition now in the GAA that . . . after a team winning an all-Ireland they're brought to Croke Park and they're introduced at half time and they're feted over the weekend. Twenty-five years after Kerry winning the 1969 all-Ireland, Kerry were brought to Croke Park. They never asked me to go, as I didn't have a medal, even though I had been playing, and that hurt an awful lot . . . I didn't make any fuss about it but a great friend of mine, Murt Galvin . . . who was treasurer of the county board for a long number of years, heard about what was happening and he kicked up rumpus. He went to the county board, and he went to Croke Park and did everything he could to rectify it . . . I'd forgive them, but I won't forget it.

Pat Spillane was only a starry-eyed boy at this time, but the events of the late 1960s had already made up his mind about his future ambitions.

My father died at a young age—I was only eight. He was a selector with Kerry in '64, and died a few days after. My first real memory was the late '60s, 'cause my uncle Jackie Lyne was managing the Kerry team, and he brought me to one of the semi-finals as part of the Kerry team group, and that was a fantastic experience and whetted my appetite.

———

Kerry were back to defend their title in 1970. Nowadays there's a lot of emphasis on how the off season can be used to have squads ready for the coming year. It was a very different policy in 1970. Tom Prendergast describes the kind of break the players had between seasons.

There was always a big break in those years when we were finished the championship in September. Really, there was no more training for the team until the following March . . . maybe there was a few National League games after the all-Ireland series until the end of October, and then nothing happened again until February or March. Kerry never did a whole lot of training for the National

League, with the exception of course of the final . . . You wouldn't be able to do anyway, because you wouldn't have the brightness in the evenings. We used get down to serious business then in March to prepare for the championship again.

March 1970 saw Kerry embark on a world tour, visiting Australia, New Zealand and the United States. D. J. Crowley has fond memories of the trip.

We had a great tour . . . We got huge receptions wherever we went. The first place we stopped was in Perth in Australia. Then we played all across Australia—Perth, Melbourne, Sydney, Adelaide—and then we went on and played in Auckland in New Zealand. We had a full month tour. We went around the world actually. We got time off from our jobs, the county board paid our salaries for that month, and we got £100 spending money. We didn't do too bad. We had a marvellous trip, marvellous togetherness.

Séamus Mac Gearailt was a principal member of the 1969 winning side, but a knee injury would curtail his involvement in 1970. He and Mick Morris were the only members of the previous season's championship-winning side not available for the 1970 opener with Limerick. John O'Keeffe and Donie O'Sullivan came into a side that would remain unchanged for the full season.

Kerry's defence of its Munster championship title got off to the smoothest of starts, with Limerick being torn apart. The Kingdom put up four points in as many minutes and led by seven to nil after only ten minutes. Limerick showed some resistance, cutting the deficit to two by the 21-minute mark. Kerry scored seven points in the closing minutes of the half, at the end of which they led by 0-15 to 1-2.

Mick Gleeson goaled for Kerry two minutes into the second period, and he also goaled two minutes from the end. Kerry 2-19, Limerick 2-5 was the result.

Cork were next up for the Kingdom, with the Munster title at stake. The provincial decider proved to be as one-sided as the previous outing against Limerick. Kerry were phenomenal from the off, as the *Irish Press* reported.

The ball was caught by Pat Griffin who placed Liam Higgins before taking a return pass and careering through for a goal. O'Dwyer quickly added a point from play but Bernie O'Neill replied with a great solo effort for Cork. Almost immediately another bad Cork clearance was intercepted by Brendan Lynch who sent Pat Griffin through for a point. The kickout was once again low and went to Lynch, who linked up with Pat Griffin, who in turn parted to Liam Higgins, whose shot gave Billy Morgan no chance and left Kerry ahead 2-3 to 0-1 after ten minutes.

Mick O'Connell had four points in seven minutes later on in the first period. The first half ended with Kerry leading by fourteen points, 2-12 to 0-4. The destiny of the Munster crown was decided at this stage.

Cork fought valiantly in the second half, however; two Denis Coughlan goals helped them reduce the deficit to 2-14 to 2-7 by the three-quarter mark. But the outcome was never really in doubt; from there on Kerry asserted their superiority. Mick O'Dwyer also got in on the scoring in the final quarter and finished the game with eight points. Kerry won by 2-22 to 2-9. That thirteen-point demolition of Cork moved Kerry one step closer to defending their all-Ireland crown.

Derry were the all-Ireland semi-final opponents. What an encounter it turned out to be! The early signs were ominous for Kerry. The Kingdom managed just one score in the first quarter of an hour. The Green and Gold also had to survive an injury scare, as described by the *Irish Times*.

The first dramatic incident of the match occurred in the third minute when Mick O'Connell, after delivering the ball, was charged by Séamus Logan. The Kerry midfielder walked to the line with an injured right knee. A point from Tom Quinn gave Derry a lead of 0-5 to 0-1 after thirteen minutes. But then, Mick O'Connell, having received some rapid treatment in the dug out, returned to the fray.

O'Connell had been off the pitch for thirteen minutes. How he was missed! Derry had dominated since the throw-in but failed to make their superiority count on the scoreboard. Brendan Lynch pulled a point back for Kerry, who then trailed five to two.

The first Derry penalty of the afternoon came in the twenty-first minute. The *Irish Press* described how

> Paud O'Donoghue fouled the full forward in the parallelogram as
> the ball dropped. Almost indifferently, Seán O'Connell stepped up
> to the spot kick, and almost casually it seemed, stroked it to the
> centre of the goalline, where Johnny Culloty grabbed the ball
> securely and quickly cleared it away.

A point by Liam Higgins for Kerry meant there were only two between
the sides. The half ended with the same gap: Derry eight, Kerry six.

Derry had the first point of the second period, from a free, to go
three in front. Kerry replied, with Mick O'Dwyer and Pat Griffin scores
putting the minimum between the teams. Eight minutes into the half,
Derry were awarded their second spot kick. Seán O'Connell, who had
missed the first-half penalty, was dumped to the ground. Confusion
reigned, as the *Irish Times* reported.

> O'Connell was fouled while in possession almost on the goal line.
> Here was his big chance to make amends. A goal at this stage might
> well have rattled Kerry; it certainly would have given a new impetus
> to Derry, whose half time lead of two points was meagre reward for
> their territorial domination over the first 40 minutes of play. But
> this time the captain decided to delegate responsibility. After some
> moments of confusion during which it appeared that a number of
> players were appealing to O'Connell to take the kick himself,
> Séamus Lagan charged in and as someone described the event
> afterwards, threw his leg at the ball, sending, with uncontrolled
> power, two yards wide of the left upright.

Donie O' Sullivan is in no doubt that fortune was on Kerry's side that
day against Derry.

> Back in 1968 Down got a goal against Kerry. I don't want to call it a
> freak. In 1970 we got a lot of breaks, particularly against Derry.
> Derry were the team that year that we were afraid of . . . Ten minutes
> after half-time, when they were up two points, they missed. If they
> had scored one of those I doubt we would have won it—even
> though we won it well in the end. But that was the breaking point.

A minute later Kerry were level with a Mick O'Dwyer free. Another O'Dwyer point, again from a free, put the Kingdom in front, ten points to nine. Kerry then had to survive a goal scare, as the *Irish Times* described.

> The Ulster side missed a golden chance of a goal in the 56th minute because Seán O'Connell held on to the ball too long. Séamus Murphy averted danger with a dashing interception and lofty clearance.

Derry faded away after that. Pat Griffin put over two points to help Kerry into a lead of fourteen points to nine. From there they tagged on nine more points. Derry's second and final point of the second half arrived seven minutes from the end, but Kerry had won on a score of 0-23 to 0-10. The *Irish Times* had little sympathy for Derry.

> It would be quite misleading to suggest that the Ulster champions were the victims of bad luck; they fashioned most of their misfortunes. Yet the extent of the losers' pressure on the Kerry line is seen in the figures of the game, which record that they kicked 15 wides and forced four 50s.

The *Irish Press* agreed that the least wasteful side deserved their victory.

> Kerry go into yet another all-Ireland final because it is a truism of football, as of any team sport, that the creation of chances is only half the work done and is worthless if not embellished with a rich translation into scores. There was often subtlety in Kerry's play, they were frequently defiantly unyielding to the point of being scornful of the opposition. But fundamentally they won this semi-final because having made their opportunities they were able to convert them into scores . . . I feel that they [Derry] would not have dethroned the champions for they were bereft of ideas in attack, had no variety in their approach work and never had the quicksilver mobility or unified smartness of Kerry.

Meath were the last barrier on the road to consecutive all-Ireland titles. They had secured their place in the final with a defeat of Galway by fifteen points to eleven.

In 1970 the eighty-minute final was introduced. For the next four years this extension of the game was applied, but in 1975 a compromise was reached, with finals of seventy minutes.

Kerry were pushed every inch of the way in one of the truly great all-Ireland finals in 1970. Twice in the opening thirteen minutes they went ahead; each time, Meath drew level. In the fourteenth minute Vincent Lynch put Meath ahead for the only time that afternoon. Ninety seconds later Éamonn O'Donoghue had Kerry level. Then, in the next minute, the same player had an opportunity to put the Kingdom in front. However, his goal-bound effort was saved. Liam Higgins fisted Kerry ahead, but Meath once more responded, and the sides were level, at four points apiece, after nineteen minutes. Mick O'Dwyer then had Kerry in front again, but only for two minutes. Meath's response was similar when Brendan Lynch pointed for Kerry. The game was tied at six points apiece with eleven minutes remaining in the opening period. Kerry edged away from Meath with two points, Mick O'Dwyer and Brendan Lynch the ones on target. Meath halved the deficit, but Mick O'Dwyer restored the two-point advantage two minutes before the break. The Kerry goal then had a lucky escape, Meath hitting the Kingdom crossbar. Fay did put over for the Leinster team, leaving the score at half time Kerry 0-9, Meath 0-8.

A point by Pat Griffin four minutes into the second half put Kerry two ahead. Meath once again replied in kind. The Leinstermen were powerless, however, during the next five minutes. Points courtesy of O'Dwyer, Gleeson, O'Donoghue and Lynch put Kerry ahead by fourteen points to nine. Consecutive points by Fay brought Kerry's lead down to three, at fourteen points to eleven.

The game was once more turned on its head, with two Kerry scores inside a minute, approaching the mid-point of the half. A point by Pat Griffin was followed by a goal, as described by the *Kerryman*.

> Gleeson's goal came after a high lob towards the square by Mick O'Dwyer. D. J. Crowley tussled with Jack Quinn and in the general confusion McCormack punched the ball away weakly. Mick Gleeson was first to get to it and from close range he stabbed a left footed ground shot to the net.

Brendan Lynch feels that Gleeson's goal was critical.

It was at a crucial stage in the second half. He pounced in a very opportunistic way and finished off a ball that broke near the goalmouth. It gave us breathing space.

The goal seemed to have put paid to Meath, as they now trailed 1-15 to 0-11. Meath added their twelfth point before Kerry once again took control. It was 1-17 to 0-12 as the teams entered the closing nineteen minutes of this eighty-minute final. Five unanswered Meath points reduced the gap to a goal for the last ten minutes. A point by Mick O'Connell again gave Kerry breathing space. Six minutes from time it was 1-18 to 0-17 in favour of the Kingdom. Still, Kerry couldn't shake their opponents off. Meath scored again, and the Kerry lead was down to three points, at 1-18 to 0-18. The game was hanging in the balance with five minutes left on the clock. Sixty seconds later the game was finally out of the reach of Meath, as the *Kerryman* reported.

> The former policeman D. J. Crowley took the law into his own hands. Taking a pass from John O'Keeffe about forty yards from the Meath goal, DJ crashed his way past two Meath tackles, flicked the ball from toe to hand twice in his own inimitable fashion and then drove a hard right footed shot to the Meath net for one of the best goals we have seen in an all-Ireland final.

Forty years later Crowley has no difficulty recalling his wonder strike.

> It was a kick-out from Paud O'Donoghue . . . John O'Keeffe caught it at centrefield. I was running outside him, and he passed it to me and I went off on a solo run. I used to practise this kick of pulling the ball back to my foot. Mick O'Connell always did: that was the natural style he played. I was trying to pull it back to my right foot, then kick it around the full-back into the left corner. It worked that day. It never, ever worked in training.

Tongue in cheek, Séamus Mac Gearailt has a different opinion of the event.

> According to D. J., himself and Pat Griffin were practising this move in training for months beforehand. I never saw them practise it. My

memory was, he took a snapshot and probably went for a point and ended up in the goal . . . That was a phenomenal run. It was only DJ could do that run, because he had the strength of an ox, and when he got moving it was very hard to stop him. He had a great rasper with the left foot too.

That final and Crowley's goal have lived long in the memory of Dónal Keenan, the renowned GAA correspondent.

That would have to be the first early memories I would have had. Even now the memory is unimpaired. You feel this charge and the power of what he did—one of the great memories.

'Take a bow, Jackie Lyne,' shouted the headline in the *Kerryman*. 'The knockers are silent now.'

Victory over Meath gave John O'Keeffe his first all-Ireland medal, emulating his father, Frank, who was part of the victorious side of 1946. Johnno's memories of the 1970 decider are scant.

I was told to mark my man very closely. I was so anxious about covering my man that it's more or less what I did for the day. I remember towards the end all right I think I set up DJ Crowley for his famous goal. He can thank me for that pass! It was great to win it, and I suppose after that the team stayed together for a while more. It was obvious that the share of the players were ageing. As it transpires, we did get to another final in 1972.

Kerry may have lost to Offaly in the replay in 1972, but Johnno's time would come once more.

Having missed out on a starting spot in 1962 and 1969, Donie O'Sullivan went one better in 1970, captaining the Kingdom to all-Ireland title number 22. His misfortune continued in that year, however, as injury forced him to retire before half time against Meath. Reflecting on his success with Kerry, O'Sullivan feels that it isn't all about the medals.

I have a personal thing about it: if you pass the age of forty you shouldn't be talking about medals. It's gone. It not so much what went with winning, anyhow. It isn't the medals: I think what went with it, and above all I think the best things is the friends that came, the genuine friends, playing with and against.

A future Kerry legend was then witnessing at first hand the impact of Kerry football. Jack O'Shea was spending time in the company of two other South Kerry men, Mick O'Connell and Mick O'Dwyer.

I was a kind of a ball boy with them. I would go down and watch them train, and go behind the goal and kick the ball back to them. Occasionally Mick O'Connell would stand away from me and start kicking the ball at me, and showing me things to practise. It was intriguing just to watch how professional the two of them were. These were the days when they didn't train with Kerry, who used to get together maybe once a week or a fortnight. These two men used to put in a couple of extra days themselves and spend their time kicking. It wasn't fitness.

One of those men, Mick O'Dwyer, had a double role for Kerry's consecutive victories. He jokingly recalls the team selection meetings.

In 1970 I was a selector. I became county selector in 1965 and continued to be a county selector right through until I finished with Kerry. That was unique in Kerry at the time, to be a player and a selector. Maybe that's why I was a player that lasted so long: I was able to put myself down at corner-forward number 1 when I'd go into meetings! [Joe] Keohane was there at the time, and when I'd go in he'd say, I suppose we'll have to put you down corner-forward. I'd say, you've no other option, I'm here anyway, and I'll know if you vote against me! I suppose I was first man on the team every time we played.

Chapter 10 ⌁

| ALL THE YOUNG DUDES

1975 was a watershed year for Kerry football. After losing to Offaly in the 1972 final, Kerry failed to come out of Munster in 1973 and 74: Cork had ended Kerry's championship hopes in both years. Hopes weren't high for 1975; and, sure enough, Kerry exited the National League at the quarter-final stage, going down to Meath, by eleven points to six, in March. In the wake of that defeat Mick O'Dwyer was appointed manager of the Kerry team.

Paudie O'Mahony, then the Kerry goalkeeper, recalls that

> there was a team meeting after that game, before we left Dublin. That's where this team changed. Dwyer made us get serious. We did twenty-seven days' training in a row coming up to the Munster championship that year. It made men out of mice. We had no clue in the world how to train properly.

O'Dwyer took over from Johnny Culloty, whose period as trainer may not have reaped rewards on the field; however, it laid the foundations for the years of glory that were to follow. Culloty was responsible for introducing such players as Paudie O'Mahony (debut 1974), Jimmy Deenihan (1973), Páidí Ó Sé (1974), Ger O'Keeffe (1973), Ger Power (1973), Mikey Sheehy (1974) and John Egan (1973) to the inter-county set-up. O'Dwyer fused those men with his own new breed of players, and the greatest team the sport has ever seen was born.

Pat Griffin, the former Kerry forward, whose last championship appearance was in 1974, says he'd love to have been part of this new side.

> The Kerry team under Mick O'Dwyer would have suited my style. I was the kind of forward that, when I saw a back get the ball, I'd move

into position looking for it. You weren't always guaranteed to get it in the early '60s.

Two men who had debuted in 1971, Paudie Lynch and Mickey Ned O'Sullivan, would be pivotal to the success of 1975. O'Sullivan was captain of the side in 1975. He's quick to dispel the notion that this team just suddenly came into being.

> I was there from '70 onwards, and then there was a transition, from an older group of Kerry players that lasted to '72, and then the new breed of Kerry players started. A lot of those young lads had been there for three or four years. There's a myth that they came overnight. I played in four Munster finals before we won one in 1975. A lot of the other lads did as well. At the same time we had won four National Leagues. Mick O'Dwyer came in 1975, and he brought a new approach of physical fitness at such a very high standard. The lads were young and they couldn't get enough of it. They were able to transfer the physical fitness onto the field. It was very exciting. I was very fortunate that I was around at the right time. All these incredible players just surfaced. In another county they might have been just ordinary players. We all had looked up to Mick as an inter-county player. We had great respect for him. He took it very serious. He instilled a new type of confidence . . . never seen before in a Kerry team.

Three members of the 1970 all-Ireland winning side remained involved for the 1975 championship: John O'Keeffe, Brendan Lynch and Donie O'Sullivan.

Jimmy Deenihan feels that it was important to have at least a degree of continuity. Of Donie O'Sullivan he says:

> Even to have someone like him there as a father figure was quite important. A lot of people don't recall that Donie was part of that panel, still playing very good football. John O'Keeffe was always a great leader. We all looked up to him, although he was just our own age. He had that experience. He was a tremendous athlete . . . Brendan Lynch as well. We brought some experience with us, but overall it was a very young team. We were full of adventure, we were

trying different things. We didn't have any fear of anyone.

Other members of the 1970 all-Ireland winning side were not so fortunate in surviving O'Dwyer's cull. Séamus Mac Gearailt was among those whose inter-county career had been cut short.

When Mick O'Dwyer took over in 1975 he got rid of a lot of us. At the time we weren't too happy about it. We thought we had some more to offer. In hindsight he was right. He went with his young cubs, surprised Dublin in 1975; they matured to a fantastic team in 1978.

Mícheál Ó Muircheartaigh has noted that O'Dwyer was keen to give youth its chance.

Some people say that he got rid of good players that had a little bit left. The team that had won in '70, they had failed against Offaly in 1972 but they had players still in their mid-twenties. Most of them were let go. He may have realised there was lots of young, good talent about; give them all a chance together. When he took charge he gave them all a chance. The result was spectacular. It was obvious in the [1975] Munster final. Cork had won [the all-Ireland] with a very good team [in 1973], as good a team as Cork ever had. They scored five goals against Kerry in the Munster final . . . They scored fifteen goals in all in that championship. [Cork] were surprised by Dublin in 1974. They underestimated Dublin. Dublin had won Leinster against the run of expectation from people outside of Dublin. They [Cork] were all set to go again in 1975 when this unknown young Kerry team came, upset them completely in Killarney.

Eoghan Corry lauds O'Dwyer's response to four seasons of failure.

Mickey Ned Sullivan and Mick O'Dwyer, when they went to a coaching course, they saw the Dublin team and the intensity with which they were training. They came across this and came back to Kerry in 1975 and said, We're not going to do the old training methods. The old fitness standards aren't going to work any more. They produced undoubtedly the greatest football team this island has ever seen out of that. Innovation is what Kerry does. Reaction is what Kerry does.

Ger Power too acknowledges the impact of O'Dwyer's appointment and how his methods have stood the test of time.

> The whole thing changed when Micko took over. The emphasis was on unbelievable physical fitness. I wasn't the greatest man to do rounds of the pitch at training. Micko would call me the hare. I might do around two laps at the start, and that would be the end. To this present day Micko's method has worked, and people can say that he ran people into the ground, but if you look at Wicklow, Kildare and all the other teams, at the end of the day Micko's system has worked.

Mikey Sheehy added his voice to those quick to appreciate the step-up once O'Dwyer had taken over.

> We were trained to win the all-Ireland. The training was savage. Micko took over in March of 1975, and I think we trained twenty-seven nights in a row. That's fact. I never in my life encountered that type of training. At that particular time it was as professional as it could have been. I think he realised he had a very good team . . . Lads were coming through at under-age level. He knew there was quality there. He wanted to get the fitness levels up. When he got the fitness up he laid down the marker. That was the main reason we won the all-Ireland in 1975.

Tim Kennelly was among the newcomers in 1975. His team-mate Jimmy Deenihan believes that Kennelly's placing at centre-back was pivotal to the success that lay ahead.

> I remember when we were building the team in 1974 and 1975 Tim was drafted in at centre-back. They were looking for a centre-back. It was difficult to get someone of the calibre that you would want for the centre-back. Tim fitted the bill. He was a great athlete himself. He was a great footballer. He had massive strength, natural strength from his farming background. He was confident and a great

competitor ... If you looked at that team, every one of us could hold down our position. That's all we had to do really. We had to ensure that we held out our own position and that we were competent and capable of playing in that position—no player depended on anybody else.

John Barry, in his *Kerryman* preview of the championship opener against Tipperary, stated:

Kerry are not likely to be suffering from any feeling of over-confidence, for the simple fact is that Kerry could find themselves making an ignominious exit from the championship at the hands of a Tipperary side that has shown excellent form in its last two outings. The memory of that depressing league display against Meath a few months back is still very fresh in the mind.

Mikey Sheehy believes that apprehension going into the Tipp match was understandable.

You could understand why, because we were hammered in the quarter-final of the National League by Meath. Things weren't right. The training hadn't been right ... Shortly after that game Micko was appointed. The whole thing changed.

Mick O'Dwyer handed championship debuts to seven players against Tipperary: Batt O'Shea, Tim Kennelly, Ger O'Driscoll, Ogie Moran, Pat McCarthy, Pat Spillane and Ray Prendeville. Also on the team that day were Paudie O'Mahony, Páidí Ó Sé, Ger O'Keeffe, Mickey Ned O'Sullivan, Ger Power, Brendan Lynch, John Egan and Mikey Sheehy. Ogie Moran wore number 9 that day.

Kerry v. Tipperary was a game that was in the balance up to the final quarter of an hour. It didn't start that way: Ray Prendeville marked his debut with a goal inside three minutes. Kerry also put over the bar to race into a four-point lead. They were five ahead by the twelfth minute; they would put over one more score between then and half time, a Brendan Lynch point close to the break. By the short whistle Tipperary had drawn level. When the teams turned around, the score read Kerry 1-4, Tipperary 0-7.

Tipperary went in front a little after six minutes into the second period. Things changed once John Egan was brought out to the forty, as Pat Spillane recalls. 'Suddenly everything changed like a switch, John Egan brought out to centre-forward, and he turned the game and we never looked back.' Egan put over the equaliser and then had Kerry in front after ten minutes. In the twelfth and fifteenth minutes goals from John Egan put Kerry in control and out of reach.

A less than convincing performance, but Kerry had negotiated the obstacle that was Tipperary: Kerry 3-13, Tipp 0-9.

Victory over Tipp secured a Munster final place against a fancied Cork team. The return of John O'Keeffe at full-back strengthened the Kingdom side. O'Keeffe felt that Cork were *the* team in Munster at that time.

> They won the all-Ireland in 1973, and they still had—on paper anyway—a very strong team. We were just a team coming out winning an under-21 championship. Brendan Lynch and myself were the two veterans. At that stage I was twenty-four.

Cork dominated early on but failed to find scores to match. Kerry replied to two points from Denny Allen with scores by Brendan Lynch and Pat Spillane. In the tenth minute a dangerous ball across the Kerry goal went narrowly wide. Cork weren't so fortunate three minutes later with a fluke own-goal. Not long after that Kerry had the ball in the net again. However, John Egan's effort was disallowed, the referee awarded a penalty instead, and this was missed. Points by Pat McCarthy and Brendan Lynch extended Kerry's lead.

After Declan Barron put over for Cork, Mikey Sheehy and Mickey Ned O'Sullivan pointed for Kerry. Kerry's advantage was six points, 1-6 to 0-3. Cork were then afforded the opportunity to halve the deficit, but Paudie O'Mahony saved Jimmy Barry Murphy's spot kick. A Mikey Sheehy free two minutes before the break saw Kerry go in with a 1-7 to 0-3 advantage.

Cork had the first point of the second period, but scores from Brendan Lynch and John Egan kept Kerry out of reach. A relatively mundane second period was lit up by a magnificent save from Paudie O'Mahony, who denied Ray Cummins a goal. Kerry, with John O'Keeffe and Mickey Ned O'Sullivan to the fore, won by ten points, 1-14 to 0-7.

Sligo were the next barrier on the road to all-Ireland glory. Paudie Lynch put Kerry in front after four minutes. Sligo equalised from a free. Paudie Lynch's brother Brendan had Kerry back in front in the tenth minute. Sligo were then handed a golden opportunity to score the first goal of the season against the Kerry keeper, Paudie O'Mahony. The westerners were awarded but subsequently missed a penalty, following a foul by Páidí Ó Sé. After Pat Spillane pointed just before the quarter hour, ten minutes passed before the next score. Consecutive points from the Lynch brothers, Paudie and Brendan, had Kerry five to one in front. Ger O'Driscoll made it six to one. The Kingdom led 0-7 to 0-2 at half time.

Points early in the second period from Ger O'Driscoll and John Egan made it 0-9 to 0-2 to Kerry. At the mid-point of the half Ger Power soloed seventy yards up the pitch and put over. It was now ten points to three to Kerry.

Sligo were torn apart in the concluding minutes. There were ten minutes remaining when the first Kingdom goal arrived, as described by the *Kerryman*.

> This followed a magnificent catch in the middle of the field by Paudie Lynch and the finishing touch was applied by John Egan who was put through by Pat Spillane.

John Egan and Pat Spillane were also involved in the second goal. As the *Kerryman* recorded, the roles were reversed on this occasion.

> One minute later came Kerry's second goal by Pat Spillane. This time John Egan returned the compliment when putting Spillane through and the Templenoe man gave Sligo keeper Cummins no chance with a powerful drive.

John Egan then pointed for Kerry before tucking away goal number 3. The Kingdom won, 3-13 to 0-5.

The other semi-final saw Dublin take care of Derry with a score of 3-13 to 3-8. Most of the GAA fraternity had felt that Dublin were likely to win against a young Kingdom team. Jim O'Sullivan in the *Cork Examiner* was one of the few to predict a Kerry victory.

Kerry against Dublin saw the introduction of one of the more unusual all-Ireland final day superstitions, that of Pat Spillane's.

I would be very religious. We would never have left home without my mother putting holy water on everything from the togs to the socks to the boots, the laces. Holy water would have been on everything. Before going out I would always like to stand in the same place in the photograph, I would always like to sit in the same place in the dressing-room, I would always like to come out in the same position. Before every all-Ireland final I would have eaten two packets of Maltesers at one o'clock. How a superstition like that starts is all imagination. It's all about keeping yourself happy. I convinced myself I was getting bundles of energy from Maltesers. Different strokes for different folk. Take semi-finals and all-Ireland, going by bus to Croke Park I would have sat alone, but I would have the eyes closed and I would be visualising in my head everything about the game. Sports psychologists now have a name for it, visualisation. I would always see the glass half full rather than half empty. I would always have been positive. I would always believe I could beat the fellow marking me. I would always believe I could score so much. Whether you did or didn't, it's important to be positive. In visualisation, what you imagined was all the positive things—getting to the ball first, rounding the opponent, kicking the ball over the bar, and I would be re-running that through my head for half an hour before going to a match.

Reflecting on the decider of thirty-five years ago, Mikey Sheehy believes that circumstances were in the Kingdom's favour.

The team was very much tuned in that day . . . It was a damp day and I think it suited us. Dublin were probably a little bit overconfident. We caught them.

Paudie O'Mahony was a keen observer of the opposition in the moments leading up to the throw-in.

My big memory of it is the parade around the field. It was a great occasion. All the Dublin players were chewing gum, and they were very tense-looking. A lot of the players on the Kerry team didn't know what to make of the occasion. We were a team of young fellows. We weren't given the chance, and Dwyer told us go out and enjoy the occasion. We had a fair idea in the dressing-room we were going to beat Dublin that day.

Dublin had the opening score, a point by Brian Mullins after two minutes. Kerry responded, with interest, inside sixty seconds, as described by the *Kerryman*.

Michael Sheehy failed to connect with a free from about 45 yards range and the ball broke off Dublin defender Gay O'Driscoll and went to John Egan—the Sneem man punished the mistake to the full; putting the ball expertly out of the reach of goalkeeper Paddy Cullen. Thirty seconds later Ogie Moran cut through to score a great point.

Dublin were blitzed in the opening ten minutes. Kerry were relentless, opening up a lead of 1-3 to 0-1. Dublin pulled back two points, leaving them trailing by that John Egan goal. Mid-way through the half Mickey Ned O'Sullivan went on a mesmerising run through the Dublin defence, before being eventually stopped in his tracks, albeit illegally. O'Sullivan has far from a total recollection of the episode.

Basically, I can remember getting the ball . . . I was psyched up to the last, and I felt I could beat Dublin on my own. That was the rock I perished on. I remember running at the defence and getting a few belts, and then the light went out. That's as far as I can remember until I woke up that night. I was in the Richmond Hospital.

Pat Spillane was the immediate beneficiary of O'Sullivan's removal on the day, but he feels that the incident had far greater ramifications for O'Sullivan himself.

He was being clattered. Four times he was clattered. They nearly took the head off him. It should have been a red card immediately . . . Mickey was a lightning-fast player—great ball-carrier. He never really came back to his form before then. It cost Mickey his playing career really, that injury.

The free following that infamous foul was pointed, and by the twenty-fifth minute Kerry had stretched their advantage to six. They led at the interval, 1-6 to 0-4.

Twice Jimmy Keaveney put over for Dublin early in the second half. On both occasions Kerry replied, as points by Mikey Sheehy and Brendan Lynch kept the Kingdom five to the good. Ger O'Driscoll then had the chance to put the game beyond Dublin. However, his shot from the edge of the area flew wide. Mikey Sheehy pointed, and Jimmy Keaveney did likewise for Dublin. A Pat Spillane point followed, and Keaveney once more did the same at the opposite end. Kerry's advantage remained at five points, 1-10 to 0-8, with seventeen minutes remaining. Thirteen minutes from time John Egan could have wrapped up a Kerry win, but his punched effort rebounded off the crossbar. Jimmy Keaveney and Pat Spillane swapped points. Five minutes from time, Ger O'Driscoll atoned for his glaring miss from earlier in the half, as described in the *Kerryman*.

> O'Driscoll put the game beyond Dublin's reach when he finished off a fine Kerry movement for a goal. The ball travelled via Michael Sheehy to Ogie Moran to John Egan and Egan's centre was cleverly deflected into the net by O'Driscoll.

As full time approached, Pat Spillane discovered that, on top of winning an all-Ireland medal, he would be making the legendary journey up the steps to collect the Sam Maguire.

> I always remember walking up to the stand with the head steward, asking him for the Irish for 'on behalf of.' '*Tá an-áthas orm an corn seo a ghlacadh ar son fhoireann Chiarraí.*' They were my *cúpla focal*. My first all-Ireland final, and I ended up getting the ultimate accolade of taking the Sam Maguire in the Hogan Stand in 1975. I've never seen it since: it certainly would have been the worst speech given by an all-Ireland winning captain. You dream about those things . . . It was a great day.

It's standard procedure for the forwards to receive much of the plaudits for a victory. However, Brendan Lynch fully acknowledges the role of the defence in that and subsequent victories.

> They were a very talented bunch. I've often said that the key was the defence, which was lightning-fast, guarded scores jealously, and in the twelve months up to the 1975 final had conceded something like an average of less than ten points. That was the foundation of the success of 1975.

Liam Higgins once spoke of the importance of defenders such as Tim Kennelly.

> By God, did he cover himself with glory in 1975! He had a tremendous game against Cork, a mighty game against Sligo in the semi-final, and I suppose another near Man of the Match performance against Dublin in the final of 1975. From then on you could just put him in centre-half-back and forget about him. He was so solid, so strong, so safe and dependable under the ball . . . He was a selfless player. Played for everybody. Played for all around him.

John Egan remembers that Kerry had travelled to the final convinced that they would be victorious.

> People talk about that as being one of the great Kerry displays. I don't think so. It was a display of fierce enthusiasm, fierce appetite. We were young and we were raw but we had no experience. Mick O'Dwyer never, ever talked about losing that match. He was so positive we didn't even worry about Dublin . . . We were flying fit, ran Dublin off their feet, an ageing team. That's where it all started. Young, fresh Kerry team, hungry, winning the first time out. People were amazed.

Kerry didn't concede a single goal during the 1975 championship campaign, their goalkeeper, Paudie O'Mahony, being responsible for that statistic.

I made a bit of history myself, because I went through the Championship without conceding a goal, and I saved two penalties along the way. That to this day is a record, and I'm very proud of that fact.

Kerry may have relinquished their title to Dublin the following season, but the significance of that victory in 1975 was not lost on the journalist Dónal Keenan.

It was extraordinary, because firstly the team was so young . . . Micko had taken a huge gamble in sending a team like that to take on the Dubs. We all got caught up fairly quickly in the excitement of this team—the way in which they played the game, the speed with which they played the game. From an early stage we knew there was something special coming through here.

| GOLDEN YEARS

Kerry's surprise success of 1975 was expected to herald a new golden era for the county. However, they were stopped in their tracks in 1976 and 77. Kerry lost the 1976 final and the 1977 semifinal, both to Dublin. They were stung by those losses. Mick O'Dwyer and his charges were under pressure. Mickey Ned O'Sullivan remembers how quickly the tide turned.

> It's amazing when you win: it's the gospel. It's accepted. If you lose, whatever methods you were using, they're not accepted. Every year the team that wins an all-Ireland, that's the yardstick going forward for the next year . . . But for the support of the then chairman of the county board, Ger McKenna, Mick would have fallen by the wayside.

Mickey Ned had missed the 1977 campaign. He took a year off after getting married. On his return he found himself attempting to displace a formidable quartet.

> The team was more or less established when I got back. I was trying to get onto two positions: Ger Power was in one of them, Pat Spillane was in the other. Mickey Sheehy was in another and John Egan was another.

O'Sullivan was not the only man who would have to play the patience game. Jimmy Deenihan was in for a rude shock in the wake of the loss in 1977 to Dublin.

> It was announced in the *Evening Herald* that four of us were

dropped for the League that year, including Spillane and myself and Ger Power and Paudie O'Mahony . . . I got a lot of injuries that summer, and maybe the selectors felt that I was too prone to injury—or that I was oversensitive about injuries . . . I recovered fully and I was in very good shape for 1978. I got the opportunity for a Munster trial in 1978, and of course for the fact I played rugby all winter my fitness levels were very high, so I was back on the team again. Both Ger Power and Pat Spillane were back on the panel.

Those consecutive defeats to Dublin raised serious doubts about Kerry's ability to incorporate a certain level of physicality in their game; the side's football abilities could never be questioned. Pat Spillane is in no doubt about the turning-point. He cites a fund-raiser for the Sister Consilio Fund in early 1978, an exhibition match in the United States, which turned out to be anything but a friendly.

It was the day we decided to lay down a marker. It was the culmination of a belief that the difference between Kerry and Dublin was the physicality and playing to the edge . . . We felt we had become soft touches; they were walking over us. That day in New York we decided to match fire with fire. We stood up to them. It was a brutal, filthy game . . . Jimmy Deenihan broke his nose; I know I broke my nose. It was a filthy game, but we won.

The side for the Munster championship opener in 1978 against Waterford was based on the majority of those who had served the county for the three previous seasons. Ten of the fifteen from the 1975 success began against Waterford: Jimmy Deenihan, John O'Keeffe, Ogie Moran, Páidí Ó Sé, Tim Kennelly, Paudie Lynch, Ger Power, Pat Spillane, John Egan and Mikey Sheehy. Pat McCarthy and Mickey Ned O'Sullivan would feature later in the season. Brendan Lynch had by now retired, while Ger O'Keeffe didn't feature in that campaign. Paudie O'Mahony was replaced in goal by Charlie Nelligan, injury curtailing O'Mahony's first-team chances.

A young man by the name of Eoin Liston, now equally well known as the 'Bomber', was selected at midfield for the game against Waterford. Liston, always acknowledged as the final piece of this Kerry jigsaw, would go on to have a debut season to savour. However, had events worked out otherwise one can only speculate about what his impact on the inter-county scene would have been. Paudie O'Mahony has revealed how one of O'Mahony's own club mates was also called in for trials.

> The interesting thing about that is the fact that Micko Dwyer brought in Tim Regan from my own club, Spa, who was an international basketball player, before he tried the Bomber. Why? Because Tim Regan was 6 ft 4 ins and he had this idea that bringing in a big player on the full forward line would be a help. Unfortunately, Tim was a bit slow so he found the Bomber and we never looked back after that. He was Dwyer's saviour because Dwyer was under pressure at the time. When he brought Bomber to us, we kind of laughed quietly because he was definitely a stone and a half over weight. I never saw a player to be as committed and he brought a certain excitement to the panel. He is an exceptional character. He is so likeable. The big soft Bomber. He was always there and he tried so hard in training. He changed around that Kerry team. He was the key to where it all happened. There was no other team in the country could handle him at the time. He could turn fast. It was a great move by Dwyer, he was a saviour no doubt. He did exceptional training because there is the belief that Dwyer trained him down in Waterville privately as well.

Liston was making the step up from an all-Ireland winning under-21 side. He admits that it took him some time to get up to speed with his senior counterparts.

> The main thing was that Micko saw something and brought me in training with the seniors that year. I was so far behind fitness-wise. If he hadn't done that I wouldn't have played with Kerry, I'd imagine. He persisted and encouraged. I got picked as a sub for the under 21s, we were to play Clare. I was a sub and Seán Walsh got injured and wasn't able to line out. They started me corner-forward. I remember that day I linked up well with Jack O'Shea. I played good enough. That was my first match and Micko Dwyer was at that match. He saw something and brought me in training then.

Eoin Liston was part of the Kerry side that won the 1977 all-Ireland under 21 championship, the county's third successive title at that grade.

O'Dwyer's persistence with Liston had stunning results later in the season, vindicating his faith in this raw talent. Liston had previously tried out when Séamus Mac Gearailt was training the county minors. He left an impression on Mac Gearailt that night.

> He stood out, in the sense that he could catch a ball from the air from anyone. His problem was when he landed with it he was a bit awkward. He was a big young fellow. Very often fellows like that they don't mature until they are older . . . Dwyer took a special interest in Eoin. We give the credit to Dwyer for taking Eoin in hand. Eoin was a big lad who needed a lot of training. Dwyer made sure he got through the training whether he liked it or not.

O'Dwyer credits Ogie Moran with the discovery of the player that he feels is the most significant in Kerry football.

> I was inside one evening and we were going to have a trial game on a Monday night. I said to Ogie, Would there be any player out there in North Kerry that you could recommend or bring in for the trial? He said, There's a big fellow in Ballybunion all right, but he's a lazy boyo. I don't know would he come in or not. Fair enough, I said, bring him in . . . I got hold of him in Waterville and I put him through the mill in Waterville and put him through the mill with Kerry. I can assure you he was the greatest find that was ever found in Kerry football.

Eoin Liston and Vincent O'Connor were selected at midfield against Waterford. Injuries prevented the pair from lining out, so Jack O'Shea and Johnny Mulvihill deputised.

Tommy Doyle and Seán Walsh, who both featured in the all-Ireland semi-final loss to Dublin in 1977, also started against Waterford. John Egan pointed in the opening minute. Kerry were four in front, with Mikey Sheehy and Ger Power both also on target before Waterford had their first score, after eleven minutes. Kerry, despite some wayward shooting, added eleven more points to their first-half tally. A Sheehy goal in the final minute of the period meant that Kerry led 1-15 to 0-3 at the break.

Pat Spillane had goals in the twentieth and twenty-seventh minutes of the second half; he finished the game with a personal tally of 2-5. Sheehy was the top scorer, with 2-8. In the end Kerry won by 4-27 to 2-8.

Eoin Liston arrived on the inter-county scene for the Munster final of 1978. His introduction at full-forward saw Seán Walsh go to midfield. Johnny Mulvihill made way in the only change in personnel since the season opener.

Cork had the ball in the net only six minutes into the encounter. That put Cork two points to the good, 1-1 to 0-2. When they pointed in the eleventh minute it was their last score of the half: Kerry were beginning to take over. Pat Spillane was denied a goal, a superb save from Billy Morgan tipping his shot over the crossbar. The Kingdom had edged one point in front when, on the quarter-hour mark, Ger Power goaled, lashing the ball to the net after a high ball into the square dropped loose. Two successive points by Tommy Doyle extended the gap to Kerry 1-8, Cork 1-2. The signs were ominous for Cork, and sure enough, seven minutes before the break, the Kingdom netted once more. Ger Power set up Liston, who unselfishly laid the ball on to Sheehy, who did the necessary.

Kerry went in at half time with an unassailable advantage of 2-10 to 1-2, but they managed only a single point in the first seventeen minutes of the second period. Cork, though, had only managed four of their own, so the gap was down to eight. In the fifty-third minute Kerry struck for goal number 3, a classic. The move began in Kerry's own square: John O'Keeffe fielded and fed out to Power. Eventually the ball was in Sheehy's possession, and he notched his second goal of the game. The score now stood at 3-11 to 1-6. Kerry conceded two further goals, but the game was never in doubt.

Tommy Doyle of Kerry, along with Tom Creedon of Cork, was sent off. The newspapers bemoaned the number of fouls: fifty-eight in total. The result was Kerry 3-14, Cork 3-7.

Kerry were unchanged for the all-Ireland semi-final against Roscommon, played at a rainswept Croke Park. John O'Gara had Roscommon in front within three minutes. A minute later the westerners seemed to be in for a goal chance, but Paudie Lynch cut off the through ball—a lucky escape for the Kingdom. Spillane levelled for

Kerry, but they were playing second-best to their opponents. Roscommon, however, failed to make their midfield domination count.

Tommy Doyle, sent off in the Munster final, went off badly injured before the twentieth minute against Roscommon.

> This high ball came out the middle. Five or six of us jumped for it. I just caught it. I thought I heard a crack or pull in my arm. I thought nothing of it. I played on . . . The next thing this high ball came again and I went for it. I knew I was in trouble: my arm just went dead. I went down, and I saw blood pouring from my arm and down my jersey and a bone sticking out through my skin. Bernard Lynch was our doctor the same day. He came out. I was down in the Richmond Hospital before the game was over.

It was not until the twentieth minute that Kerry had their second point of the afternoon, a stunning sideline kick from Sheehy landing over the bar. The next scores, after twenty-five minutes, were more telling. After Liston pointed, the Roscommon kick-out was mis-hit and sent along the ground. Ger Power pounced and fed Pat Spillane. Spillane, closing in on goal, spilled the ball but subsequently smashed it beyond the goalkeeper. Kerry were leading 1-3 to 0-1. The teams swapped ends with Kerry ahead 1-4 to 0-2.

The rain at half time was so heavy that the Artane Boys' Band performed in the Nally Stand instead of on the pitch.

Only a fine save by Charlie Nelligan prevented a Roscommon goal in the opening stages of the second half. Two Ger Power points put Kerry 1-6 to 0-3 to the good. Power's hat trick of scores arrived in the forty-fourth minute, this time with a goal to his name. With the gap now at nine points, 2-6 to 0-3, Roscommon's race was run. The Connacht champions refused to lie down, however, and they kept pressing. They brought the gap down to six before a narrow escape for Kerry ten minutes from time. A shot from John O'Connor seemed destined for the net, but Nelligan tipped it onto the crossbar and over for a point.

Roscommon's chance of catching the Kingdom was now gone. Sheehy put over three points from frees in the closing minutes. The sub Pattie O'Mahony also left his mark on proceedings, goaling two minutes from time. Kerry were through to the all-Ireland final once more, defeating Roscommon 3-11 to 0-8.

For the fourth consecutive season Kerry were to face Dublin in the championship. Kerry had won the 1975 final, lost the 1976 decider, and in 1977 went down to Dublin at the semi-final stage. This season Dublin eased past Down, 1-16 to 0-8.

Jimmy Deenihan feels that this coming game was to be a watershed in Kerry football.

> We were always confident. That was one of the strong points of that team ... At that stage we knew it was the end of the team if we didn't win; it would have been three losses in a row to Dublin ... There was a move on within the county to have Dwyer removed after 1977 ... That's Kerry football! If you're not winning in Kerry football, they want your head.

Injury meant that Tommy Doyle was omitted from the Kerry side for the final. Ogie Moran moved to centre-forward. Paudie Lynch was moved from the corner to wing-back. Pat Spillane's brother Mick was faced with the daunting task of making his championship debut in an all-Ireland final.

This was not the first time that Ogie Moran had led his county out at Croke Park: he was team mascot for the 1960 final, in which Kerry lost to Down. Early on in the match it seemed as if Moran would once more be leaving Croke Park a loser. Kerry managed only one score in the opening twenty-five minutes, a Mikey Sheehy point. During that time they played second fiddle and looked as if they would be on the receiving end of a heavy drubbing. Jimmy Keaveney had put over five points by this time for Dublin, with Bernard Brogan adding a sixth. Five points down with ten minutes to half time, Kerry were looking for a lifeline. John Egan provided it, as the *Kerryman* recalled.

> Bobby Doyle was penalised for over holding the ball and Eoin Liston counter attacked; the bearded Ballybunion man found Jack O'Shea who in turn slipped the ball to Pat Spillane. Once Spillane got possession a goal was on, because John Egan had managed to slip inside the defensive cover and Spillane duly gave him a perfect pass, it was now up to Egan and the Sneem man applied a grand finishing touch by flicking the ball over the head of the advancing Paddy Cullen and into the net.

Ger Power is fully appreciative of the chance given to the team by Egan's goal.

> We were really being beaten, and being beaten well. John got a break and got a goal. All the goals are important, but that goal got us back into it.

Egan and Jack O'Shea pointed, to draw Kerry level seven minutes from the break. Jimmy Keaveney put Dublin back in front, 0-7 to 1-3. Three minutes before half time, in what became one of the most famous Irish sporting moments, Kerry took an unlikely lead. Mikey Sheehy's instinctive goal, from a free kick following a foul on Ger Power, is still talked about when so many other incidents are forgotten. There's hardly a Kerry fan alive who hasn't witnessed the incident, either on the day itself or on that most played of videos in the Kingdom, *Kerry's Golden Years.*

All parties involved have maintained that there should never have been a free in the first place. To this day the victim of the Paddy Cullen foul, Ger Power, has his doubts.

> I think I had my back to the ball. He touched me or something like that. I can't recall; there was an incident before it, and he didn't give a free. Maybe he made up for it there. It was a crucial decision anyway.

Sheehy, the main benefactor of this apparent foul, agrees with Power's statement, adding that

> there was an incident with himself and Paddy Cullen earlier on. Power probably went in a bit late. Paddy drew a side kick at him. He did it again a second time, and the referee didn't see it. The Kerry crowd in the Hogan Stand did, and then a couple of balls came in to Paddy. The referee knew he had missed it, the linesman missed it. The Kerry crowd were half-jeering Paddy when he got a couple of balls. This famous one came in to him, and he picked the ball clearly. I've seen it so many times now . . . The referee gave a free, and Paddy was as baffled as anybody else. I was baffled myself. Robbie Kelliher was more baffled than anybody else. He handed the ball to me, disgusted.

John Barry of the *Kerryman* felt that the free should have been given the other way.

> The funny thing about that is that it was a crazy decision to give Kerry a free because Paddy Cullen did absolutely nothing to Ger Power. In fact if anything it should have been a free out to Dublin. The Kerry crowd had got onto him for some decision he had made against Kerry. He decided to give Kerry this totally unwarranted free. Fair play to Mickey. Mickey was a genius who was always thinking three or four moves ahead of everybody else. Mickey put it in the net. It was a score that everybody who was there that day will always fondly remember, everybody from Kerry that is.

Sheehy admits that he's still at a loss to explain why he took the kick.

> There certainly was a gap, and I said, Here goes. I suppose to this day I don't know what made me do it. Maybe just an instinct. Paddy— we've often spoken about it. In fairness to Paddy, we're great friends, but it took him a long time to talk about that goal. I wouldn't blame him. I get fed up about talking about it, and I scored it!

Sheehy's goal has understandably become part of GAA folklore. The journalist Dónal Keenan was among those fortunate enough to witness it in person.

> It was only a player of the brilliance of Sheehy would think of that. That's what made the likes of himself and Egan stand out. They did things others wouldn't even think about. Whether it was a legitimate goal or not I'm not too sure. Mickey always smiles when you ask him. Paddy Cullen even smiles when you ask him. It was just the audacity of what he did.

That goal was the last score of the period, after which Kerry led 2-3 to 0-7.

The Kerry dressing-room at half time was a happy place to be, given the events in those closing minutes. It's hard to believe, given what had just happened, but Sheehy says that his goal never featured in O'Dwyer's half-time chat.

I could see what he was thinking. He gave a wink over at me . . .
Micko was always saying 'Take the points, the goals will come.' I
would have said that it was a chance that if I'd missed it he'd have
shot me. He'd have said, Why didn't you take the point? Silently, that
was going through his head.

Eoin Liston was perplexed by the sudden change at the end of the first
half of what was his first senior all-Ireland final.

I knew Dublin were good. I had seen them playing. Brilliant team.
This was their fifth all-Ireland final in a row. They had won three. It
was a defining match . . . Have no doubt about it, they were just
destroying us. We hadn't played at all. The next thing, I remember, a
high ball came in and I caught it and a goal came off it. I felt at least
I had done something. Then I remember there was confusion, and I
saw the ball going into the net . . . I went in at half time and I didn't
know whether the goal was allowed or not. Here we were inside at
half time and I think we were two points up . . . It was very hard for
them to come back after it.

The second half was barely ninety seconds old when Liston stamped his
authority on the match. According to the *Kerryman*, 'he was perfectly
positioned to take a centre from Jack O'Shea and he gave Paddy Cullen
no chance form close range.'

Eoin Liston, in search of an all-Ireland medal, feels his job was made
easier by the events at the end of the opening period.

All that was in my head was to win that match. I didn't care if it was
by a point or ten points. I just wanted an all-Ireland medal. That was
the motivating thing, I wanted to have an all-Ireland medal. When I
was so close to it we were prepared to put our head on the line. I
knew Dublin were as well but we were highly motivated. We were
very well prepared. I think the psychological damage that was done
to Dublin must have been very hard for them to come out in the
second half.

Kerry had by now scored as many goals as points. They led 3-3 to 0-7, a
five-point advantage. Jimmy Keaveney then pointed for Dublin to make

it a four-point game. Kerry hit back, scoring three times to consolidate their match-winning position. The pick of those was Liston's second goal, scored after a one-two with Power. It was now Kerry 4-5, Dublin 0-8. Sheehy then scored two points and Liston another, before the big man goaled again a quarter of an hour from time, as described in the *Kerryman*.

> Ogie Moran sent the ball down into the right corner where it was collected by Ger Power; the Stacks man parted to John Egan who punched a great ball across the face of the goal—and there rising two feet above Seán Doherty was Liston to connect with his right fist and send the ball crashing to the net.

Kerry won, 5-11 to 0-9. This demolition of Dublin meant that the disappointments of the previous two seasons could be forgotten. This side had proved also that they were no one-season wonders. For Pat Spillane,

> winning in 1978 was always going to be fantastic. Two years of failure, you knew what failure was like in an all-Ireland semi-final in 1977, you knew what failure was like being beaten in a final in 1976. You were filled with emotion and drive: this wasn't going to happen again . . . 1978 was great, because you banished so many demons. You were able to prove, as a team and individuals, that 1975 wasn't a flash in the pan, and we were as good if not better than Dublin.

People have asked him about a watershed moment in Gaelic football.

> My one incident will always be Mickey Sheehy's chipped goal against Paddy Cullen in 1978 . . . It was a piece of absolute genius. You can't coach fellows to do something that's spontaneous. Off the cuff and just showing initiative . . . From then on Kerry had a dominance over Dublin.

O'Dwyer believes that his tenure in charge of the side would have come to an end had Kerry lost to Dublin in 1978.

> Dublin had beaten us in two previous years. They beat us in the 1976

final and the 1977 semi-final. Then we came along in 1978 and beat them. That was one victory that really stands out in my mind . . . We hammered them that day, actually. I think it was the finest display of football I've seen in Croke Park for many a long day.

Séamus Mac Gearailt is quick to acknowledge Eoin Liston's role in the success of 1978.

I think he was the final cog in that team. In 1975 I think their fitness and athleticism caught Dublin by surprise. I think Dublin proved in 1976 and 1977 that they were still a good team. That particular Kerry team matured in 1978 when the Bomber arrived.

Mick Finucane, a Kerry player of the 1940s and 50s, feels Liston was more than just a target man and that his inclusion brought the Kingdom to a new level.

The man that made the greatest difference to that team was the Bomber. That team was a good team, but it wasn't a great team. When they brought the Bomber on, they were unbeatable . . . He gave them height inside. He was the first of the target men inside. But he was better than that. He could play out the field.

Liston's team-mate Seán Walsh also believes it's important that people understand the role Liston played.

He was a big influence in our team, because he could take the ball high, low—it didn't matter. Very versatile, very skilful for a big man . . . If you were under pressure out the middle, he had a habit of going behind the full-back, and he'd put his hand in the air if he wanted it high. He'd give you the options always.

One question remains from 1978: Just where did the Bomber Liston get his nickname?

It was many years ago, playing soccer on the beach in Ballybunion. There was a lazy fellow that used hang around the square, Gerdie Muller—he was known as the Bomber. I was a heavy, fat young fellow, I suppose, and sometimes I was called, instead of Pele, it was 'Bele'—'Belly', kinda. More used call me 'Bomber'. 'Bomber' stuck, anyway.

Kerry were searching for two in a row in 1979, having put paid to Dublin in the previous year's final. They opened with a victory of thirty-six points over Clare, a game that has gone down in history as the Milltown Massacre.

There were two changes from the previous year's all-Ireland final for the meeting with Clare in Milltown Malbay. Vincent O'Connor was a late replacement for the injured Seán Walsh; Tommy Doyle started in place of Ogie Moran.

Kerry and Clare were level after ten minutes, at two points each. The first goal for Kerry came from Vincent O'Connor, after eleven minutes. The Kingdom still led by only 1-7 to 0-4 twenty minutes in. Ten minutes from half time Pat Spillane punched home a cross from Tommy Doyle for goal number 2. Tim Kennelly set Ger Power up for the third goal six minutes before the break. Liston also goaled before the short whistle. Kerry were now leading 4-9 to 0-6.

The Kingdom had the ball in the net five times in the second period: Mikey Sheehy in the sixth minute, Eoin Liston after thirteen, Pat Spillane seven minutes from time, then Ger Power, and finally Spillane again for his hat trick. It ended 9-21 to 1-9.

Strangely, when people refer to the Milltown Massacre one thing that's forgotten is that Clare's tally was the highest recorded against Kerry that season. According to Pat Spillane,

> great teams have ruthlessness. Like Kilkenny hurlers, it's one of the qualities you like to see in a team, ruthlessness that you never ease up. The ruthlessness by Kerry was . . . that there was as many fellows on the sideline as good as you. Micko selected on form, and if you didn't take your chances against Clare and somebody else came in and banged in three goals he'd be in pole position for the Munster final; so it was fear. You got your opportunity and you were going to avail of every chance that came your way.

Not surprisingly, the selectors for the Munster final gave a vote of confidence to the fifteen from the Clare win. Seán Walsh, who had missed the season opener because of an ankle injury, was again off the starting fifteen. He recalls the hard training methods the team faced at the time.

It was rough stuff, looking back on it. I think modern trainers mightn't agree with his methods, but it made us mentally very tough. He was big into stamina work and rounds of the field— bringing us over the edge, his type of training, I mightn't be able to do the same type of training as John O'Keeffe would, or wouldn't be as good at it, but I was brought over the edge at a certain level, and Johnno was brought over at another level. That's what Micko was very good at.

In the final, Cork registered a point and two wides inside the opening five minutes. Kerry hit back in the best possible fashion, with a goal from Ger Power. Mikey Sheehy and Pat Spillane then pointed. Tommy Doyle did likewise, his shot going over off the crossbar, as Kerry raced into a 1-3 to 0-1 lead. Cork were given the perfect chance for a goal of their own in the thirteenth minute, but John Courtney's penalty went over the bar. Three Spillane points and another from Sheehy made it Kerry 1-7, Cork 0-2.

After Denny Allen put over for Cork, the Rebel net had a narrow escape. Ger Power palmed over the advancing goalkeeper, Billy Morgan. The ball seemed destined for the net, but it just cleared the crossbar. Cork did manage a goal before the break, through Jimmy Barry Murphy. At half time Kerry led 1-8 to 1-3.

Cork were to the fore early on in the second period, their pressure leading to the second penalty of the afternoon for the Rebels. Denny Allen was entrusted with taking it. Charlie Nelligan dived to his right to save. A Cork point followed, and the next score also belonged to the Rebels. This time Cork finally breached the Kerry rearguard, Denny Allen netting. The goal left the minimum between the teams, Kerry 1-8, Cork 2-4. Cork, though, would not score in the remaining twenty-six minutes. Kerry in the meantime racked up the points: Mikey Sheehy, Ger Power, Pat Spillane, Ger Power, Power again and the sub Seán Walsh.

Power, the Man of the Match, netted his second goal in the closing minute. He finished the day with a tally of 2-4, the same as the entire

Cork team. Kerry had registered 2-14.

There was one change to the Kerry team for the semi-final against Monaghan: Seán Walsh came in at centre-forward for Tommy Doyle. Kerry had this game in the bag by the quarter-hour mark. They had opened up a lead of eight points by this stage, 2-3 to 0-1. The goal-scorers were Liston and Power. The Kingdom led 2-5 to 0-4 at half time.

Kerry had three points in the first five minutes of the second period. Thirteen minutes into the second half Sheehy had his first goal of the encounter. Ten minutes later he repeated the trick, and he went on to complete his hat trick before the end. He also had time to put over a free from fifty yards, and he finished the game with 3-5 to his name. This defeat of Monaghan by 5-14 to 0-7 meant that Kerry were through to yet another all-Ireland final.

Joe Keohane, a Kerry selector and former full-back, proclaimed this set of Kerry forwards to be the greatest ever to represent the county.

With the Papal visit on the horizon, the all-Ireland final was to be played earlier than usual, on 16 September. That meant that the Dublin forward Jimmy Keaveney, sent off in the Leinster final, would miss the decider, as his two-month suspension would not be over until the following Saturday. Kerry's Tommy Doyle returned for the final. Ogie Moran also started; Ger Power and Vincent O'Connor didn't. Seán Walsh went to midfield, with Moran at centre-forward.

Mikey Sheehy pointed inside the first thirty seconds. Tony Hanahoe replied for Dublin. Kerry then kicked into gear, adding two points, before Mikey Sheehy goaled after being set up by Ogie Moran. Kerry 1-3, Dublin 0-1, after ten minutes. That blistering start was followed by a more mundane period. Kerry went back on the attack, but Liston had a goal disallowed.

Spillane and Sheehy did register scores as the Kingdom moved ahead by 1-6 to 0-2. Dublin then pointed, but the half ended as it began, with Kerry in the ascendancy. The gap at half time was seven: Kerry 1-7, Dublin 0-3.

Sheehy struck the Dublin bar, before points from Spillane and Egan stretched Kerry's lead to 1-9 to 0-3. Kerry were strolling, but they were in for a rude awakening. Dublin brought the gap back to 1-10 to 1-5, and Kerry also had to cope with the sending off of Páidí Ó Sé half way through the second half. The difference was still five points, with the clock reading fifty-six minutes, when Kerry pressed for the attack. The

Kerryman describes those match-clinching moments.

> John Egan was brought down as he careered through on one of his
> many dazzling runs and the referee pointed to the penalty spot
> without hesitation. Mikey Sheehy coolly stepped up to the spot kick
> and without taking his gaze off the ball he unleashed a blinding shot
> which rose as it thundered into the left rigging of the net.

Double scores now: Kerry 2-10 to Dublin's 1-5. Kerry were making light
of Ó Sé's dismissal. Dublin were a beaten team. Kerry weren't letting up,
however, and eight minutes from time Egan sealed the victory with
Kerry's third goal. Sheehy had two points for Kerry in the closing
minutes. In a 3-13 to 1-8 defeat of Dublin, Sheehy's personal tally was
2-6.

Sheehy feels that it's not all about personal glory.

> People would still talk about records. You don't ever think about
> them out on the pitch. You don't even think about it. All you're
> doing is playing for the team. Individual things are fine to a point,
> but I mean, the main thing you want is the team to win, and get your
> all-Ireland medal. That's all you think about.

Mick O'Dwyer had by now well and truly moulded this Kerry team into
what he had envisaged for them. Liston knew that O'Dwyer was keen to
make the most of the vast playing area.

> The one thing he wanted was to create space . . . Quick movement
> of the ball and space. He'd pull us up loads of times in training if we
> were all coming together instead of staying out to the wings . . .
> From playing together you develop understandings. We got the idea.
> Spillane was usually gone back helping out at the back, so there was
> extra space, and if Mikey or John Egan moved out, that corner was
> free, and they knew then the ball would be played into that corner. I
> made sure I'd stand at that side of my man. If they were in trouble
> then they'd put it into that corner. You developed a lot of that
> between the players themselves. Micko gave us the guidelines and
> got us fit.

Kerry and Dublin met every season in the championship from 1975 to
'79. John Egan feels that the rivalry was mutually beneficial.

> I think that Dublin brought us on, made us better . . . What took
> Kerry and Dublin away from the rest of them was that Dublin had
> to get better to beat us, and we had to get better to beat them, so it
> became a confrontation, and all the other counties slipped a way
> behind.

Kerry received a bye to the Munster final in 1980. They had thirteen of
the previous season's all-Ireland winning fifteen on the field when they
began against Cork in the provincial decider; Jimmy Deenihan and
Paudie Lynch were the odd men out. Ger O'Keeffe came into the side at
centre-back and Ger Power as wing-forward. Ogie Moran reverted to
the half-back line.

Kerry beat Cork 3-13 to 0-12 in a match described by the *Kerryman* as
'the worst final for many years.' Kerry were leading 7 points to 1, with 25
minutes on the clock.

A goal just three minutes shy of half time, with the scores 8-2, led to
an already one-sided affair becoming a rout. Eoin Liston was the scorer,
and Kerry led 1-8 to 0-5 at half time. Just as they finished the first period,
the Kingdom opened the second. Two minutes after the resumption,
Liston netted once more. There was no stopping Kerry, and certainly no
way back for Cork.

The remainder of the mach was memorable only for two further
incidents. The first was Kerry's third goal of the final, which arrived a
little after the quarter-hour mark in the second half, courtesy of Ger
Power. The second incident of note was an own point by the Kingdom!
Tim Kennelly was that day responsible for one of the most bizarre
scores ever seen on a GAA pitch. Attempting to halt a Cork attack,
Kennelly lashed out at the ball, only succeeding in kicking it over his
own crossbar.

Kerry were the kingpins of Munster once more, having beaten Cork
3-13 to 0-12 to clinch a sixth successive provincial crown. An all-Ireland
semi-final against Offaly awaited.

Kerry went with the fifteen who had accounted for Cork. They
registered four goals and missed as many more chances in a game that
was to produce thirty-three scores. They lost the midfielder Seán Walsh

through injury only six minutes into the match; Jimmy Deenihan was introduced, at corner-back. Ger O'Keeffe moved out, Ogie Moran went to the forty, and Tommy Doyle was brought back to partner Jack O'Shea at midfield.

John Egan and Eoin Liston had early points as Kerry took the game to their opponents. Mikey Sheehy was then off target with a goal opportunity. In the twelfth minute Kerry did have the ball in the net, thanks to Pat Spillane. They were ahead by 1-4 to 0-3 entering the twenty-second minute, when an Offaly goal cut the deficit to the minimum. Offaly threatened to take over, but the Kingdom brought Liston out from full forward. The big man's presence at midfield worked a treat, as Kerry put over five unanswered points. Egan, Sheehy and Tommy Doyle all registered scores, as did Ger Power and Ogie Moran, leaving Kerry with a lead of 1-9 to 1-3 at half time.

Spillane had the first score of the second period, but Matt Connor responded for Offaly. Seven minutes in, Offaly halved the deficit with a goal by Gerry Carroll. Kerry hit back with points by Spillane, Egan and Power to bring the gap back up to six. It was now Kerry 1-13, Offaly 2-4. Two goals from Sheehy and Spillane well and truly put paid to Offaly. Kerry had the advantage, 3-13 to 2-5, with twenty minutes remaining. The gap was eight as the game entered the closing minutes. Matt Connor then goaled for Offaly, but Kerry were quick to respond, with Egan finding the net at the other end. The eighth goal of the afternoon arrived thanks to Gerry Carroll of Offaly, but Kerry's superiority in the second half was never in doubt. The game ended Kerry 4-15, Offaly 4-10.

Roscommon came through the other side of the draw, beating Armagh 2-20 to 3-11.

Eoin Liston was a late withdrawal from the Kerry side for the all-Ireland final in 1980: he missed the game after being taken to hospital on the Wednesday before the match to undergo an operation for acute appendicitis. With Liston out injured, changes were necessary in the Kerry line-up. Tommy Doyle was handed number 14, and Ogie Moran moved to the forty. Ger O'Keeffe took Moran's wing-back position. Jimmy Deenihan, brought on against Offaly in the semi-final, started against Roscommon. So too did Paudie Lynch, in his first championship appearance of the season. As well as Liston, Mick Spillane also lost a starting spot.

Kerry and Roscommon were to play one of the most instantly forgettable finals in recent memory. Roscommon goaled in the very first minute, through John O'Connor. The westerners had the platform to take the game to Kerry. And, initially, they did. Points by Séamus Hayden and John O'Gara gave them a 1-2 to 0-0 advantage after twelve minutes. Ger Power believes that the Kingdom were there for the taking.

> They totally had us on the rack. And I think they had us through the whole game. But I think they just threw it away, being a little bit too physical on the day.

Kerry pulled two points back, Sheehy on thirteen minutes, then Ger Power after seventeen. The Kingdom were level in the twentieth, as noted by the *Kerryman*.

> Tom Donnellan, the Roscommon centre half back, struck a free badly and the ball went to Tommy Doyle; Doyle found Pat Spillane and the Templenoe man went haring for goal; when challenged, he found the unmarked Mikey Sheehy inside him with a perfect pass, and Sheehy completed the move by expertly flicking to the net.

Each side would score just once more in the first period, Dermot Earley for Roscommon after twenty-two minutes, then Sheehy four minutes later.

Half time arrived with the game level, 1-3 apiece. Kerry went ahead for the first time when Sheehy pointed a free in the third minute of the second period. However, it looked as though the lead would be short-lived. Only a tremendous Charlie Nelligan save, both acrobatic and reflex, kept the Kerry goal intact. Nelligan plays down his heroics:

> It was one of those things, really it was a kind of reflex more than anything else. He hit it on the volley, I was lucky to get a hand to it, but we had met Roscommon in the under-21 final in Dr Hyde Park in 1978 and they beat us by a point and we were badly handled that day. There was a bit of jostling going on there on the field and off the field and we didn't forget it. We should have won that game and we didn't and the players that were involved that day in 1978 in the under-21s were reminded of that. It was time to get revenge. We

stuck with the football in 1980 and it paid off in the end.

Kerry moved into a 1-6 to 1-4 lead after fifty-three minutes. Roscommon were back on level terms within five more minutes.

Ten minutes from time, Kerry pulled ahead once more, but the real drama was yet to come, as recalled in the *Kerryman*.

In a goalmouth tussle the ball ran loose to Dooley and from the position he was in it seemed that he simply could not miss. But dramatically to the rescue came Páidí Ó Sé, who managed to get down and cover the shot.

The game would see just two more scores as Sheehy took his tally for the day to 1-6. Those points, in the sixty-fifth and seventieth minutes, helped Kerry grind Roscommon down, and the Kingdom prevailed 1-9 to 1-6.

It's not a victory that Pat Spillane remembers fondly.

Ah, it was a horrible game of football . . . I suppose it was the precursor to what modern-day football has now become, where Roscommon just set out their stall to stop us from playing football. It was negative, it was cynical, it was dirty . . . But there are days that you have to grind out victories, and it was a grinding day, and it wouldn't have been a good performance, I suppose, as all-Ireland final performances go.

Dónal Keenan, whose father won two all-Ireland medals with Roscommon, feels the 1980 decider was one that Kerry got away with.

It was the one final that Kerry shouldn't have won. Not everyone in Roscommon will subscribe to the theory that Roscommon played the wrong game, tried to be dirty, tried to knock Kerry off their stride. Roscommon players to this day would deny that was the approach, but certainly they did get a blistering start to the match— and with so many good players. There were tremendous footballers who didn't perform on the day as they could have and still were within touching distance of beating Kerry.

Tim Kennelly was named Man of the Match following his display in the 1980 final. It was a well-deserved accolade, according to Mikey Sheehy.

> I think his performance in the 1980 all-Ireland final against Roscommon was absolutely awesome . . . Any time the ball came in the half-back line Timmy was there to mop it up. They were hopping off him. The Roscommon guys were tough; the tougher they were the better Timmy liked it, and he was brilliant.

Jerry Savage, a Kerry supporter, goes a step further when recalling the 1980 final.

> Tim Kennelly carried us through that period . . . Kerry went on and won their match, and I would say, totally, Tim Kennelly was responsible for it.

All the talk for the 1981 season was of the Kingdom's attempt at the four in a row. In 1981 a third member of the Spillane clan, Tom, joined the Kerry squad.

Kerry opened against Clare. Tim Kennelly, Man of the Match from the 1980 all-Ireland final, was out with a hamstring injury and would also miss the Munster final. Seán Walsh was also to start, but injury excluded him. Tom Spillane came in for his debut, after playing a club match the previous evening. Eoin Liston returned with a vengeance after missing the previous year's final and was responsible for three goals and three points.

Clare led by two points to one early on, the Bomber opening Kerry's account after two minutes. He then set up Pat Spillane for the equaliser after a quarter of an hour. Tom Spillane then marked his debut with a point for the Kingdom. The first Kerry goal came in the eighteenth minute; Liston sent to the net, taking advantage of a ball from John Egan that was misjudged by the Clare defence. Kerry were now ahead by 1-3 to 0-2, and six unanswered points followed by half time.

Four minutes into the second half Clare hit the Kerry crossbar, through Tom Killeen. Three minutes after that Bomber got his second goal. The Kingdom had a 2-14 to 0-4 lead. Three penalties followed. Pat McNamara of Clare had his spot-kick saved by Charlie Nelligan. Mikey

Sheehy then sent his penalty over the bar, following a foul on Ogie Moran. George Fitzpatrick for Clare followed Sheehy's lead.

Bomber's hat trick arrived six minutes from time, making for a score of 3-16 to 0-6. John Egan got goal number 4 in the final minute, and Kerry had won, 4-17 to 0-6.

Kerry were going for their seventh Munster crown in a row when they met Cork; but there was more drama in the week before the match than in the game itself. Mikey Sheehy escaped unhurt from a car crash in Limerick, the car somersaulting and landing on its roof. Sheehy knows well he had a lucky escape.

> We were just very, very lucky to get out alive, I can tell you now . . . and walked out of the car and actually went training that night in Killarney; and, you know, you'd be thinking of it for a while, all right. But thankfully the game worked out fine.

The match referee, Pat Lane of Limerick, was also involved in a car crash and couldn't take part.

Kerry recalled Seán Walsh for the Munster final, with Tom Spillane making way. Spillane was not too put out about being dropped: 'If they asked me to bring the bottles, I would have.' Tommy Doyle was at midfield alongside Jack O'Shea. Walsh was at centre-back. Cork mustered only three points in the Munster final, losing by eleven.

After winning the toss, Kerry opted to play against the wind. That turned out to be wise decision, as Kerry held Cork to a single point in the opening period. A Mikey Sheehy free in the thirteenth minute had Kerry in front. Pat Spillane doubled the advantage after nineteen minutes. The twenty-first minute saw Cork's one and only point of the first period. Both sides then had goal chances. Charlie Nelligan denied Tom Creedon, while at the other end Tommy Doyle was foiled by the Cork keeper, Billy Morgan. With the wind behind them, Cork registered seven wides in the first half. At the short whistle they trailed two points to one.

The referee had whistled Kerry for illegal hand-passing on numerous occasions. This was the season in which the hand-pass rule had been altered, and they hadn't yet got used to new the rule. Rule 148 (*a*) now read (with the alteration in italic type):

A goal is scored when the ball is driven, played *or deflected by hand*
(1) by either team between the goal-posts and under the crossbar, except when thrown, carried or passed by hand or fist
(2) by any of the attacking side . . .
Rule 169 now stated:
. . . (2) (*d*) When caught, the ball may be kicked, struck with the fist or open hand or hopped once against the ground with one or both hands. *In the case of the Open Hand Pass, there shall be a visible striking of the ball by the hand, and where the striking action is not visible the Referee shall deem the pass as being foul.*
(3) The ball may not be thrown.

The wind had risen for the start of the second period. Kerry were quickly into their stride, and within five minutes Mikey Sheehy and John Egan had put over. It was now Kerry 0-4, Cork 0-1. An unfortunate tenth-minute collision between Eoin Liston and Billy Morgan led to Morgan being stretchered off. Thirteen minutes into the half, Liston punched over to make the game five points to one. Cork doubled their match total twenty minutes into the second half, thanks to a Dave Barry point. Consecutive points by Sheehy increased Kerry's advantage further.

The only goal of the game came ten minutes from the end, as recalled by the goal-scorer, Mikey Sheehy.

> John Egan, who had unbelievable vision, a bit like the Bomber . . . He put it onto my chest . . . and, you know, I absolutely didn't have to break stride. I think that would have to be a goal remembered clearly only because of his pass and his vision.

That score made it 1-7 to 0-2. Pat Spillane and Sheehy then added a point each. Six minutes from the end Denny Allen scored Cork's third point, before points by Pat Spillane and Jack O'Shea completed Kerry's scoring. The match ended Kerry 1-11, Cork 0-3.

The final fell short of the expectations of the *Irish Times*, which proclaimed that 'there have been many more cheerful funerals.'

It was an unchanged Kerry side that took to the field for the semi-final against Mayo. A second-minute point from Adrian Garvey had Mayo ahead. Mikey Sheehy equalised from a free. Joe McGrath put

Mayo in front again, in the seventh minute, but Pat Spillane had Kerry back on terms a minute later. Points in the eleventh and twelfth minutes from Ogie Moran and Sheehy had Kerry two ahead. A Ger Power goal sixty seconds later put five between the sides, with a point from Eoin Liston coming hot on its heels. Pat Spillane then put over, to which Jimmy Burke replied. Mayo, down by 1-6 to 0-3, cut the Kingdom's lead in half with a goal of their own on twenty-three minutes.

Kerry were afforded some much-needed breathing space ten minutes later, as described in the *Kerryman*.

> What a beauty it was, Paudie Lynch cleared a great ball downfield to Doyle who sent it to Mick Spillane. The latter duly passed it to Egan on the left of the Mayo posts and he dummied and then transferred the ball to Liston coming in on the right. The Mayo rearguard had no chance as the giant-like full-forward all but tore the rigging with a tremendous shot into the left corner of the net.

A Mayo point in the thirty-fifth minute proved to be their last score not only of the half but of the entire match. Kerry led 2-7 to 1-6 at half-time. Mayo were kept scoreless in the second half, while Kerry tagged on twelve points to win by 2-19 to 1-6.

Kerry's final opponents were to be the side they beat in the previous season's all-Ireland semi-final, Offaly, winners over Down by twelve points to six in the last four.

A knee injury forced Pat Spillane to miss the final.

> They left it up to me to whether I was fit to play or not in '81 . . . I always knew in the back of my head that my knee wasn't right . . . I remember doing a fitness test . . . on the Saturday evening . . . and I passed it. You know, the boys thought I was great, and I kind of knew in my heart and soul that I wasn't . . . Too many fellows with injuries for selfish reasons declare themselves fit when they know they're not fit. . . . Micko, he always left it to the players. I mean, the one thing about that bunch of Kerry players . . . they were mature, solid guys. At least they weren't guys who put self-interest before the team.

Mikey Sheehy was in danger of joining Spillane on the sideline.

I got injured in the county championships playing with the Stacks against Shannon Rangers, and I had a serious instep injury. I couldn't train. In fairness to Micko, he would always give you every chance of playing in a final—you know, he would trust you to be honest with him. . . . So I went kicking. I said, This isn't going to work at all, but I kicked a few along the ground; eventually I got into range, and I said to Micko, I told him, but he said no, we'll start you. And even though I got a pain-killing injection before the game—I think the first free from what I can remember that day—I don't think I got it airborne at all, but I got a couple of points during play, believe it or not. I've seen the clips of the all-Ireland, and you can see I was limping clearly, and I didn't play football for about six months, I'd say, after it. They didn't discover the seriousness of the injury until the following March.

Tim Kennelly was finally able to return from injury for his first appearance of the season. He came in at centre-back, Seán Walsh moved to midfield, and Tommy Doyle went to half-forward.

Before the all-Ireland final Mick O'Dwyer called on the referee to visit the Kerry training camp.

We had asked him to come down to explain the hand-pass and the pick-up and all that to us, which I think was a great move from our point of view . . And, would you believe, we weren't whistled for one bad hand-pass in that all-Ireland final.

John Egan has an opinion about why the hand-pass rule was changed.

They were trying to change the rules from top down. Now, having played football all my life, and I heading into thirty years of age, and the referee coming down to show us how to pass the ball, that was quite extraordinary: you couldn't believe it. And he was on about the modified version of the hand-pass, and you do this . . .

A wet and windy day contributed to a poor affair in the final. Two scores from Matt Connor in the first five minutes had Offaly ahead. Between the tenth and thirteenth minutes Kerry had three points of their own through Ogie Moran, Páidí Ó Sé and Mikey Sheehy. Sheehy and Ger

Power then made it five points to two. With Kerry remaining scoreless for the rest of the half, Offaly drew level by the break. Firstly, Seán and Brendan Lowry reduced the gap to the minimum. Then just before Tomás Connor grabbed the equaliser, Martin Furlong denied Eoin Liston from a definite goal-scoring opportunity. The game was tied at five points apiece at half time.

There was an eventful start to the second period. Two minutes in, Gerry Carroll of Offaly struck the crossbar. The Kerry goal remained intact, spurring the side into action. Seán Walsh put Kerry in front, and John Egan and Mikey Sheehy made it 0-8 to 0-5 going into the twentieth minute. Ogie Moran then put four between the sides. Offaly were forced to wait until twenty-five minutes into the half for their first score of the period, Seán Lowry's point making it nine points to six. Sandwiched between points by Mikey Sheehy and Tommy Doyle was an Eoin Liston effort on goal, which would have finally killed Offaly off. The nail in the coffin was not too far away, however. Entering the thirty-third minute the score was twelve points to seven. The *Kerryman* best describes the clinching goal.

> Jim Deenihan, in front of his own goal, found Tim Kennelly outside him on the right; Kennelly drove a powerful ball outfield and it was won brilliantly by Tommy Doyle, the Annascaul man passed to John Egan and then Egan engaged in a beautiful one-two near the Hogan Stand sideline with O'Shea before racing on, tapping the ball a couple of times on his toe and then firing a lovely ball into the centre to Mikey Sheehy . . . Jack O'Shea had come up to form an overlap and . . . Sheehy slipped the ball into O'Shea and the Cahersiveen man sent a marvellous shot which was just the right height and completely beat Martin Furlong.

Jacko remembers having to work his own way up from one end of the pitch to the other.

> I was actually quite close to the corner-back when the ball was back there . . . I just kept going up along the Cusack Stand side, and I knew eventually the ball would come across. These are the golden moments you dream about, being able to do that. Achieving that was probably one of the highlights for me.

That goal put the seal on a win of 1-12 to 0-8, and Kerry had once more secured the four in a row. It was a victory that saw John O'Keeffe emulate his namesake Danno: the pair were the only two men to have won seven all-Irelands.

The new jersey that Kerry wore that day was yellow on top to a little under the armpit, with the remainder green. John Barry in the *Kerryman* declared:

> About those new style jerseys; it took a while to become accustomed to them, and the numbers on the back could have been a little easier to read—but who's complaining!

To this day the numbering on Kerry jerseys remains problematic.

Achieving the four in a row meant that Kerry had emulated the county's side of 1929–1932 as well as the Wexford side of 1915–1918. Dónal Keenan feels that this achievement, along with that of 1975, set this side apart.

> I suppose if you're looking at sheer football ability, natural football ability, then the strength of people like Kennelly, Deenihan, you know, the flair of Spillane, the flair of Ger Power—there was just so much. Then the arrival of the Bomber was massive, to me probably the final crucial link in making that team the four-in-a-row team it was.

Murt Kelly, who served as a county selector, was among the watching crowd as Kerry won their four in a row. Murt's son Colm recalls his father's thoughts on how the game had evolved since Murt's own playing days of the 1930s and 40s.

> I think when the hand-passing game came in the late '70s, early '80s, he didn't like it. You know, he always said fellows are throwing the ball around the place; they should be fisting the ball, they should be kicking the ball, and he felt that it was almost like the basketball game—but I think when Kerry won the four in a row from '78 to '81 he seemed to forget it.

Eugene McGee was manager of the Offaly team in 1981. He would have his revenge twelve months later against a side that he felt was beginning to show signs of wear and tear.

'81 is significant, because the scoring statistics suddenly began to change dramatically. This was the first time that no Kerry forward scored a goal. Now that, in my opinion, was hugely symbolic. We had played them seven or eight times over the previous three or four years, and it was usually three or five or six goals. And this time there was no goal, except for Jacko's goal near the finish . . . No-one remembers the '81 final . . . but for us it was crucially important, because when we reassessed it a few weeks later, we saw that we were closing the gap quite a lot, a lot more than most Kerry people had figured. Kerry had just regarded that as a vehicle to get you into the fifth in a row.

Alas, it was not to be: the name Séamus Darby will for ever send a shiver down the spines of Kerry GAA folk.

| FAR FROM FINISHED

Kerry went into the 1984 season following two heartbreaking last-minute losses: one against Offaly in the 1982 all-Ireland final and another against Cork in the 1983 Munster championship. The newcomer Ambrose O'Donovan remembers that the final whistle had barely blown on Kerry's 1983 season when thoughts turned to the coming year.

> I was on the panel in '83 as well, and I remember coming out of Páirc Uí Chaoimh, and I don't know who said it inside in the dressing-room after but it went along the lines of 'Now, guys, it's make-your-mind-up time. What do you want to do?' And I remember—I think it was P. Shea and Bomber, I think Spillane was involved as well as Mikey—they said, 'Lads, we're going to have one more cut, and'—I believe that was the first time 'Centenary' was mentioned—'we'll have to win the Centenary final' . . . In a way, I suppose, '83 was a godsend, because fellows got revitalised that time. There was no back door or nothing, your championship was over . . . I think there was a big effort put into '84, and I think that is why it kept the team together.

Tommy Doyle feels that the time off after the early exit in 1983 afforded the players a chance to recharge the batteries.

> I think possibly in '83 the team took a break . . . I remember getting a phone call from Micko, and we all convened in Ballybunion . . . The gang of us went out, we were actually like kids again, because we hadn't seen one another for a long time . . . We were told to bring the gear. It was pouring rain, and we togged out . . . We had a bit of a

kick around and a bit of soccer and that caper. But we all convened down in Bernie's hotel. O'Dwyer was there, and Frank King [County Board chairman], God rest him, was there as well. And the next thing was we had a meeting anyway . . . O'Dwyer stood up, and he made a statement . . . He wanted to win the '84 title, because it had been the Centenary year, and I think it was important to Kerry for us to do that, for our tradition as well, I think.

Before starting their provincial campaign the Kingdom secured the League title, beating Galway in the final in Limerick. The journalist Martin Breheny was in the Kerry dressing-room after that success. He recalls O'Dwyer attempting to play down the Kingdom's chances for the coming championship season.

Micko started spinning this line about being in transition. I said, 'By the way, Micko, you had eleven of the team that won all these all-Irelands.' He looks at me, and a big scorch of a laugh, and disappears.

John Kennedy attended that League final as a spectator. On the way home he and his friends discussed a potential Kerry team for the championship. Little did he know that his name would be added to that list.

I had played minor and under-21 for Kerry, and I was actually down in Limerick at the League final . . . And I was with a few friends— John Joe O'Carroll, P. J. O'Connor. We travelled to matches together, if I didn't go with my late father . . . That night I got a call from our chairman in Ballylongford, Alan Kennelly, to say I was called in to Kerry training on Tuesday night. And that was the start of my senior inter-county career . . . Complete surprise, to be honest. I was playing reasonably good football with the club . . . but to be called into the Kerry senior squad—you know, initially I thought it was just for training, just to be part of a panel for the championship . . . But, as things turned out, it was better than that, and I actually got my place on the team.

The nucleus of the Kerry squad remained from the four-in-a-row winning teams of 1979–81. Gone were Jimmy Deenihan, Tim Kennelly and Paudie Lynch. New blood—Ger Lynch, Timmy O'Dowd, John Kennedy and Diarmuid O'Donoghue—was introduced for the season opener against Tipperary.

Kennedy still remembers his first night joining the squad.

It was a very strange feeling going into the Fitzgerald Stadium . . . Getting out of the car, there was a reluctance to go in. From the very first introduction the guys were fantastic: they welcomed me and made me part of it. Those guys sheltered us and explained things as we went along, and they were great for young guys coming into the team.

Tom Spillane, having previously represented his county at midfield and centre-forward, found a new position for 1984, having missed the previous year through injury. He had the unenviable task of taking over the number 6 jersey from Tim Kennelly.

The game against Tipperary was a walk in the park, Kerry winning by twenty-three points to six. The biggest cheer of the first period came two minutes before the break when the Tipp goalkeeper, Anthony Colville, saved a Jack O'Shea penalty.

John Kennedy feared that his championship debut was at an end following a slow start in the Kerry jersey. However, he would soon repay the faith shown in him by O'Dwyer.

The first thirty-five minutes, things didn't go particularly well for me. At half time I was expecting to be taken off. O'Dwyer said to me, 'That's the first thirty-five over, it's time to do business.' Early in the second half Jacko got a ball, an easy score on, and he actually turned back and gave it to me, and I kicked it over the bar. I didn't look back from then on.

Six points from John Kennedy stood out as particularly memorable in the second half. There was also an audacious attempt on goal by Timmy O'Dowd, on sixty-four minutes. The players may not remember that effort of twenty-six years ago, but it's preserved for ever, thanks to the *Kerryman*.

Colville's kickout from the Tipperary goal was caught by Timmy O'Dowd about 40 yards from the goal. The quick-thinking O'Dowd immediately lobbed the ball towards goal as Colville made a frantic dash back to his line. The ball passed over Colville's head as he ran, but to the dismay of the crowd it clipped the crossbar and went over for a point.

The seventeen-point demolition of Tipp was John O'Keeffe's last championship match of forty-nine for Kerry. He was among the subs for the Munster final and subsequently announced his inter-county retirement.

With O'Keeffe out of the picture, Seán Walsh was moved to the pivotal position. It was not a switch that he was keen on.

I felt that I had ended up full-back very early . . . at twenty-six. I felt that I had another few years at midfield, but John O'Keeffe had retired, so I was asked to go back.

There was to be a new midfield combination for the Munster final against Cork and a new team captain. Diarmuid O'Donoghue's omission for the final would ultimately give Ambrose O'Donovan the honour of leading out his county. First, however, O'Donovan had to secure a spot on the starting fifteen. He explains the circumstances.

O'Dwyer put it very straight to me. We had a trial game, Jacko and myself, against Vincent O'Connor and Dermot Hannafin. Micko put it that it's either you or Vincent, and ye mark each other in the trial game. I must have done all right, 'cause I got the nod. I remember Dwyer coming out after training, and he winked at me.

So, in O'Donovan's first championship game for Kerry he captained them in the 1984 Munster final. He was proud to lead his team-mates into the match, but he also knew not to get carried away by the accolade.

I was told that the captaincy of this team means very little. You go up and toss and say a few words in the dressing-room beforehand. You had experienced fellows who took the pressure away. They'd be telling you what to say and what not to say, people to talk to and not to talk to. There were certain members of the media looking for the big headlines, but the boys would steer you away from them.

Ger Power and Willie Maher were also drafted in for the Munster final. Out went John O'Keeffe, Timmy O'Dowd and Diarmuid O'Donoghue. This game was also Maher's first Munster final.

Cork raced into a lead of four points to one after only ten minutes. Liston and Mikey Sheehy made it a one-point game. Cork then went two in front, but Kerry soon took over: three quick points saw them move into a lead they would never surrender. Kerry then goaled on twenty minutes, Maher finishing off the good work of Liston. Rather than serve as a wake-up call for Cork, that goal drove Kerry on, and seven minutes later they doubled the dose, Pat Spillane the benefactor of a pass from Mikey Sheehy. The Kingdom led 2-9 to 0-7 at half time.

Three minutes into the second period Kerry put further daylight between themselves and Cork as Pat Spillane sent in their third goal. With Kerry leading 3-10 to 0-8, the match was all but over. However, a bout of Kerry inaccuracy, combined with equally wayward defending, let Cork in with a chance. Two late Cork goals—by Barry Coffey and Dave Barry—meant that with eight minutes remaining the gap was reduced to five points. But late scores from Jack O'Shea and Tom Spillane consolidated Kerry's lead, and the game finished 3-14 to 2-10.

Kerry recorded sixteen wides that day against Cork. John Kennedy was responsible for seven of those, but nonetheless he impressed with his four points. Ambrose O'Donovan had safely made it through his first Munster final. Eoin Liston never had any doubts about him.

> It didn't faze him one bit . . . He was an experienced man . . . and he was a great leader. He was totally selfless, and on the field he gave in a fabulous ball and great trajectory always. It was a great pleasure to play inside him, with his deliveries, and you knew that Ambrose would empty the tank every time he would go out, especially against Cork.

There were two changes for the all-Ireland semi-final. Ogie Moran, a sub in the Munster final, retained the centre-forward position. John Egan was brought in at corner-forward. Out went Ger Power and Willie Maher. Maher's season had ended prematurely with an unfortunate leg break sustained the week after the victory over Cork.

Galway were the second-last hurdle as Kerry sought to regain the Sam Maguire. Mikey Sheehy had Kerry's opening point in the third minute. That was sandwiched between scores for Galway from Gay McManus and Pádraig Conroy. After Galway went further ahead through Val Daly, the Kingdom responded to make it three points apiece.

Eighteen minutes in, Kerry launched another attack on the Galway goal, and Jack O'Shea was denied a goal by a fine save from the Galway netminder. Kerry took the lead for the first time in the twentieth minute and then doubled the advantage. Ten minutes from half time Pádraig Kelly cut the lead in half. Kerry's advantage was five points to four. The remainder of the half was all Kerry: Mikey Sheehy, Ambrose O'Donovan and Tom Spillane all pointed before Kerry's first goal arrived. John Kennedy remembers the strike well, and his role in the proceedings.

> There was a lot of space being created above by our forwards, they were always running off the ball. I got a ball maybe 50 or 55 yards out, I looked up and I remember Egan pointed. I kicked into space, he couldn't actually pick up but he first timed it to the net, a fantastic finish. At half time in the game John came over, said A fantastic ball, a superb pass. Things like that meant an awful lot, when you're going out with nerves at Croke Park, on my first competitive match at the venue.

Half time arrived, Kerry 1-8, Cork 0-4.

Tomás Tierney put over three points for Galway in the opening quarter of an hour of the second half. Each time Kerry responded with one of their own: from Eoin Liston, Pat Spillane and Jack O'Shea. Approaching the half-way point of the period, a Kerry goal settled the issue once and for all. The *Kerryman* reported how Páidí Ó Sé

> triggered off the movement when he glided the ball to the waiting Liston and he in turn found Egan. With panther like speed the latter flicked the ball down onto the path of Sheehy and Mikey reminded his onlookers one and all of the heady days of yesterday when he blasted a furious drive into the net.

The rest of the game was academic. The closing minutes were notable, however, for the scoring prowess of Jack O'Shea, who had each of the Kingdom's final three points.

Kerry had beaten Galway 2-17 to 0-11. Charlie Nelligan, the Kerry goalkeeper, was thrilled to be back in the final, which he felt Kerry were capable of, despite their earlier shortcomings against Offaly and Cork.

> That was a heartbreak, that time, '82 and '83. It was great to get back up there again, 'cause we thought it would never happen. The great team had broken up a little bit. We were on a new mission again, and it was the start of it. Although people around us didn't see it, the players themselves could see that, with the extra players who came on, there was the makings of another good team.

It wasn't all roses, though, with Mikey Sheehy unable to play in the final against Dublin.

> My Achilles tendon gave out in training about ten days before the all-Ireland final. Micko was very good to me . . . Why I togged out . . . I don't know. In fairness to Micko, he said to me, We won't rule you out until the end of the week. My mother was praying for miracles, and so was I . . . I didn't ring Micko until the Saturday morning, before we met in Killarney, and I said, Micko, I'm gone. He knew deep down, but I'd say he was only trying to keep me going and keep my spirits up. I was never going to play in that all-Ireland final, any part in it.

With Mikey Sheehy ruled out of the final, Ger Power, his Austin Stacks clubmate, started instead.

Despite Kerry's achievements from 1975 to 1983, winning five all-Ireland finals, it was widely believed that they were in decline. The Kingdom had proved their detractors wrong in the past, but Dublin were seen as the ultimate test. The men from the metropolis were the defending champions, and they expected to take over the mantle of greatness from the Kingdom. Kerry's captain, Ambrose O'Donovan, noted that O'Dwyer used this sentiment to their advantage.

> I think it was the RTE *Guide,* he plastered that all over the wall in the

Grand Hotel in Malahide. That night we went for a walk down the beach, and when we came back: 'This Kerry team is over the hill, the sell-by date is up.' That's all he wanted us to see, this is what they think of us, lads, and this is what'll be written after us if we don't win. Every fellow got very conscious of the fact that there is a lot of people against us who would like to see us fail. From that point of view, it was a great spur on.

In a journey reminiscent of the Kerry fans of old, one Kingdomite, John Curtin of Castleisland, opted to cycle to the 1984 all-Ireland final. He also wanted to mark the fact that it was the hundredth year of the GAA.

In his first all-Ireland final, Ambrose O'Donovan once more had the honour of leading his county into battle.

I would normally be cool enough before a game, but I remember, before the all-Ireland final in '84 the hair stood on my neck. My legs went like jelly, the first three steps I took onto the pitch . . . It's a fantastic feeling. But at the time it can be frightening and nerve-racking. The one thing the lads said . . . they felt it was getting harder and harder and they got more and more nervous.

O'Donovan may have been one of the Kerry newcomers in 1984, but his team-mate Seán Walsh has revealed that the Gneevgullia man's speech before the match set the tone for what lay ahead.

He spoke with passion—a fantastic speech-maker before games. I'll never forget the spirit before we went out to play Dublin and the speech that Ambrose made. I've never been in a dressing-room that electric before going out on a field.

The final against Dublin was dominated by Kerry from the off. Eoin Liston opened the scoring, then two John Kennedy points made it three-nil. It was the fourteenth minute before Barney Rock opened Dublin's scoring. Pat Spillane cancelled that effort, but Rock put over again. With twenty-two minutes gone it was Kerry 0-4, Dublin 0-2. Spillane pointed for Kerry, which Dublin responded to with a point of their own from Tommy Conroy. Kerry it was who brought the first half's scoring to a close, through John Kennedy and Pat Spillane. Kerry's half-time advantage was four points, 0-7 to 0-3.

As the second period began, Kerry continued from where they had left off, Eoin Liston and John Kennedy extending the gap to six points. There was a clear gap between the sides now, Kerry 0-9, Dublin 0-3. Dublin gave themselves a fighting chance with a Barney Rock goal nine minutes in. But Ogie Moran and Kennedy quickly made it 0-11 to 1-3. Consecutive Barney Rock points meant that there were three between the teams with thirteen minutes remaining. Two scores in a three-minute spell, by Pat Spillane and Jack O'Shea, finally finished Dublin off. With nine minutes left on the clock, Kerry were now in front 0-13 to 1-5. Rock and Liston swapped points before the end.

Kerry had banished those memories of 1982 and 83: they were all-Ireland champions once more. John Kennedy remembers:

> We were good value on the day. We really beat Dublin all over the field, maybe not on the scoreboard, but we were on top in most areas. We dominated the game right through and were never in danger of losing the game.

And he describes what it meant to him to claim his first all-Ireland medal.

> The final whistle was something that'll stay in my mind for ever, realising that I had won an all-Ireland with Kerry. When the final whistle went and the celebrations began, it was then you realised you had done something special.

Ambrose O'Donovan now had to compose himself for the presentation and for the speech.

> There's a man in Croke Park who makes a bee-line for you to go up for the cup. He caught me by the shoulder, and I says, If you don't take your hand, one of the two us will be going to hospital, and it won't be me. I wanted to meet the Dublin captain, Tommy Drum, and shake hands, because I knew well how Kerry felt in '82 . . . It's a lovely walk up but a far nicer walk down when you've your speech made. I remember Dr Paddy Hillery was the President at the time, and he shook hands and said, Well done, must be a great honour,

and take your time, now, relax and enjoy the moment . . . I was black and blue by the time I reached the dressing-room, from all the well-wishers. I had a couple of great men helping with the speech. Seánie Walsh—I can remember the Saturday night, walking down the beach, and Seánie was asking me if I had a few words put together. I said I have—not being cocky in any way, but I know what I want to say. He said, Run it by me, which I did. The one thing he said is, it's important to mention Diarmuid O'Donoghue, the hard luck. It'll ease the burden for him. You must remember he could've been going up there for that cup if we win it.

Winning the Centenary all-Ireland was always going to be memorable. Pat Spillane, however, had more reason than most to appreciate this victory. Two seasons previously, such a scenario seemed an impossibility for him.

'84 was fantastic for me, 'cause I was told in '82 that I would never again play football. because of rupturing my anterior cruciate ligament. It was like the end of the world, being told that, being told you'd never again play, then trying to prove them wrong and slogging for two years and coming back. I never thought I'd be playing football, not to mind playing in an all-Ireland final.

Two future Kerry stars have fond memories of the big day. Declan O'Keeffe remembers: 'I got to the final with my dad, I got in over the turnstiles. It was a fabulous memory. My dad is a Gneeveguilla man, so a very proud day for him.'

It's the customary visit of the cup to the local national school that Séamus Moynihan recalls: 'Ambrose coming to the school, I'd say I was in fifth. I can remember the excitement it brought.'

When Kerry took to the field for the 1985 opener against Limerick they did so with thirteen of the all-Ireland winning side of the previous year. Eoin Liston was unavailable, as he was abroad. John Egan was also missing. Mikey Sheehy was back in after missing the previous season's all-Ireland final. Timmy O'Dowd, a sub in that final, also started against Limerick. Seán Walsh returned, having been out since February with an ankle injury.

Kerry eased to a 2-18 to 0-9 win over Limerick, a score that doesn't tell the full story of the encounter—of its first half, anyway. The Kingdom were only two points ahead, five to three, entering the final ten minutes of the period. But a Jack O'Shea goal, scored after a one-two with Timmy O'Dowd, put Kerry five in front. Further scores from Ogie Moran, Pat Spillane and John Kennedy had Kerry ahead 1-8 to 0-4 at the break. They had recorded twelve wides in that half and should really have been out of sight by the short whistle. Seán Walsh's injury woes returned, however, and he was forced off soon after the restart.

O'Shea got his second goal approaching the quarter-hour mark of the second half. Once again he played a one-two with O'Dowd before goaling. The game petered out after that, with Sheehy continuing to add to his high tally of seven points.

Before the Munster final against Cork, Kerry played a match of As v. Bs to mark the opening of the Kilcummin pitch. O'Dwyer felt that such outings were as good as any challenge matches.

> We rarely played a challenge game . . . You can have great games here in Kerry, because you can get a second team in Kerry that would play for any other county. We had very, very competitive games in Killarney, trial games on the Monday night before the all-Ireland or Munster final. They were played like championship games. Players gave one hundred per cent, and that's the reason, I suppose, they were so good. Massive crowds—we never closed the gate in Killarney or Tralee. They came from all over the country; we had no secrets.

Eoin Liston was back in for the Munster final, Timmy O'Dowd making way. Seán Walsh's injury ruled him out, so Tom Spillane moved to full-back, with John Higgins coming in for his debut.

Kerry opened the scoring through Eoin Liston, but Dave Barry and Teddy McCarthy had Cork ahead on twelve minutes. Kerry then went in front again, but twenty-three minutes in Dave Barry equalised, at three points each. Cork, though, were level for only one minute. As the *Kerryman* reported, Pat Spillane was the architect of the opening goal.

> Spillane set off on a solo run down the left flank. When the ball eventually came back to Jack O'Shea the Cahersiveen man unleashed a ferocious shot and the ball came back down off the

underneath of the crossbar, with goalkeeper John Kerins not knowing where he was and as the ball hopped in front of him up rose the Bomber Liston majestically to knock it into the net for a smashing goal.

Cork hit back, with scores by Coffey and Kerrigan making it a one-point game: Kerry 1-3, Cork 0-5. A Mikey Sheehy score two minutes from half time was responded to by another Coffey point. There was the minimum between the sides at the break: Kerry led 1-4 to 0-6.

Sheehy was not having the best of days, with many of his frees failing to find the target. But he more than made amends in the third minute of the second half with a classic Sheehy strike, as described in the *Kerryman*.

Mikey bestrode the scene like a colossus to hammer home the second and most important of Kerry's brace of goals in this decider. And he did it with a flair and a flourish that is peculiarly the hallmark of this great player. John Kennedy it was who triggered off the defence splitting movement—he transferred the ball to the Bomber Liston and it passed quickly from him to Pat Spillane and Ogie Moran. The Beale man could have essayed a score on his own in front of the Cork posts but instead he slipped the ball to the waiting Sheehy and quicker than it takes to tell, Mikey sent goalkeeper John Kerins going the wrong way as he stabbed the ball to the open net. A goal worthy of champions and befitting the skills of the men who helped to weave it.

Jack O'Shea then pointed to make it 2-5 to 0-6. Tony Nation pulled it back to 2-5 to 0-7 in the forty-second minute. Ambrose O'Donovan's Munster final ended prematurely when he was stretchered off following an off-the-ball incident with Teddy McCarthy.

O'Donovan says that he was knocked unconscious.

I was out for a while and I just woke up, and Dr Dave Geaney was with me. Dr Dave said, I think you've nothing broken, anyway . . . I had a couple of stitches under the jaw but I was hit perfect—it was on the button, as the fellow says.

Subsequent points from Pat Spillane and Ogie Moran gave Kerry some much-needed breathing-space. It was now 2-7 to 0-7. After Cork put over, Kerry did likewise, with the Kingdom goal once more under threat. Fortunately for Kerry, the shot struck the crossbar, and Cork pointed. Had the goal been scored there would have been only three points in it. That point, though, meant that Cork were five adrift, 2-8 to 0-9.

The gap was down to four when Cork registered their tenth point in the fifty-eighth minute. Three minutes from time Mikey Sheehy brought the gap up to five. One minute later John Kennedy made it a six-point game. Kerry had weathered the Cork storm and retained their Munster title with a score of 2-11 to 0-11.

It emerged in the wake of the final that John Egan had confirmed his inter-county retirement to the county board.

Kerry were unchanged for the all-Ireland semi-final against Monaghan. Seán Walsh was among the subs, after missing the Munster final through injury. Monaghan raced into a four-point lead before Kerry finally got on the score-sheet sixteen minutes after the throw-in. Monaghan made the most of their early advantage, and Kerry were fortunate not to be further behind. In the eighteenth minute a Charlie Nelligan save denied Monaghan a goal, but they then went ahead by five points to one. The lifeline Kerry were looking for arrived twelve minutes before half time. Ger Power collected the ball and drove home after a John Kennedy effort came back off an upright. A defensive mistake gifted Monaghan a goal of their own three minutes later. A sideline ball towards the Kerry square was fielded by Tom Spillane, whose attempted hand-pass to his brother Pat was poor. The ball came loose, and Michael O'Dowd for Monaghan was on hand to shoot home. There was no scoring in the closing nine minutes of the half. At the break Monaghan led 1-5 to 1-1. Kerry were lucky to be just four behind, such was Monaghan's dominance.

Timmy O'Dowd was brought on for the second half. The *Kerryman* reported that O'Dowd got the call to go to the Kerry dressing-room only after Monaghan had reappeared on the pitch for the second half. O'Dowd pointed three minutes after his introduction, doing so after Mikey Sheehy had already put over the opening score of the period. Kerry had made it a two-point game. By the sixth minute of the period Kerry had reduced the gap to a single point. They were then afforded the chance to go in front for the first time. However, a Timmy O'Dowd shot was saved when, had O'Dowd opted to pass to Eoin Liston, a goal seemed a certain outcome. After forty-three minutes Liston pointed to bring Kerry level. But within a minute Monaghan responded in the best possible fashion: the northerners' first score of the second half, which came nine minutes after the restart, was a goal. Three minutes later Mikey Sheehy put over from a forty-five. Kerry added two more points and were back on level terms. It was Kerry 1-8, Monaghan 2-5, after fifty-two minutes.

Two minutes later it looked as if Kerry had taken the lead, Ger Power was sent clear by Eoin Liston, evaded two Monaghan defenders and then collided with the Monaghan goalkeeper before kicking the ball to the net. The umpire raised his green flag, but the referee disallowed the goal.

With that score ruled out the sides were level entering the final quarter of an hour. Those closing minutes were tit-for-tat. A Pat Spillane point on fifty-six minutes had Kerry ahead for the first time. Éamonn McEneaney then tied proceedings. With the sides level at 1-9 to 2-6, and with five minutes remaining, the game was there for the taking. Jack O'Shea put Kerry back in front, but Monaghan equalised from a free after the Kerry goalkeeper, Charlie Nelligan, was ruled to have picked the ball off the ground. It was now 1-10 to 2-7 with only three minutes to go. Yet again Jack O'Shea pointed, and Kerry once more held the advantage. However, McEneaney for Monaghan restored parity. With two minutes left the score read 1-11 to 2-8. A little more than fifty yards out Ger Power earned a free for Kerry; Mikey Sheehy sent over. Kerry were a point in front, 1-12 to 2-8, as the game went into injury time. Kerry were within touching distance of the all-Ireland final, when, according to the *Kerryman*,

> the ball was outside the 45 metre line, the breeze was against the free taker Éamonn McEneaney and all a Kerry player had to do was gain possession if the ball dropped short. But the ball didn't drop short. McEneaney's kick had perfect distance and perfect accuracy and it was well worthy of taking this all-Ireland semi-final to a replay.

The match finished Monaghan 2-9, Kerry 1-12. Ambrose O'Donovan was in awe of that Monaghan equaliser.

It was a fantastic kick, to be fair to him, it was a great free, fantastic free. Tommy Doyle was marking him that day, I'll never forget Tommy Doyle's face. He said to me, 'If he's here for another twenty years, he won't kick it.' They had a good team: it was no flash in the pan that they won a league title, but I mean they put it up to us in '85.

Despite Monaghan needing that late chance to equalise, John Kennedy feels that they should have won.

Kerry were very lucky to come out of that, to get a draw, really . . . After getting the fright, Kerry won [the replay]; and they were probably always going to win it, because Monaghan had probably lost their chance. But that was a very good Monaghan side, they had some fantastic individual footballers, you know. They had come through Ulster, which was always tough, and on the first day they probably should have won and got to an all-Ireland final . . . As had been proved with Kerry through the years, when you get a second chance, Kerry take it.

O'Donovan argues that Kerry knew full well what to expect from Monaghan that day.

People said that we nearly got caught by Monaghan. We didn't . . . They had trained very hard. Word was out here that they had gone for weekends away . . . That was totally and utterly new for Ulster teams . . . We were under no illusion at all about them; but they gave a good performance.

For the replay Kerry drafted in Seán Walsh and Timmy O'Dowd. Walsh was back after injury and had come on in the drawn match against Monaghan. Tom Spillane was released from full-back duty, and John Higgins dropped to the bench. O'Dowd came in for John Kennedy. Kennedy has no qualms about his omission.

It was a policy with Dwyer, if you were going well, he picked guys in form . . . I didn't really perform in the Monaghan game and, deservedly I think, was dropped for that.

The replay was very different from the drawn encounter. This time Kerry took the game to their opponents. Two Pat Spillane points put the Kingdom in front. The tally was added to nine minutes in, as the *Kerryman* reported.

> Tom Spillane and the Bomber triggered off the movement, Ger Power got in on the act before the ball again came Liston's. With python like swiftness, he fired a ground shot underneath the body of goalkeeper Paddy Linden to send the champions surging into a 5 point lead.

Liston then turned provider for Pat Spillane to point. Monaghan were shell-shocked. After only ten minutes Kerry led by six, 1-3 to nil. The tide seemed to be turning, however, as the half wore on. Kerry lost Tommy Doyle through injury. Worse was to follow in the twentieth minute, with Eoin Liston sent off. The *Kerryman* described how

> the 2 men went tumbling out over the line like a pair of acrobats and as the ball continued in play McCarville is alleged to have hit the Kerryman as they were getting up off the ground and this in turn led to Liston retaliating and hitting his opponent.

Ambrose O'Donovan believes that Liston's sending off actually worked to their advantage and kept them focused.

> I felt Bomber was very hard done by that day . . . I thought it was a real injustice, because he wasn't that type of player . . . I think everyone stepped up the game that little bit more when we saw Bomber being sent off.

Monaghan had yet to score, and Kerry made it a nine-point game in the twenty-sixth minute. Ger Power goaled, and it was now Kerry 2-3, Monaghan 0-0. Under normal circumstances it would be seen as game over; but Kerry had the handicap of a missing player. Players and supporters alike could recall Monaghan's never-say-die attitude of the drawn match. And, sure enough, they finally imposed themselves on the game: they had four points in a row to close the gap to five. Kerry didn't score again in this half, and so at the short whistle it was 2-3 to Kerry, 0-4 to Monaghan.

Monaghan failed to capitalise on their extra man in the second period. Kerry it was who began the second-half scoring, courtesy of Mikey Sheehy. Monaghan didn't register a score until the tenth minute. Ger Power responded to that, and Kerry maintained their six-point advantage. The Kingdom didn't score again until the twenty-third minute of the period. That point followed two from Monaghan, with the scoreboard now reading 2-5 to 0-8 in Kerry's favour. Another Kerry point kept the northerners at a distance in what was a relatively low-scoring half. Monaghan then brought the gap down to four; but whatever chance they may have had disappeared when, with three minutes to go, Hugo Clerkin was dismissed for striking Ger Power. The honour of closing the scoring fell to Mikey Sheehy. The result was Kerry 2-9, Monaghan 0-10.

In the *Kerryman*, Frank King, chairman of the county board, denied that a deal had been done to allow Eoin Liston and Ogie Moran to line out for Kerry against Monaghan in the replay. Liston and Moran's club, Beale, had asked them not to play, in protest at the board's treatment of the club. They were at loggerheads over disciplinary issues that arose from a county championship match between Beale and South Kerry. According to Eoin Liston,

> I think it was a kind of personality thing between our chairman and the chairman of the county board, and we had to make a decision . . . We knew we had the backing of a lot of the players and the members for the decision we took.

Dublin also needed a replay to progress to the all-Ireland final. On the second day they saw off Mayo, 2-12 to 1-7.

Ambrose O'Donovan was relishing the prospect of facing the Dubs once more.

> There was something about a Kerry-Dublin clash that time, you know, it was special . . . People said that in '84 Dublin had underachieved and underperformed and, you know, Kerry weren't as good as people thought they were. That hurt, it hurt a lot of fellows on the team . . . I suppose we don't see it as much now, because they don't get to all-Ireland finals as much, but there was ferocious hype about that Dublin team.

1985 was the year of the notorious washing-machine advertisement, and Kerry also wore a particular brand of gear, causing controversy. The *Kerryman* reported before the final that the selector Joe Keohane refused to pose for the team photo because of his disapproval of the GAA's association with a foreign company.

For the 1985 final Kerry gave the expected vote of confidence to the fifteen who had seen off Monaghan. Kerry went in front within seconds of the decider. Barney Rock equalised after two minutes. But the opening minutes of this final were only about one man: Jack O'Shea. He soon had Kerry back in front. In the tenth minute Kerry got a penalty after Ger Power was fouled. According to the *Kerryman*,

> the stadium was fraught with expectancy. As a hush descended up stepped Jack O'Shea and the big South Kerryman fired an unstoppable volley high into the left hand corner of the net with John O'Leary beaten all ends up.

After ten minutes it was Kerry—or rather O'Shea—1-2, Dublin 0-1. Points from Tommy Doyle and O'Shea had Kerry leading 1-4 to 0-1 by the quarter hour. Two Mikey Sheehy frees and another point by Ogie Moran stretched the lead to nine. Tommy Carr then got Dublin's second point of the half. Spillane had the final point of the period, and the score stood at 1-8 to 0-2 in Kerry's favour.

Dublin kept Kerry scoreless for the first thirteen minutes of the second period, tagging on three points of their own. The deficit was down to six points. Then came the second Kerry goal, scored by Timmy O'Dowd. The *Kerryman* described how

> the dynamic Ger Lynch came surging up field with the ball. He passed it to O'Donovan and then took a return pass as he careered his way goalwards. Like a flash he spotted Timmy O'Dowd and when he passed the ball to the young John Mitchels stalwart the latter showed all the coolness of a veteran as he clipped a right footed shot at goal and the ball angled away to John O'Leary's right and into the net for a memorable goal.

That goal should have been the beginning of the end for Dublin, who were now trailing by 2-8 to 0-5. However, their time was coming. The

Kingdom wouldn't score for the next sixteen minutes, and in the meantime Dublin were chipping away at that nine-point deficit. A ball in towards the Kerry goal was misjudged, and Joe McNally sent it home.

Two Dublin points made it a four-point game with ten minutes remaining. Kerry were on the ropes, and four minutes later they suffered another potentially fatal blow, a Dublin goal, fisted home by Joe McNally. Kerry had been nine points up approaching the middle of the second half; now, with seven minutes remaining, the difference was a single point: Kerry 2-8, Dublin 2-7.

The Kerry goalkeeper, Charlie Nelligan, admits that what happened in 1982 and 83 was on his mind.

> It was bound to be. The Dubs were a machine—they were like Cork, you know—if things start going wrong for you at all, they could go drastically wrong . . . Things were inclined to slip that day, all right.

Ger Power was confident that the team had the personnel to recover.

> I think the team that time wouldn't panic, anyway, they'd relax . . . You had six forwards had the ability to get the vital scores at the vital time.

The Kingdom's ship indeed steadied a minute later. Kerry's first point—only their second score of the half—arrived from a Mikey Sheehy free. Dublin went down to the other end, Barney Rock putting over a free to make it a one-point game once more. In the thirty-first minute Kerry led 2-9 to 2-8. And then, just when one of those vital scores was most needed, Pat Spillane confirmed his reputation as one of the all-time greats. He went on a run after collecting the ball just inside the Dublin half; after three solos, as he made his way along the field in front of the Hogan Stand, he gave a quick glance towards the posts; he steadied himself, then kicked high and straight between the posts, doubling Kerry's advantage.

Kerry now had a precarious lead of two points. Dublin would need a goal if they were to prevail. It was not to be. The Kingdom ensured victory when Timmy O'Dowd and John Kennedy added further points.

Consecutive titles had been secured. Now, could the Kingdom emulate the side of 1978–1980?

The Kingdom returned in 1986 to attempt the most unlikely three in a row. Kerry had been written off following their last-minute defeats in 1982 and 83. Victory in 1984 was seen as a bonus for a supposedly over-the-hill group of players, and the following year was another season of glory, defying the odds. 1986 provided the opportunity for Kerry to win the all-Ireland title for a seventh time in nine seasons.

Twelve of the starting fifteen from the 1985 final took to the field in the opener against Tipp. Tommy Doyle was missing because of an ankle injury; Mick Spillane, though selected, failed to line out because of injury; and illness prevented Ambrose O'Donovan from taking part.

John Kennedy, a used sub in the 1985 all-Ireland decider, reclaimed the number 10 jersey. John Higgins came in at corner-back, and Stephen Stack was brought in at half-back. Stack discovered that he would be playing only hours before the game.

> I'd say I only found out maybe two hours before the game, so I didn't really have much time to prepare my mind for it. But I think they were hoping against hope that Mick would be able to make it, but I think he might have had a late fitness test that morning and he didn't make it, so that was it really.

Kerry won 5-9 to 0-12 against Tipp. With an emphatic five goals securing their victory, Pat Spillane was free to spend the closing minutes signing autographs!

> The game was nearly over, I suppose. I remember actually signing autographs on the sideline, 'cause Clonmel was quite close; and they sat on the sideline as well—there were seats along the sideline.

Willie Maher was a used sub that day against Tipp, making his first championship appearance since breaking his leg on his debut against Cork in 1984.

A Munster final against Cork awaited, following that success against Tipperary. Three changes were made for the provincial decider. The defenders Mick Spillane and Tommy Doyle returned to take over from John Higgins and Stephen Stack. With the midfielder Ambrose O'Donovan also returning, Timmy O'Dowd was named on the forty in place of Ogie Moran.

O'Donovan's impact was evident within four minutes. The *Kerryman* related how

> Cork launched a blistering attack with Jimmy Kerrigan, Colm O'Neill and Kerrigan involved again before the ball went to midfielder Martin McCarthy; the Youghal man shot from close range and the ball hit off goalkeeper Charlie Nelligan's leg and seemed to be bouncing over the goal line when Ambrose O'Donovan popped up from nowhere to sweep it off the line and avert a certain goal.

O'Donovan feels that, had Cork goaled, it could have been a different story.

> It would have steadied Cork, it unnerved them when they didn't score. They were getting better and better, they were getting closer and closer to us—they were competing harder and they were getting more physical with us, in a good way. We weren't going to over-run them; you could see they were going to make it harder on us later on.

John Kennedy had the first two scores of the day. Twelve minutes in, the Kerry goal was in danger of falling, but Nelligan's save thwarted Cork this time. Dave Barry pointed the resulting forty, Cork's first score. Barry made it two points all with a free in the nineteenth minute. It was a low-scoring encounter, but the efforts of the Kerry half-backs stood out. Tom Spillane and Ger Lynch provided the springboard for attack while also keeping Cork at bay.

Cork managed only two points in that opening period. Kerry went back in front three minutes after Cork equalised, and they went on from there. They had six points in total in the last fifteen minutes of the first half, to lead eight to two at half time.

Cork ate into Kerry's advantage right from the start of the second period, reducing the gap to four. Six minutes into the half Ambrose O'Donovan placed Jack O'Shea to kick Kerry five in front, but they were finding scores hard to come by. Points by Cork in the thirteenth and seventeenth minutes cut the deficit to three, Kerry 0-9, Cork 0-6. But Cork never got any closer. Kerry went on to win by four points, 0-12 to 0-8.

The *Kerryman* felt that this was John Kennedy's best game for Kerry, and Kennedy agrees.

It was the most consistent display I had, and I kicked four very good long-range points at the end—good moves . . When you're kicking from long range, you know, some days they'll go over and other days they won't. That day they did, and I was particularly happy.

There was just the one change for the all-Ireland semi-final against Meath: Ogie Moran came into the half-forward line, replacing Timmy O'Dowd.

Moran had Kerry in front early on, but Colm O'Rourke's long-range effort cancelled that out. By the tenth minute Meath were two in front through two frees from distance by Liam Hayes. Bomber levelled after a quarter of an hour, before Bernard Flynn restored Meath's two-point advantage. Approaching the eighteenth minute, Ger Power saw an opportunity to put the Kingdom ahead, as described by the *Kerryman*.

Ogie Moran sent in a probing centre from about 40 yards and, as it hopped ahead of him, Ger Power chased it for all he was worth; it seemed as if the Meath backs had it covered but suddenly there was a cruel collision between the advancing McQuillan and full backs Joe Cassells and Mick Lyons. All three Meath men fell stricken to the ground and the ball broke loose. Ger Power looked behind him in the confusion and could not believe his eyes when he saw the ball bobbing in front of him, he ran and grabbed it, turned just on the left of the parallelogram and, with wing back Terry Ferguson trying vainly to get to him, blasted it into the net for a great opportunist goal.

Charlie Nelligan believes that Power's goal was crucial. 'For me that was a turning-point at the match, because we were on the rack before half time.'

Power's goal had Kerry leading 1-2 to 0-4. Play was held up for the Meath players to be treated; but the injury time at the end of the half would prove costly for them.

There was no score again until just before the half-hour mark, Bernard Flynn pointing to make it all square, 1-2 against 0-5. Two quick

Meath points, by Flynn and Martin O'Connell, had them two in front once more. Kerry trailed 0-7 to 1-2 entering the final minute of the half. Eoin Liston halved the deficit. During the three minutes of injury time Kerry put over as many points.

Soon after the restart a point from Pat Spillane put three points between the sides. Jack O'Shea made it four with a superb long-range effort. Meath's first point of the half came from a Flynn free. The substitute Willie Maher pointed for Kerry, making it 1-9 to 0-8 in the Kingdom's favour. Another Spillane point a minute after the quarter hour put five between the sides. The gap was three following two Meath points, courtesy of O'Rourke and Murtagh. After one more point from Liston the Meath dream would be crushed. The *Kerryman* describes how in

> a dazzling movement, starting in the middle of the field, Ogie Moran kicked the ball onto Pat Spillane who in turn hoisted a pass in the direction of Jack O'Shea; the midfielder gauged it perfectly, and seeing Willie Maher lying free just to his right, fisted a gem of a pass to him. The Milltown man grabbed the ball with alacrity and, sidestepping left fullback Pádraic Lyons, he promptly picked his spot and hammered the ball to the net, leaving keeper McQuillan groping in its wake.

The Kingdom was on its way to another all-Ireland final, eventually overcoming Meath, 2-13 to 0-12. Stephen Stack, the Kerry newcomer, felt that this display against Meath was an eye-opener for the Kingdom's critics.

> A lot of people that year were writing the Kerry team off, because Meath were the coming team in Leinster and Tyrone had been very good in Ulster . . . I think everyone kind of thought that Kerry were gone and that they were really on their last legs. But the game for me that really proved how hungry they were for it was the Meath game, because they really came out of the blocks like greyhounds that day, and they absolutely blew Meath away . . . They made a huge statement of their continued desire to keep winning and keep being successful.

For Ambrose O'Donovan it was a very good performance by Kerry,

> because that was a good Meath team, and they had very good
> footballers—again they had experience and they had youth . . . We
> were lucky to get out. . . . It was the up-and-coming Meath team, but
> when the old heads put it together again that day there was only
> going to be one result, and that was a Kerry victory.

Seán Walsh believes that Kerry caught Meath at the right time.

> That Meath team was just emerging, and we were lucky that we met
> them when, possibly, we were on the way down and they were just
> starting to come up. A few years after, they proved to be a great team,
> so I think we just met them at the right time.

Kerry's all-Ireland opponents were Tyrone. They had defeated Galway
in the other semi-final, 1-12 to 1-9. Willie Maher's substitute
performance in the semi-final saw him selected against Tyrone in place
of John Kennedy. Kennedy had been taken off early against Meath.

> I went for a few balls, misjudged them, and I was in front of the
> Kerry bench and got called ashore. Willie came on, and I think he
> ended up with 1-1. Willie was in pole position. I'd have to say I was
> disappointed I didn't get started in the all-Ireland final, because I
> had been playing particularly well in training . . . It was
> disappointing not to get on, but you know, at the end of the day the
> county and the team is bigger than any individual, and we won the
> all-Ireland . . . I still have an all-Ireland medal, and that's the most
> important thing.

Tommy Doyle, the Kerry captain, felt honoured to lead the team out for
the final.

> The pride coming out with the team and leading them on the pitch
> at the time was fantastic, you know, brilliant. You just think back at
> the legends that went before you, that's all you've got to do, and back
> to John Dowling and these people . . . You're following in those
> footsteps and the traditions that are in Kerry, and I think that is why

... in Gaelic football we have the most traditions. We stick by them, we play the game in the traditional way that it should be played ... We can adapt our style and change, like we did in the '70s and '80s. We didn't play too much of the football that Tyrone's come on with in the last couple of years, which I am delighted we didn't do.

The first half of the all-Ireland was barely a minute old when the stage was set for one of the most remarkable finals of all time. A penalty to Kerry, following a foul on Ambrose O'Donovan, was missed by Jack O'Shea. Despite that miss Kerry stayed on top, dominating the first ten minutes. They went three in front, but Tyrone were on level terms by the middle of the half. Nineteen minutes in, Kerry were back in front through Eoin Liston. Seán McNally then equalised, and Tyrone took over for the next few minutes, with points from Mickey Mallon, Damien O'Hagan and Mallon again. Tyrone were leading seven points to four. Kerry had managed just one score since the tenth minute, and that was to be their last of the half. At half time it remained Tyrone 0-7, Kerry 0-4.

Timmy O'Dowd then came on for Ambrose O'Donovan. An ankle injury sustained in that second-minute penalty incident put paid to O'Donovan's participation.

There was no way I would have done the second half of that game, and I suppose it worked out. It was just as well, because we were dead and buried at half time. There was worry in the Kerry dressing-room at half time.

O'Dowd recalls a stirring half-time team talk from O'Dwyer.

The lads were on their last legs, and in fairness to them ... they had nearly eleven years on the road now. But we thought we were beaten ... Micko worked the magic at half time. There was a lot of sympathy for Tyrone that time—you know, it was their first all-Ireland—and I remember Micko saying at half time, Now, lads, there's 31½ counties against ye here; and the lads just rose up, and ... we played exceptionally well in the second half.

Kerry had barely settled down for the second half when Tyrone came at them. Inside the first minute Paudge Quinn goaled for Tyrone to make it 1-7 to 0-4. Worse was to come for Kerry as Tyrone were awarded a contentious penalty after three minutes. Kevin McCabe, the scorer of a spot kick in the semi-final, stepped up. He kicked the ball over the bar, although he said afterwards that he did go for a goal. For the Kerry goalkeeper, Charlie Nelligan,

> Tyrone were very unlucky that year. They had a penalty . . . Kevin McCabe, he'd taken one in the semi-final before, I think, and when he was taking the penalty he'd intended to kick it to my right-hand side, but I'd say he changed his mind, because he was probably thinking what I was thinking . . . He kicked it over the bar. But one thing amazing about that side of the pitch—Croke Park—a lot of players who were taking penalties they drove them high and over that bar . . . It was amazing. There was a little hump in the fourteen-yard line. It was only a small little thing, but it's a thing that goalkeepers remember.

It looked as if the young guns from the North were too much for the ageing legs of the Kingdom: it was 1-8 to 0-4, and Tyrone were the ones playing like champions. For the Kerry substitute John Kennedy, going down by seven points to Tyrone was hard to believe.

> When you go seven points down . . . you're wondering will you get a call to come, if you're on the bench, and can you do something if you do come on; and then, all of a sudden, it was like you'd turn a switch, Kerry really turned it on.

The supporters must have been concerned that the Kingdom's hold on the title was slipping. But Ger Power wasn't quite as worried.

> I think most of the panic was up in the stand, most of the supporters thought the game was all over at that stage; but I don't think it took us too long to get back two goals. I think that was one of our finest victories, '86.

Tom Spillane feels that Kerry's previous experience of all-Ireland finals stood to them in the coming minutes.

I think we were probably very fortunate against Tyrone in the final. We didn't play well at the start, but fellows took the game by the scruff of the neck in the second half . . . I think [his brother] Pat had a particularly good game that day. But every fellow had to pull the finger out. We were down seven points . . . We were at sea, but we pulled it back, and we got out of jail, really, I think, that day. I think maybe playing Kerry in an all-Ireland final, they probably hadn't the confidence to follow through on it, whereas you can see the fellows today, they have no fear of anyone, the Tyrone team that are there today—whereas at the time Northern football was coming up . . . I think maybe they had a little bit of respect for the jersey, and when Kerry came at them they didn't have an answer for it.

Kerry needed someone to step up to the mark—and quickly. Five minutes into the second half Pat Spillane pointed. Two minutes later the same player was on hand to send home Kerry's first goal. The *Kerryman* reported that

> Timmy O'Dowd, though falling, whipped the ball out to Ger Power on the left. The ace Austin Stacks man sped goalwards, cut inside to his right and sent the ball across the face of the Tyrone goal where Pat Spillane was waiting to make a salmon leap and fist the ball to the right-hand side of the net.

For Spillane, with that goal

> I did something that I never did in a game in my life before . . . I dived and palmed the ball the opposite way. And why did I do it? . . . I've no idea. It's like Mikey Sheehy's chipped goal again, it's just instinct . . . It would be my best all-Ireland ever. It was one of those days that just everything went right.

Kerry were back in it. It was now a three-point game, Tyrone 1-8 to Kerry's 1-5. Within two minutes Mikey McClure had Tyrone back in front by four; but they would score only once more in the game. Mikey Sheehy then pointed for Kerry, making for a score of Tyrone 1-9, Kerry 1-6. By the thirteenth minute Kerry had wiped out the seven-point deficit. Charlie Nelligan remembers the goal well.

I caught an oul ball inside, and I ballooned it out the field, and Ger Power gave it a bit of a nudge, and he drove it in to Mikey. Three kicks and it was in the back of the net—and their heads went down then. It was like ourselves in '82, when the goal came . . . the head goes down . . . it was the same with Tyrone that day.

The Tyrone fans were shocked. The sides were now level, 2-6 to 1-9. Could Kerry push on and maintain the momentum? Or would Tyrone respond as they had when coming from behind in the first half? Experience was to have the upper hand over youth and exuberance as the Kingdom dismantled Tyrone. Six points in an eight-minute spell ensured that there would be no Northern fairytale. The Kingdom were now six points in front, 2-12 to 1-9. Ogie Moran had the final say in the closing minute, Kerry ultimately victorious by 2-15 to 1-10.

Ger Power feels that the players could have kept going.

I will always remember . . . even though the players were coming to their end, I think when that game finished, Kerry could have kept playing for another fifteen or twenty minutes at the way they were going. The one thing surprising about that whole set-up in 1986 is that there was only about nineteen players on the panel. We won in '86; when was the next year we won after that? Eleven years. You could see it happening, because there was no young people inside in the panel: there was a panel of about nineteen to twenty, where usually there was twenty-five.

After the match there was one final battle to be won: the race for the match ball. The contestants were Páidí Ó Sé and Jack O'Shea.

I just saw the ball came out over my head and said, I better get a hold of this, I might be able to keep this if I get a hold of it . . . I was running to get the ball, you know, nice and leisurely . . . and the next thing this fellow flew past me—I never saw Páidí running as fast, it was the biggest sprint he did in the match on the day, I think, getting out past me to get the ball.

The honour of lifting the Sam Maguire Cup fell to Tommy Doyle. The Annascaul man feels that he was representing a county.

When you lift the cup, you see you are lifting it on behalf of
everybody . . . The players who helped you get there, obviously the
management, county boards, and the people on the pitch . . . You are
realistically up there representing your county with a Kerry jersey on
you, and that's what it's all about . . . And it's an honour you will
always have . . . But you must think of the people that are on the
pitch in the pouring rain, or the sunshine, cheering you on, and the
lads who went there and got it with you.

Pat Spillane considers 1986 to be among his favourite memories. For
him, on some days

you go and everything you do turns to gold, and in '86 I would have
my best all-Ireland final ever. That three in-a-row team were a bit
like the Kerry team now: there were bits and pieces of youngsters
and a bit of old fellows.

Five Kerry players were winning their eighth all-Ireland medal. Stephen
Stack was winning his first.

The players that time were so experienced it was almost a given, but
they never took it for granted. They always prepared very
professionally. A journalist interviewed Ger [Power] one of those
years and was trying to nab him going into the dressing-room
before the all-Ireland . . . Ger turned around and said, 'Yerra, put me
down for whatever I said last year.'

Chapter 13 ∾

| THE RENAISSANCE MEN

Kerry won their thirtieth all-Ireland senior football championship in 1986. Nobody could have envisaged that more than a decade would pass before the Sam Maguire Cup would reside in the county again. The closest Kerry had come in those barren years was 1991, losing the all-Ireland semi-final to Down, and 1996, when the Kingdom fell to Mayo in the last four. The aim in 1996 was to reclaim the Munster crown, which they achieved. Nonetheless, it was widely believed that Kerry didn't do themselves justice in that year's all-Ireland semi-final.

Kerry didn't wallow in too much self-pity following that defeat. In fact, as Séamus Moynihan recalls, preparations for the following season had quickly begun.

> When we got beaten by Mayo in '96, Páidí had us back in again in October, and we had a serious amount of work done, even pre-Christmas. We lost one game that year, and that was to Meath in Navan . . . and I think we went thirteen months then without being beaten by any team. You get out of football what you put into it, and that year, definitely, the work that was put in was second to none, and thankfully we got the rewards for it.

While the drought in the senior grade continued, the county had experienced success at the under-age level. A minor all-Ireland in 1994 was followed by under-21 victories in 1995 and 96. This meant that players such as Mike Frank Russell came into the senior set-up with a winning mentality.

> We were coming in with no fears; we had grown up on a diet of

success at under-age. It was a new senior team; we came in with no baggage and were able to have no fears when we played. It took off from there.

Stephen Stack was the only member of the '97 team who had already won an all-Ireland medal. He feels that the promotion of young players was vital.

What I found more than anything else was that the younger players that came through to the squad in '97 just came with a great freshness and weren't a bit intimidated by the fact that it was so long since we had won one. They brought a great impetus to the squad . . . they had a kind of devil-may-care attitude.

Of the players who took part for Kerry in the 1997 championship opener, the following had won the all-Ireland under-21 championship in 1995: Barry O'Shea, Killian Burns, Darragh Ó Sé, Dónal Daly, Denis O'Dwyer, John Crowley, Liam Hassett and Dara Ó Cinnéide. Killian Burns, Darragh Ó Sé, Denis O'Dwyer, Liam Hassett and Dara Ó Cinnéide were part of the side that retained the title in 1996. Other members of that team were Morgan O'Shea, William Kirby and Mike Frank Russell. That trio also played in the 1997 senior championship opener.

Liam Hassett saw similarities between the 1997 panel and that of the golden years.

Having won two all-Irelands, in '95 and '96, the crop of players that came into the senior panel were a confident bunch. I suppose you kind of look back to '74 and '75, those players that came onto the Kerry team then. Maybe it was similar in that way, young players full of enthusiasm, full of hunger.

Despite a shaky start Kerry went on to win the 1997 National League. Liam Flaherty believes that this gave them the confidence to challenge on a bigger stage.

After Mayo beating us in the ['96] semi-final, the team felt there was something left to prove . . . We said we're going to have a cut at this

League. Now, I remember the first couple of games didn't go off great. Towards the end of the League we were putting wins together, and we got to the quarter-final. Then against Down—we beat them. After that we beat Laois handy enough, and we got Cork in the final. We gave them a bit of a drubbing, and after that the team felt, we're on a bit of a roll ... We could have a good cut at this championship.

The championship opener against Tipperary seemed to be in the bag after a quarter of an hour. However, after five points in the first fifteen minutes Kerry failed to get on the score-sheet again until the closing minute of the half. They were paying for their nine wides in the first half hour. Tipp scored three points to cut the gap to two, at 0-5 to 0-3. Two scores in injury time gave Kerry breathing-space, and they led seven points to three at half time.

Kerry doubled that lead in the opening minutes of the second period. Tipp's first score of the half saw them find the net. By the fifteen-minute mark Kerry, aided by a John Crowley goal, led 1-10 to 1-4, a seemingly safe six-point margin, even allowing for the fact that there were twenty minutes to go. In minutes, however, Tipp had reeled off five unanswered points. With ten minutes remaining there was a single point separating the teams: Kerry 1-10, Tipp 1-9. A minute later Kerry eventually put the game beyond Tipp's reach, when a Denis O'Dwyer goal was followed by a point from Liam Hassett. Kerry won by 2-12 to 1-10.

Surprisingly, Clare were to be the Munster final opponents for Kerry, following their last-minute victory over Cork. Clare's victory may have been dismissed as a fluke in some quarters, but John Crowley says that Kerry approached the game with the utmost respect for their opponents.

Clare had beaten Cork with a last-minute goal, and they had a few fine players at the time. We were not taking them for granted, by no means.

In the match Denis O'Dwyer put Kerry 2-1 ahead after eight minutes. A minute later Kerry fans were celebrating what they thought was a goal; however, Maurice Fitzgerald's shot had merely rattled the side netting. Clare equalised, then Kerry went three in front. 5-2 became 5-3. After Pa

Laide made it double-scores, Clare put over consecutive points to put the minimum between the sides: it was six points to five after half an hour. Kerry closed the first half scoring and led 0-8 to 0-5 at half time.

The decisive score arrived in the fourth minute of the second period, as reported by the *Kerryman*.

> Liam Flaherty pumped a centre up the middle. Laide jumped for it with an opponent and got it. Then, finding at least three opponents closing in on him, he swung left, and made a few vital feet of space for himself before blasting a powerful left footed shot which saw the ball rocket into the top of the net.

That opened up a six-point gap, 1-8 to 0-5, a deficit that Clare cut in half by the eleventh minute of the period. Twice Clare got the gap down to two points; each time Kerry answered with a point of their own. The score read Kerry 1-10 Clare 0-11 with five minutes to go. The Kingdom kept the Clare forwards scoreless up to the final whistle, while adding to their own tally. It concluded at 1-13 to 0-11.

Fittingly, fifty years after contesting the all-Ireland final at the Polo Grounds in New York, Kerry and Cavan met in the all Ireland semi-final. Whatever other memories the match offered, Liam Flaherty says that he'll never forget the parade before the match.

> I never in my life heard such a noise, or a crowd, and I was playing a good few years with Kerry at this stage. I never heard noise like the Cavan people were making when we went around by their area of the field.

After Cavan took an early lead, Kerry hit back in style with points from Darragh Ó Sé, Denis O'Dwyer and Pa Laide. Three points to one to Kerry inside five minutes. They would have to wait eleven minutes for their next score, however. In the meantime Cavan took over. The northerners forged ahead, four points to three. Brian Clarke had Kerry level on sixteen minutes, before Cavan went in front by two. Maurice Fitzgerald then stamped his mark on the game with three scores. These edged Kerry in front, with thirty minutes on the clock. Cavan tied the game within a minute. Kerry then had the ball in the net—but to no avail. Éamonn Breen was the goal-scorer, but the referee ruled the strike out, as Kerry had taken a quick free. Maurice Fitzgerald pointed the subsequent free, and in injury time Éamonn Breen put Kerry two in front. The first-half scoring was not yet done, however. A Cavan goal, on the half-time whistle, was a sucker punch, leaving them ahead at the break, 1-7 to 0-9.

Stephen Stack was not too put out.

> We felt we weren't playing that badly at the time. Cavan did get a run on us for the goal, but we felt at the same time, in a lot of positions we were going much better than we were the previous year. At half time there was no sense of panic, no sense of disappointment . . . We certainly did learn an awful lot from the experience of being in the semi-final the year before. It gave us that little extra bit of confidence that we weren't going to panic, and, if things were going poorly, we were going to play our way out of it—and we did.

Liam Hassett restored parity in the third minute of the second half. Then Maurice Fitzgerald once more came to the fore with two points. Kerry were two to the good, 0-12 to 1-7. Within three minutes Cavan were level, but Kerry responded with interest, after which the score read Kerry 0-15, Cavan 1-9, with sixteen minutes on the clock. At the mid-way point of the half Cavan put over to reduce the gap to two. This was to be their last score of the match. They did have their chances but failed to make the most of the opportunities. The Cavan goal was not as fortunate in the thirtieth minute: Maurice Fitzgerald was the provider, and the scorer was the substitute Mike Frank Russell.

> You've no inhibitions when you're a young fellow, so I was just happy to get on the field the same day. I was . . . just screaming for the ball, to be honest, and thankfully I got a chance.

With the score now at 1-15 to 1-10, Kerry were out of reach and on their way to their first final in eleven years. Maurice Fitzgerald and Mike Frank Russell tagged on points in the closing minutes as Kerry won by 1-17 to 1-10.

Injury had curtailed Billy O'Shea's early-season contribution, but he got an unexpected call up in that first half against Cavan.

I came on towards the end of that at wing-back. Early '97 I got injured with the club . . . I was out for quite a while but lucky to make it back for the Munster championship . . . I remember Denis O'Dwyer taking a ferociously bad knock. He knocked himself out catching a great ball, fell awkwardly on his head . . . I'll remember that day for a long time, because not only did I enjoy the game but the roar from the crowd that day—both from the Cavan and the Kerry side—was phenomenal. They were two teams vying for an all-Ireland final for the first time in a long time, particularly the Cavan people. It was deafening. I remember the final whistle . . . you couldn't hear yourself think.

Victory over Cavan meant that Kerry's all-Ireland journey would extend into September. For Mike and Liam Hassett it was a journey in every sense of the word. The brothers were travelling to and from Leinster throughout the summer for training.

Mike was teaching in Greystones, I was teaching in Dublin. You'd travel down and train and be back up again for maybe half one or two o'clock and go into work the following day. It's something you just did, you didn't think about it. All you were focused on was football, and coming up to the all-Ireland final, you'd do anything.

The county was now busy planning for a first final in eleven seasons. All-Ireland fever had well and truly swept through the Kingdom. For many, supporters and players alike, it was a new experience. For Billy O'Shea,

you didn't want to be getting too caught up in the whole lot of it because . . . you still have to go and win the game. I remember Maurice Fitzgerald being interviewed after the game and saying he couldn't go into school the Friday beforehand because he was getting so much attention and well-wishers. The whole town of Killorglin was euphoric, because not only did we have the captain but there was four of us from the club on the panel. There was a huge amount of good will towards the players that were representing the club.

O'Shea's Laune Rangers club-mate Liam Hassett was also well aware of the hype.

> It was the age when Kerry supporters really donned the green and gold. You had the younger supporters coming on board wearing jerseys. We had the press night and a lot of media attention, but in fairness to Páidí, we knew we had a job to do, and he gave us good advice. He knew that a job had to be done, and the only time to be in the media, as Páidí says, is after the final.

Russell's goal-scoring performance off the bench against Cavan had led to calls for the sharpshooter to be considered for a starting spot for the final, but ultimately he was felt to be too young. He wasn't the only Laune Rangers man who would find himself consigned to the substitutes' bench for the final. While his clubmate Billy O'Shea did get the nod to start, the Kerry captain, Mike Hassett, was omitted from the side to face Mayo. His brother Liam recalls that it was on one of their many long trips from training that he discovered that his older sibling wouldn't be starting.

> It was a long drive back up to Dublin, because Mike had put in a lot of dedication and commitment and sweat since he debuted against Limerick in 1993. Mike got injured, so I was captain for the Cavan match [semi-final]. . . . It was disappointing for Mike [not to be selected for the final], for the family . . . When everything died down, around January of '98, we just didn't have the heart to go back, and we didn't play in '98. It was difficult. I thought Mike could have got some bit of pitch time that day [against Mayo].

Of Mike not getting a medal, Liam says that

> this was the real nail in the coffin for him. Back then there was only twenty-one medals given out. Thankfully, through association with the GPA, that rule is changed, and everybody who puts in an effort is rewarded.

The team veteran Stephen Stack believes that Kerry's preparations for the decider were very focused but very relaxed. Perhaps things weren't as relaxed for Liam Flaherty the night before the match.

> I used to room with Éamonn Breen. The same night they had radios
> inside in the lockers by the bed. There was Breen with the bloody
> radio on full blast and he sound asleep, snoring. I said, Breen, is
> there any chance you'd turn that thing off? And he wouldn't wake up
> for me . . . I said to myself, how in the name of God can this man
> sleep the night before an all-Ireland?

Séamus Moynihan feels that Kerry were in an ideal position going into
the final, thanks to the previous year's loss to Mayo at the semi-final
stage.

> Mayo probably reckoned we weren't as good as what we were. They
> were in the all-Ireland final in '96 . . . They probably felt we would
> have been an easy touch after the year before, after they hammering
> us.

In the final, Mayo kicked five bad wides in the first quarter of an hour.
Kerry were far more economical in possession. The first three points all
went to the men in green and gold. In the sixteenth minute Billy O'Shea
suffered his infamous match-ending injury.

> It was one of those incidents that's very difficult to describe. Myself
> and Maurice were going for the one ball. He told me after he was
> trying to fly-kick it over the bar. I remember meeting my brother in
> the hospital afterwards; he started giving out to me. He says, Fitzie
> was going to fly-kick that over the bar on the volley, we'll never again
> see something like that. I remember at the time Maurice came over
> and asked if I was okay. I said, I'm fine. He was getting a bit
> emotional, and in the end I was trying to cool him down, because he
> had to go on and play the game.

Séamus Moynihan felt for his colleague.

> Billy was absolutely flying for the first fifteen minutes of the game;
> he had Flanagan beaten and had won every ball that was kicked in
> to him. In fairness to Maurice, he must have said something in his

own head, because the performance he gave after that was something unbelievable. No doubt part of that was for Billy.

With O'Shea departing the scene, the Kerry management was forced to bring on a sub much earlier than anticipated. John Crowley got the nod. Fitzgerald composed himself, and he kicked Kerry four in front after twenty-two minutes. A minute later Mayo had their first score of the decider. Fitzgerald and Maurice Sheridan then exchanged scores, to leave Kerry in front by five points to two after half an hour. Kerry extended their advantage to seven points to two. First-half injury time saw Maurice Sheridan register Mayo's third point. Fitzgerald had the final say of the period, and at half time Kerry led 0-8 to 0-3.

Liam Flaherty recalls that, despite what had happened to Billy O'Shea, the dressing-room remained focused on the job in hand during the half-time talk.

> Believe it or not, there wasn't one word mentioned about that in the dressing-room at half time. First thing that anyone said was from Páidí: He's okay, he's gone away to hospital. That was it. Everyone else was focused: we won the first half, let's win the second half.

After Mayo opened the second-half scoring Kerry hit back to go seven up. Nine minutes into the half Kerry led by eleven points to four. Mayo pointed to put six between the teams, and a penalty on fourteen minutes gave them the perfect chance to halve the deficit. They duly obliged. John Crowley feels that Mayo should have been put to bed by then.

> We knew we were very close to it, 'cause Mayo weren't performing great. We knew if we could just get going at all that we had it. There was a few chances, I got through and I had a great chance of a goal, and I tried to keep it low . . . The goalie blocked it. They were hanging in there. Next thing they got the penalty, and they were coming back at us, without even playing great.

Mayo added two points. Their one goal and three points without reply meant that Kerry's seven-point advantage had been whittled down to the minimum. After sixteen minutes of the second period Kerry led by

0-11 to 1-7. The next score didn't arrive until the twenty-fifth minute, Kerry doubling their advantage. The score remained Kerry 0-12, Mayo 1-7, entering the final moments. Fittingly, it was Maurice Fitzgerald who had the final say, a historic moment for Radio Kerry, which was about to report its first all-Ireland final victory for the Kingdom. The match commentator that day was Liam Higgins.

> Maurice Fitzgerald out near the sideline, he's going to have a big one. It's fifty-two yards out; by the time he kicks it it's fifty. He's dropping it in, dropping it in, and it's gone over the bar. That's a marvellous point from Maurice Fitzgerald—unbelievable.

Stephen Stack could now relax, safe in the knowledge that he had secured a second all-Ireland medal.

> They attacked us; their half-forward line and their midfield took over for a little bit in the second half. Teams in games that big are always going to have a spell. It was just a case of trying to weather the storm. They had about fifteen or eighteen minutes when they were very, very good. Eventually we got to grips with it again, and we finished that little bit stronger. And Maurice kicked that point from the sideline, which was just out of this world altogether.

These sentiments are shared by Séamus Moynihan.

> There was one passage of play that will always stick in my mind. A Mayo defender had cleared the ball under pressure. Liam Flaherty took it from nowhere. Liam that day had a massive game. Only for Maurice doing what he did, Liam was no doubt the second-best player on the field. He caught a great ball, played the ball in nice and low, and the ball actually hit over the line. After that Maurice—it was the last kick of the game—he kicked it from sixty yards. I knew, once that ball floated over the bar, that it was curtains. We had the all-Ireland, we had the Sam Maguire. It was just a great feeling.

The eleven-year drought had ended, with Kerry beating Mayo, 0-13 to 1-7.

Among the many thousand pitch-invading Kerry fans was Kieran

Donaghy, the future Kerry star.

> I won a ticket in the Stacks [Austin Stacks club] draw, for the Nally Stand—not the best view, but good enough to see Maurice Fitzgerald kick his points. I went down onto the pitch afterwards and went up to Dara Ó Cinnéide and asked could he get us into the dressing-room. Dara, being Dara said, Not a bother, went up to the steward and said, My two cousins are behind me. It was myself and Andrew Dinneen. Andrew had the full Kerry gear on, and they actually thought he was a player, 'cause he was about six foot at the time. I got in behind him, and I just remember being in the dressing-room, champagne being cracked, the Sam Maguire in there, and fellows on top form, as I now know what it feels like.

Emotions were running high after the match for the Kerry players. Declan O'Keeffe:

> I can't believe it. I'm shocked, really—the happiest day of my life. I just met my mother and father outside, and they're crying, they're crying with happiness.

Pa Laide:

> Myself and Liam Flaherty have waited a long time for that, since 1988, since we left the minors. We didn't think it'd take us nine years to get back here.

Liam Flaherty:

> Breaks came my way today. They didn't in the semi-final—not really, anyway. I got a lot of criticism after that semi-final performance. People didn't understand I was marking a great player in Ronan Carolan.

Liam Hassett was the recipient of the Sam Maguire Cup in 1997. Liam felt for his predecessor, his brother Mike, who had been omitted from the team for the final.

He didn't get a run that day. I ended up lifting the cup. Myself and Mike have spoken about this several times. That time there was only one man lifting the Sam Maguire. You see now that there's maybe two fellows. I invited Mike up. He didn't want to come up, 'cause he felt he didn't partake in the final. It's a thirty-second decision, and I ended up lifting the Sam Maguire, which I'm very proud of, of course; but if we could turn back the clock it'd be easier on all of us if the two us lifted the Sam Maguire in '97.

Mike Frank Russell admits that he mightn't have grasped fully what Kerry had achieved.

I was only eighteen, and I was just coming onto the scene. At the time maybe I didn't realise how much it meant, because I had come up under-age and won a few things. Just to see people afterwards— old people crying . . .

Many in the county may have been rejoicing in their first title in more than a decade, but Billy O'Shea was on his way to the operating theatre.

It only started to kick in when they were going over the little bumps in the ambulance. One of the doctors at the hospital was a Kerryman, and he rolled me into this room so I could watch the rest of the match. They wanted to bring me to the theatre straight away, but this fellow intervened. He put on the match, so the two of us ended up watching it. It was kind of cool that they had delayed an operation because of a football match! I saw most of the second half. It was kind of a frustrating thing to do, because I don't think we played to the best of our ability in the second half. Mayo went through a period of dominance, and it looked like they were coming back. Thankfully the boys steered the ship. That Fitzie point at the end probably summed up the whole year for him, because that year he was giving an exhibition of football.

Jack O'Shea agrees.

I said it to the lads in the stand, all the hard work Maurice puts in in Cahersiveen that nobody sees came to fruition today. Today the public have seen Maurice Fitz at his greatest.

For the journalist Jim O'Sullivan,

> Maurice was an absolute genius, there's no other way of saying it. He
> had such a tremendous influence on that team. I think back to Billy
> O'Shea's unfortunate injury and how another player, it might have
> upset him. Maurice just overcame that and kicked some tremendous
> scores. That was an important breakthrough.

Billy O'Shea was not forgotten amidst all the celebrations. Liam Hassett
was among the many visitors to his hospital bedside.

> The following day I went in and got a little replica of the Sam
> Maguire. I gave it to Billy. I think he appreciated it, and he put it up
> on his little locker where he was inside the hospital.

Meanwhile a county awaited the celebratory homecoming.
Stephen Stack can remember the flight down from Dublin.

> When we came back it was fantastic. I could see bonfires blazing.
> The whole week was fantastic. When things like that happen to you
> in life you have to take them in and enjoy them. They're memories
> that are locked away for ever. In '86 people were so used to it, it was
> a case of whoever was in Tralee turned up. '97 was very different, for
> a lot of reasons. Real colour started to come into the game from the
> supporters' point of view. It was my first time remembering a
> massive number of people wearing county jerseys, and not just from
> Kerry. There was a huge crop of young Kerry supporters that
> actually hadn't seen Kerry win an all-Ireland.

Billy O'Shea was pleased that Kerry had reclaimed their place at the top.

> People refer to the '97 team as the renaissance team, because that's
> when it all seemed to start off again. But I suppose the whole start
> of it was when Páidí came along in '96, because he was bringing on
> a lot of his under-21 players . . . We beat Cork in the Munster final,
> which was what we had set out to achieve . . . We didn't focus too

well after that. If we had gone into the all-Ireland semi-final against Mayo in the same form as the Munster final against Cork, we probably would have given a better account of ourselves. The only consolation is that I think there was a great learning curve from '96 that followed on to '97. That's why we had the success of that year.

O'Shea finally got his hands on the real Sam Maguire Cup later that week.

I actually got to lift the Sam Maguire the Friday night after at the reception in Listowel. I was asked would I make an effort to get out there. I played with Emmets when I was a young fellow, under-twelve and fourteen, so it was nice to be able to make it out to the town that night . . . I was able to put my two hands on the cup and lift it up. The success of a team and the way it's judged will be on the number of all-Irelands it wins. If you're going to be seen as a team that can get out of Munster but can't come back with the all-Ireland—you don't want to be recognised like that. That's why '97 was a very successful year . . . Our focus on the championship that year was one hundred per cent on winning the all-Ireland. There was a game every four weeks, so everything was disciplined and constructed in such a way that you knew you were going to be doing the heavy training in the first two weeks, the ball training in the third week, and then the winding-down period. Páidí knew that at the start of the year and had set out an agenda for what he wanted to achieve.

The Kerry goalkeeper Declan O'Keeffe wants people to appreciate that 1997 was far from a soft all-Ireland.

We'd a great win over Cavan in the semi-final. People said that was an easy all-Ireland. We barely got out of Limerick against Clare before that. We had a tough enough journey to the final. There was a palpable sigh of relief when we won that final. It wasn't about the performance. The team performance wasn't the best in the world. Maurice's contribution was unbelievable that day, and the reality is we won our first all-Ireland in eleven years, and the place went hopping mad.

After winning that title in 1997 Kerry seemed destined for another stint at the top table. But it was not to be: Kildare put paid to the Kingdom in the semi-final in 1998, while Kerry surrendered their Munster crown on a wet summer's afternoon in Cork in 1999.

The placing of Séamus Moynihan at full-back for the 2000 season divided the county. An injury to Barry O'Shea had him on the sideline for the season. It was felt that moving Moynihan back to the number 3 slot would curtail those legendary inspirational bursts forward. However, there was also a belief that Moynihan was the best man for the full-back job, as would be made more and more clear as the year progressed.

Declan O'Keeffe was more than happy to have his colleague and friend at full-back.

> We had been on the road since 1990 together. The communication there between the two of us was great, but there was trust there as well. I think there has to be a trust between your full-back and your goalkeeper, because high balls coming in, or who's staying, who's going, or whatever—that was never an issue with Séamus.

Kerry's toughest provincial test was in their first match. They hosted Cork in Killarney in the semi-final. The Kingdom went five points in front a little after twenty minutes. After twenty-three minutes, with the lead at seven points to two, Kerry were awarded their first penalty of the afternoon. Dara Ó Cinnéide tucked it away and did likewise in the thirty-second minute to leave Kerry with a half-time advantage of 2-9 to 0-5.

The first half an hour of the second period saw Kerry manage only three points, while Cork added on 1-8. The gap was down to two points, 2-12 to 1-13, with four minutes remaining. A Mike Frank Russell point, sandwiched between two from Dara Ó Cinnéide, saw Kerry home.

Clare were the opponents in the millennium Munster final. The sides were tied at two points apiece after ten minutes. In a twelve-minute spell from the quarter-hour mark Kerry broke Clare's resistance, scoring a goal and four points. Eight minutes from half time Kerry were ahead 1-6 to 0-2. The sides swapped ends with the Kingdom ahead by 1-7 to 0-4.

Clare outscored Kerry by three points to two in the first twelve minutes of the second half. Five points was as close as they got, however. Once more, Kerry took over. In fifteen minutes they scored two goals and six points. Clare had the final say: a late point. Kerry won by 3-15 to 0-8.

The all-Ireland semi-final was against Armagh. Kerry led from the off, scoring a goal, courtesy of Dara Ó Cinnéide, and a point, by Mike Frank Russell, in the opening ninety seconds. The advantage grew, and Kerry had a 1-3 to nil lead. The clock showed seven minutes before Armagh registered a score, but they were level by the quarter-hour mark at 1-3 apiece. The northerners were taking over, Kerry unsettled by their tactics of sitting deep and forcing the Kingdom into long-range efforts. Mike Frank Russell restored Kerry's lead after twenty-six minutes with what was Kerry's first score since the sixth minute. As the game became more open it was Kerry who benefited. Three points had the Kingdom in front by four, 1-7 to 1-3, with two minutes to half time. Play went to the other end. Oisín McConville pointed, but it could just as easily have been a goal. Armagh closed the scoring. The sides retired with Kerry leading 1-7 to 1-5.

Two Armagh points in the first three minutes of the second half had the teams level at 1-7 each. Six minutes in, Kerry launched an attack. Like Oisín McConville before the break, Aodán Mac Gearailt pointed when a goal would have been possible. Kerry weren't in front for long, and the sides swapped further points. With a quarter of an hour remaining the sides were tied at 1-9. Two scores in sixty seconds seemed to have finally turned the game in Kerry's favour. A Noel Kennelly point and a goal by Maurice Fitzgerald had Kerry four to the good with thirteen minutes remaining. Armagh reduced the gap to three, then missed two scoring chances. The warning signs were there for Kerry, and one minute from time the Northerners goaled. The game was tied at 2-10. Who could find the match winner? Armagh looked like they had. And then, entering the fourth minute of added-on time, it was desperation stakes for the Kingdom. Kerry were awarded a free over fifty yards out. Maurice Fitzgerald duly converted.

The Kerry goalkeeper, Declan O'Keeffe, was shattered after the drawn affair.

We were exhausted after the first Armagh game. I can remember going to training, and Páidí called it off after ten minutes. And I said,

Look, the wheels are falling off the wagon here now. We actually hardly played any football in the week before the replay. But it just worked, we were totally rejuvenated and had time away from it. Armagh seemingly trained hard. We hit the ground with a spring, then, the second day.

It's hard to believe, but the replay would exceed the drawn affair. Kerry started well enough. With the replay being a more open encounter than the draw, the game suited the Kingdom. They went into a lead of three points to one within ten minutes. Four unanswered points put Armagh in control, but the Kingdom hit back. Twenty-seven minutes in and Kerry led by six points to five, but they failed to score for the rest of the half, allowing Armagh to nudge in front. Then, just before the break, the northerners netted. The goal saw Armagh take a four-point lead into the second half, 1-7 to 0-6.

It had been a relatively poor first period by Kerry. The backs coped well enough with the Armagh forwards, but the Kingdom midfield and attackers were second-best in the first thirty-five minutes. They introduced Maurice Fitzgerald five minutes into the second half. However, it was Armagh who had the first say of the period, Tony McEntee pointing to make it 1-8 to 0-6.

With nine minutes gone in the second half, Kerry trailed by a goal, 1-8 to 0-8. The two Fitzes then edged Kerry closer to Armagh. Points by Fitzgerald and Éamonn Fitzmaurice brought the gap down to the minimum. Twelve minutes to go and it was Armagh 1-8, Kerry 0-10. Armagh hadn't scored in eighteen minutes, as the Kingdom dominated proceedings. Oisín McConville, with eleven minutes remaining, finally had Armagh's second point of the half. Kerry hit back within three minutes. The super-sub Maurice Fitz set up Mike Frank Russell for a goal.

The Kingdom was a point in front with eight minutes on the clock. Oisín McConville drew the sides level at 1-10 apiece. In the thirty-second minute there was a chance for Kerry to go in front, and Dara Ó Cinnéide duly obliged. The next few minutes went by slowly for Kerry, who were eager for the full-time whistle, and quickly for Armagh, who were in search of an equaliser. And there was to be one more score: for Armagh. Game over, 1-11 apiece. Extra time was necessary.

The Kerry forward Noel Kennelly was confident as they prepared for those extra minutes.

> We knew we had the legs on them, actually. We said in the huddle . . .
> before extra time that we seem to be a bit fresher. Páidí had said that
> . . . even though they were coming at us, they seemed to be a bit
> more heavy-legged, and it turned out that way.

The early, decisive stages of the first period of extra time belonged to
Kerry. John Crowley and Dónal Daly pointed, followed by a Mike Frank
Russell goal. Having trailed for so much of normal time, Kerry were five
points in front after only four minutes of extra time. But they failed to
register another score in that first period, and Armagh got three
unanswered points. At the turnaround, Kerry led 2-13 to 1-14.

The half-way mark of the second half of extra time had passed before
the next score arrived. A Maurice Fitzgerald point put Kerry ahead; now
it was Kerry 2-14, Armagh 1-14. Each would add only a solitary point
from there to the finish, allowing Kerry to progress to the all-Ireland
final.

Galway were the last obstacle to all-Ireland success in 2000, an
obstacle that Kerry seemed to have overcome with little difficulty,
following a tight start to the final. After ten minutes they led by two
points to one. They then reeled off six successive points. Those scores
meant that Kerry led by seven points with twelve minutes to the break.
Liam Hassett felt that Kerry may have suffered from their policy of 'total
football'.

> There is a danger when you come out of the traps flying . . .
> Fortunately, or unfortunately, Kerry are an attacking football side,
> and we always look to push forward . . . That Galway side, they had
> a full-forward line of Derek Savage, Pádraig Joyce and Niall
> Finnegan . . . they would trouble any defence in the country.

Galway set about reducing the deficit. Points by Pádraig Joyce and Niall
Finnegan were followed by Galway's first from play, after twenty-nine
minutes. After half an hour it was Kerry 0-8, Galway 0-4. Dara Ó
Cinnéide made it nine to Kerry. Galway put over two in a row to make
it a three-point game. Noel Kennelly and Niall Finnegan swapped

points in the last minute. Kerry, ahead by seven points twelve minutes earlier, went in at half time with a three-point advantage, ten to seven.

The Kingdom extended the gap by two after the break. Those scores were cancelled out by Galway, leaving it Kerry 0-12, Galway 0-9, after seven minutes of the second period. Mike Frank Russell then pointed to put four between the teams. That was to be the Kingdom's last score for nearly a quarter of an hour. In the meantime Galway put over three points and missed two further scoring chances. It was now Kerry 0-13, Galway 0-12. There were only three points in the closing thirteen minutes, as Galway had to come from two down to secure the draw.

The sides reconvened on Saturday 7 October. Fifteen seconds into the replay Kerry pointed through John Crowley. Galway's opening score came on seven minutes, when a goal put them in front. Ó Cinnéide and Finnegan then swapped points, and after fourteen minutes the scoreboard read Galway 1-1, Kerry 0-2. Points by Mike Frank Russell and Dara Ó Cinnéide brought Kerry level. Michael Donnellan nudged Galway ahead in the nineteenth minute. The next score came in the twenty-fifth minute, and Kerry finally began to convert the many chances afforded them in that half. They tagged on three points and were now ahead by 0-7 to 1-2. Joe Bergin for Galway, after half an hour, and Dara Ó Cinnéide, in the final minute, closed the half's scoring. Kerry went in leading by 0-8 to 1-3.

As they had at the start of the match, Kerry pointed from the second-half throw-in. They were now three in front. Michael Donnellan and Tommy Joyce brought Galway to within one by the eighth minute. The Kingdom squandered its next two scoring chances, kicking badly wide on both occasions. Galway were far more clinical, and they moved into a 1-7 to 0-9 lead. Entering the seventeenth minute Kerry found their scoring boots in some style. Three unanswered points saw them move into a two-point lead with a quarter of an hour remaining. Kevin Walsh of Galway put over, and then Liam Hassett did the same for Kerry. The gap remained at two. From a free, Niall Finnegan for Galway left the minimum between the sides. There were eleven minutes to go, and the tie was delicately poised. A three-point scoring burst in eight minutes finally put Kerry out of Galway's reach, and they ended all-Ireland champions for the thirty-second time on a score of Kerry 0-17, Galway 1-10.

Liam Hassett had secured his second all-Ireland medal, and there was a first medal for his brother Mike. Liam was delighted to play such a big part in the victory.

> It was, I think, one of my best performances for Kerry. I was playing centre-forward and full-forward and . . . it was great to kick four points. It was great to get on the scoreboard, and it's great that Mike was part of that all-Ireland winning team, and he played very well as well that day.

The goalkeeper, Declan O'Keeffe, reflecting on the 2000 season, has revealed how despondent he was in the wake of the drawn final with Galway.

> I remember drawing the first game and feeling so dejected and feeling . . . a sense of anti-climax and being pissed off really, and going out to the function, the day-after function. The two teams were there, and I remember saying to Páidí, do you know, how pissed off I was, and he turned around and said, Jesus, I'd love to be facing another all-Ireland final, two all-Ireland finals in the one year . . . and when he said that to me . . . I realised we got back on the ship again, and we knuckled down; and that final was played on a Saturday, I think it was the first all-Ireland to be won on a Saturday because the Australians were playing Ireland the following day in Croker; so not alone to win, to play in two all-Irelands in one year, to win it eventually and to win it on a Saturday—'twas absolutely tremendous altogether.
>
> I went straight to Séamus after the game . . . If there was ever justice in Gaelic football, it's a player like Séamus Moynihan lifting the Sam Maguire . . . I think he epitomised the spirit of the team all year by his displays, and I think everybody around him rose to the occasion.

Maurice Fitzgerald:

> It's a great honour . . . It's been a long, difficult campaign, I think, for everybody. Every championship game brought up different tests, and though every test was stern, things worked out very well. I think

the character came through in the team today. We came up with a strong belief that we could win, and I am really delighted for the whole twenty-seven players and management and everybody and particularly, obviously, for Séamus Moynihan.

Chapter 14 ❧

| STARS IN THE MAKING

Páidí Ó Sé's time in charge of Kerry came to an end in 2003. Jack O'Connor was appointed to the manager's position in October that year. O'Connor, a South Kerryman, had served with Ó Sé as a selector as well as having taken over from him at the helm of the county under-21s. Jack's brother Joe has since revealed the poignant moment when their late mother was told he had the job, and she said, 'Johneen, don't take it, because they'll be at you,' that the media would be giving out to him if things didn't work right for him, that they'd be blaming him.

O'Connor drafted in Johnny Culloty and Ger O'Keeffe to serve with him as selectors. Pat Flanagan was also brought on as the team trainer. Mike Frank Russell firmly believes that the appointment of Flanagan was crucial.

> He was very thorough in his preparation . . . He was very scientific. He seemed to tell you what you were training for, and he explained everything. I thought he was very good, and he brought a lot of freshness as well, and new ideas . . . Kerry reaped the benefits of it.

Going into the 2004 season, Kerry had endured three significantly low years. They had been hammered by Meath in the 2001 all-Ireland semi-final, lost the 2002 final to Armagh, and were then beaten by Tyrone in the 2003 semi-final.

The Kerry forward Colm Cooper was determined to make up for the previous years' shortfalls.

> We made a conscious effort that we were going to leave no stone unturned in trying to bring this all-Ireland back to Kerry . . . We

prepared as best we can and we went to levels we hadn't maybe done before as players.

Jack O'Connor's first game in charge ended in defeat, Kerry being beaten by a last-minute goal in Longford. According to Liam Hassett,

> you were saying, Is this the start of our year, 2004, where we can't even beat Longford? But Jack really was able to talk to the players, and he really analysed things afterwards . . . We had a great physical trainer then as well—Pat Flanagan.

A Munster championship quarter-final away to Clare raised the curtain on Kerry's 2004. The first score came to Clare, a point after three minutes. Kerry's first offering was more telling, a goal after five minutes. That John Crowley strike set Kerry on their way. After twenty-eight minutes it was Kerry 1-4, Clare 0-1. Clare's second point arrived on the half-hour mark. Eoin Brosnan and Colm Cooper extended Kerry's advantage. The Kingdom led 1-6 to 0-3 at half time. Already the game was beyond Clare.

By the middle of the second half Kerry were ahead by 1-10 to 0-5. An Eoin Brosnan goal on twenty-two minutes was the only incident of note from there to the end. Kerry prevailed by 2-10 to 0-9.

The old firm of Kerry and Cork met in the Munster semi-final. The sides were level on two points after sixteen minutes. Kerry then fired off five points in a row. With six minutes to go to half time Kerry led seven points to two. Cork pointed four minutes from half time.

In the very first minute of the second period Cork reduced the gap to three. Kerry put over four unanswered points to go seven in front by the fourteenth minute. In the seventeenth minute Kevin McMahon had Cork's fifth point of the day. Kerry went on another scoring spree. After twenty-nine minutes Kerry led by fifteen points to five. The game ended 0-15 to 0-7.

Limerick, led by Liam Kearns, were Kerry's Munster final opponents. They had the first two points of the final before Kerry sprang into action. A Mike Frank Russell goal and point put the Kingdom in front. However, four points in nine minutes had Limerick on top, 0-6 to 1-1. Worse was to come for Kerry in the twenty-fifth minute: a Limerick goal. The score was Limerick 1-6, Kerry 1-1. Gooch Cooper and Muiris

Gavin then swapped points. Two scores in injury time saw Kerry move within touching distance. At half time the score read Kerry 1-4, Limerick 1-7.

A low-scoring second half ensued. The sides exchanged points; it was Limerick 1-8, Kerry 1-5. Kerry then moved to within a point, 1-8 to 1-7, entering the nineteenth minute. Eoin Keating put the Treaty County two in front. Kerry were level by the twenty-fifth. 1-9 apiece became 1-10 with seven minutes to go. Kerry had survived, and Liam Hassett knows they were lucky to do so.

> I suppose Limerick had their homework done for us in the Gaelic Grounds of Limerick, and we were poxed lucky to get out of that with a draw. They brought great intensity to that game.

Mike Frank Russell believes that game against Limerick and the subsequent replay worked to Kerry's advantage that season.

> I just remember vividly, Limerick were very aggressive the same day . . .I definitely think those two games helped us though as well . . . They watched Tyrone and Armagh, and they seemed to bring that kind of approach to it, but thankfully we came out the right side of it in Killarney at the replay.

Jack O'Connor too feels that Limerick were a team on the rise.

> Limerick had a right good team . . . A lot of people underestimated them and kind of gave us no chance of winning the all-Ireland that year after having struggled against Limerick, but . . . Kearns had done a great job with them. . . He had them playing a very aggressive brand of football. As well, they were big, strong men—the likes of Jason Stokes and John Galvin . . . They put it right up to us both days, and we were just hanging on by our fingertips.

There was a dramatic start to the replay in Killarney, with Stephen Kelly goaling for Limerick inside twelve seconds. Before Kerry could recover from that shock they found themselves trailing by six. An eleventh-minute Dara Ó Cinnéide free was Kerry's first score of the afternoon. Limerick maintained their control, however, and led 1-6 to 0-2 after twenty minutes. Kerry were approaching fifteen minutes without a score. They were looking for inspiration; an Eoin Brosnan goal provided it. Paul Galvin followed that with a point. After thirty-one minutes it was 1-6 to 1-3. Kerry pulled level by the break, a Dara Ó Cinnéide penalty almost on the stroke of half time doing the necessary. Half time: Kerry 2-3, Limerick 1-6.

Four minutes into the second half Eoin Keating put Limerick ahead once more. Dara Ó Cinnéide soon equalised. Kerry then hit the front through an unlikely source, when one of Tomás Ó Sé's legendary forays forward ended with the Kingdom half-back rattling the Limerick net. That eighth-minute goal was added to as Kerry exerted their superiority. It was now 3-6 to 1-7, in Kerry's favour, with thirteen minutes gone in the second period. The next ten minutes yielded just one point apiece. Limerick were then handed a lifeline: a goal. One minute later Limerick scored again, a Muiris Gavin point leaving a solitary score separating the teams: Kerry 3-7, Limerick 2-9. Limerick wouldn't manage another score that afternoon, however, as Kerry secured a hard-earned win, 3-10 to 2-9.

Dublin were next up for the Kingdom, in Croke Park. Colm Cooper feels that it was an experience like no other.

> It was a huge game . . . That day I'll never forget the volume coming from Hill 16. I had heard all about it, but until you are actually out there—you can't actually hear the guy two feet away from you, it's that loud. . . Having beaten Dublin in the quarter-final, that certainly gave us the confidence to go on to bigger and better things, and the team really stepped up to the mark that day.

The all-Ireland quarter-final against Dublin had Kerry starting like a house on fire, snatching two quick points. Dublin, though, had four points in a row after that to go into a lead of 0-4 to 0-2 after seventeen minutes. Kerry spurned a goal chance one minute later. They had to wait until the twenty-fifth minute for their third score of the day. That point, Kerry's first in twenty-two minutes, meant that they trailed by the minimum with ten minutes to half time. Kerry had Diarmuid Murphy to thank for keeping the lead at that single point, a superb double save keeping his goal intact. Colm Cooper had Kerry level on the half-hour mark. Senan Connell then put Dublin back in front.

On the stroke of half time Dara Ó Cinnéide pointed. Kerry, despite a lethargic first half, went in level at the break, at five points each. Dara Ó Cinnéide put over twice in the first four minutes of the second period to send Kerry into a lead of seven points to five. Senan Connell quickly halved the deficit. Twelve minutes into the half came the decisive moment: a Dara Ó Cinnéide goal. That gave Kerry a four-point advantage, and they built on it. Having outscored Dublin 1-4 to a single point in the opening sixteen minutes, Kerry had moved into a lead of 1-9 to 0-6. Dublin hit back for a point of their own, but Kerry were relentless. The last of five points gave them a lead of 1-14 to 0-7 entering the thirty-third minute. Dublin goaled by the end, but come the final whistle it was Kerry who prevailed, 1-15 to 1-8.

Derry were the final barrier between Kerry and a place in the all-Ireland decider. The sides exchanged points early on before Kerry took over. It was four points to one in Kerry's favour thirteen minutes into the proceedings. The game was tied two minutes later, then Derry went two points in front. Worse was to follow for the Kingdom, as Darragh Ó Sé limped out of the game after twenty-one minutes.

When Paddy Bradley pointed for Derry in the twenty-seventh minute to make it 1-4 to 0-4 in their favour, Kerry had now gone a quarter of an hour without registering a score. They made up for lost time in the remaining minutes of the half, however. A burst of four unanswered points gave Kerry a slender lead come the break, 0-8 to 1-4.

The Kingdom began the second half as they had ended the first, making light of Darragh Ó Sé's absence. Six points in a row put Kerry well on the road to another all-Ireland final appearance. They were now leading by 0-14 to 1-4, double scores with twenty minutes to go. Kerry's final score of the day arrived on the half-hour mark. Derry registered five points in the closing minutes to give the final score a more respectable look of 1-17 to 1-11.

Kerry could now plan for an all-Ireland final, but they had to do so without the services of Darragh Ó Sé. The injury that forced him off against Derry brought a premature end to his season. At first it was hoped that he might make a speedy recovery, but Jack O'Connor knew they had to admit defeat.

If you had said to someone at the start of '04 you would win an all-Ireland without Darragh Ó Sé or Séamus Moynihan starting—who

were our two best players at the time—you would have said that
there wasn't much chance of that; but we just got a great bit of spirit
and a great bit of momentum going throughout the year, and we
finished up with a midfield of William Kirby and Eoin Brosnan, and
we did very well and obviously around that area in the final.

The all-Ireland final was to be against a Mayo team who required a
replay to see off Fermanagh in their last-four encounter.

John Crowley got the nod to start for Kerry against Mayo, as the
Kingdom set about exploiting the Mayo defence. Colm Cooper notes
that in the weeks before the match they had explored the possibility of
testing Mayo's resolve under the high ball.

> Jack . . . felt that these guys might not have been tested too much
> over their head . . . We felt that . . . particularly with Dara Ó Cinnéide
> and Johnny Crowley—who were particularly good over their
> head—we felt that that was an avenue that we could explore . . . We
> tried it in training a bit . . . we talked it through . . . Whatever it was
> on that day, we just seemed to grab every ball that came in, and the
> team were pretty ruthless with any of the chances we got.

Jack O'Connor admits that the decision to drop Mike Frank Russell in
order to start John Crowley was not a straightforward one.

> It was a funny year again, because John had a patchy year. He'd been
> taken off in that Limerick game in Killarney, and I suppose he was
> putting in a big sacrifice, because he was living up in Cork and he
> had a young family and, you know, I just told him to keep the head
> down and that eventually his break would come. And he started
> coming into form four or five weeks before the all-Ireland final . . . I
> suppose it was very hard on Mike Frank, but we felt that we could
> do with Crowley inside there, because he's an awful strong man, and
> he's able to create a lot of room for himself.

Kerry settled into the game better, registering two points in the first two
minutes from Dara Ó Cinnéide and Marc Ó Sé. Mayo weren't to be
outdone, however, and after Ciarán McDonald pointed the westerners
went in front. Four minutes into the decider, Mayo were ahead by 1-1 to

0-2. But Kerry didn't trail for too long. Two scoring bursts in the first half put them on their way. The first began in the twelfth minute, and with seventeen minutes gone the Kingdom led by 0-8 to 1-2. Ciarán McDonald pulled a point back for Mayo, but to no avail, as Kerry came to the fore again. A Colm Cooper goal, even at this early stage, was the final nail in the coffin.

Cooper says that the goal was on his mind from the moment he gained possession.

> Éamonn Fitzmaurice launched another one in, and it just came out, and I knew I had a yard on my man, so I just leaped up in the air, and the ball stuck, and I think he probably jumped a little bit behind me, and I knew I had hit the ground a second or two before him, so if I got away before him I didn't think he would catch me, so I had a goal on my mind going in along the Canal End. The corner back came across, so if I tried to lash it or drive it he would possibly have got a block on it, so I tried to make it as easy as possible. It was the obvious thing to do, to step back inside and just keep it down. Peter Burke was a good goalie, so I thought for a split second, to just keep it down and not to lash it and let it just roll away into the corner.

Kerry had racked up 1-11 inside twenty-seven minutes to Mayo's 1-3 and led 1-12 to 1-4 at half time.

In front by eight points at the break, Kerry continued to keep Mayo at a distance. Fourteen minutes into the second period it was Kerry 1-16, Mayo 1-5. There was no danger of Kerry being caught, and the four-year gap was about to be bridged. All-Ireland number 33 was secured on a score of Kerry 1-20, Mayo 2-9.

Mike Frank Russell, dropped for the final, closed the scoring that day after coming on as a sub. He feels it was a fitting end to what had still been a successful season for him.

> I was still actually happy enough, the way I played that year. I ended up top scorer in the championship. I came on in that game as well. I think a lot of the players' mentality is changing nowadays. You can still have a role to play; there are players coming in the whole time, 'cause the game is so fast now as well . . . It's nice to get a point at the end of a game, and the final whistle blowing, and see the Kerry

supporters coming on. It's something you will always bring with you.

For the Kerry manager, Jack O'Connor, the success was a dream fulfilled, as he revealed after the full-time whistle.

It doesn't get much better than this. This was our dream all the year. See those young fellows up there lifting that cup? They worked so hard for it. We felt all during the week, and this morning, we wouldn't be beaten. You know, they deserve it. This team has taken a lot of criticism over the last three years, but, look, it's all worth while.

Colm Cooper was among those winning a first all-Ireland medal in 2004. He feels that the victory answered their critics.

I suppose the special one is probably always your first one. I remember things going so well against Mayo in 2004. We had been beaten in the final in 2002, and well beaten in 2003 in a semi-final, so there were probably question marks over the team coming into the final. It was just an unbelievable feeling; you could kind of go numb when the final whistle goes, you know. You think to yourself, Has it really come true? And just making your way over to the stand, and seeing your family and your parents, and just roaring laughing . . . Only when you look back at it a couple of months later, or a couple of years later, you realise how special it was.

After he had brought the Sam Maguire Cup back to the Kingdom the Kerry captain, Dara Ó Cinnéide, felt that the disappointments of the previous seasons only added to the joy on this occasion.

It's unbelievable scenes of joy and jubilation here, I think, and relief on top of everything else. It's a huge outpouring of emotion between young and old, and it's just great to see . . . Unfortunately, I suppose in Kerry three years is a long wait. It's very long coming around. We've been very, very low for the last couple of years, with results that went against us. But I think, in a strange kind of way that makes the high all the higher.

Johnny Crowley was in agreement.

> People are delighted after the defeats of the last couple of years. The
> Armaghs and the Meaths and Tyrones . . . has been so heartbreaking
> for a lot of lads. As I say, if we lost yesterday it was the finish of a
> good few lads. But it was a great victory, and very comprehensive
> and decisive, I'd say, so that's the most satisfying part of it. Today was
> the best we have played all year. That was the day to do it.

Séamus Moynihan, a sub in the final after missing much of the
campaign through injury, believes that Kerry's first-half display against
Mayo was as good as he'd seen from that bunch of players. And the
Kerry selector Ger O'Keeffe had some choice words for the side's critics.

> We had the homework done since last October. We had only one
> thing on our minds at the start of the year: we knew that this team
> was good enough. Over the last couple of days we'd been very
> calm—no pressure. The build-up only started just about five
> minutes before we got on the bus coming to Croke Park—nothing
> major; these guys knew what they were at. There's been three years
> of disappointments, and to hell with all those pundits who didn't
> give us any plaudits. We're Sam Maguire winners, and we deserve it.

Jimmy Magee, the legendary broadcaster, was among the watching
crowd as Kerry reclaimed the all-Ireland title.

> What a day for the Kingdom! What a day, one hundred and one
> years since they first won it. They've won it thirty-three times now,
> so that's once every three years—class is permanent, boy. They won
> it in the first half, of course; they played brilliantly in the first half,
> they won midfield. I don't think Mayo won a kick-out all day, did
> they? Kerry got every ball—they got every breaking ball, and then of
> course there were individual displays. Ó Cinnéide, I was delighted
> for him, he was terrific. Kirby, William Kirby, at midfield—what a
> game he had! He was terrific. Not alone did he patrol his own area
> and do it well but he scored three very good points when they were
> needed and when things were going bad for them.

Reflecting on that first year in charge, Jack O'Connor admits that

> you don't feel it when you're in the thick of it, because you're just so
> focused on it. But it's a difficult job. It's every minute of your waking
> day you're thinking about it, and you're planning things, and you're
> trying to get fellows motivated and all the rest of it . . . The players
> have it that bit easier, when you think about it, because they only
> have to think of themselves, whereas the manager and the
> management have to think of the whole set-up, not just the players
> but the background team . . . But sure there's great satisfaction as
> well when it comes together then, because there's nothing like
> winning in Kerry. You're a hero when you win.

2006 began in relatively straightforward manner. However, with
winning scores of 0-16 to 0-8 against Waterford and 0-17 to 1-5 against
Tipperary, Kerry weren't fully convincing, and they were hardly in their
best form going into the Munster final against Cork.

Cork opened up a three-point lead inside seven minutes. Colm
Cooper had Kerry's opener on ten minutes, but Cork had the next two
scores. That put the Rebels five to one up after a quarter of an hour. It
was seven to one by the half hour. Cork then suffered a potentially
fateful setback as Anthony Lynch was given the red card. Kerry took
immediate advantage, scoring three points before half time. The last of
those, which came in the thirty-sixth minute from Declan O'Sullivan,
was their first from play. Cork led 0-7 to 0-4 at half time.

Four minutes into the second period Bryan Sheehan pulled a point
back for Kerry. James Masters had two in reply for Cork, who now led
nine points to five approaching the ninth minute. Sheehan pointed
once more, then his team-mate Darren O'Sullivan did likewise. After
eleven minutes Kerry trailed by only two points, 0-9 to 0-7. The next
notable incident didn't arrive until the nineteenth minute, the second
red card of the afternoon, Kerry's Kieran Donaghy the recipient. The
sending off had no effect on Kerry, who had the next three points. They
had edged in front, ten points to nine, with just four minutes remaining,
but they couldn't hold on: Cork equalised, and a second day out was
necessary. Despite his sending off in the drawn game, Anthony Lynch
succeeded in having his suspension overturned.

Speaking to Radio Kerry before the throw-in, the Kerry selector Ger
O'Keeffe was

hoping that 'we'll step up our performance a lot from the last day; if we don't, we'll find ourselves in trouble.'

Kerry and Cork had a point each in the first quarter of an hour. Paul Galvin put Kerry in front on eighteen minutes, despite the fact that Cork were the dominant side. Darragh Ó Sé doubled Kerry's advantage on twenty minutes. Cork were ahead sixty seconds later, 1-2 to 0-3. They added a point on twenty-eight minutes before Colm Cooper and Donncha O'Connor exchanged points. A score in injury time from Bryan Sheehan saw Kerry go in at half time trailing by 1-4 to 0-5.

They opened the second half scoring, but Cork then had three points in a row to move four in front, 1-7 to 0-6. Sixteen minutes into the second half Declan O'Sullivan was withdrawn from the action to a chorus of boos. Jack O'Connor believes that O'Sullivan may have been made the scapegoat for a side that was struggling.

> I felt aggrieved, to be honest with you, because I felt that this was an amateur player who was captain of the team, and he didn't deserve what happened to him that day, and I didn't shy away from telling people that they were wrong. I would tell them to my dying day that they were wrong . . . The team in general wasn't going well at the time, and he just happened to be the fall guy, I suppose [by] association with myself being from the same club . . . I felt very aggrieved because no player deserves that. It's one thing being booed by the opposition, but it's a different story altogether being booed by your own.

Turning to the match itself, he felt that

> you can be talking about the delivery until the cows come home, but it's just that we possibly need to get a ball-winner in the full-forward line, a ball-winner that you can just kick ball into, that wins primary ball. That's our biggest problem. We're going out into corners and carrying the ball too much; we just need a bit more direction up there.

Cork were able to answer every Kerry point, and they went on to win by 1-12 to 0-9.

After the match the team bus set off without Jack O'Connor and Declan O'Sullivan. Séamus Moynihan, though, makes light of a supposed public spat in Killarney that night, in which he was forced to step in as a peacekeeper.

> You wouldn't want to believe everything you hear. The bus scenario was a total mistake. It was just an oversight. The incident in Killarney, only raiméis!

Kerry regrouped, and the draw for the qualifiers paired them with Longford. More importantly, perhaps, Kerry had home advantage. The Kingdom fans turned out in force for the tie in Killarney. Mike Frank Russell felt it was important that the supporters now got behind the side.

> There was a big crowd there the same day . . . Everyone turned out to support us, which is good, you know; and the fact that it was in Killarney, we needed a big lift from supporters, and they didn't leave us down.

Kieran Donaghy was moved to full-forward for the game against Longford. Three goals in the first sixteen minutes against Longford marked the dawn of a new star. Donaghy helped create two goals for Eoin Brosnan and another for Colm Cooper. Those three goals allowed Kerry to build up a half-time advantage of 3-7 to 0-7, rendering the second period all but irrelevant. Kerry progressed 4-11 to 1-11, with Brosnan completing his hat trick in the second half. Some doubts persisted about Kerry, but they had booked their place in the all-Ireland quarter-finals.

For Kieran Donaghy it was an opportunity to continue playing alongside one of his idols, Séamus Moynihan. The man they call Star declared in the minutes after the win that

> I'd really like to do it for Séamus Moynihan. He's been a stalwart. I told him there today I want to play a few more games with him, not just one.

Reflecting on that now, Donaghy opens up further.

We lost to Cork, and I was saying, Oh no, it's not going to end the way I want for this fella. But we came out against Longford, and we all played a good game, and we knew we had Armagh next . . . I suppose that was my main goal, to play in Croke Park with him, and I was lucky enough to get to walk on an all-Ireland final day with him . . . To play with him was a great privilege and a great honour, and he's the best footballer I have ever played with. That day after the game I put my arm around him and said, I want to play four more games with you. He was laughing and said, Oh look, we will take the one next week and we will move on, and I said, Séamo, I want to play four more with you, and he was, Alright, we'll see, we'll see.

Armagh were the opposition in the last eight. The Kingdom went in as underdogs. After twenty minutes the sides were tied, Kerry 1-3, Armagh 0-6. Armagh goaled in the twenty-third minute, and a point put them four to the good. Colm Cooper was a central figure as Kerry sought a way back into the game, approaching half time. At half time it was Armagh 1-7, Kerry 1-5.

The Kingdom were level within two minutes of the restart, and worse was to come for Armagh. A cross-shot from out on the right wing by Seán O'Sullivan dropped towards the Armagh square. Kieran Donaghy fielded and slammed the ball home. Kerry went from two down to three up in those early second-half minutes. Aided by two Marc Ó Sé points, they were leaders by 2-10 to 1-8 after the opening fifteen minutes of the second period. There were still twenty minutes to go, but a five-point advantage looked comfortable even at this stage. Only three points separated the sides as they entered the final twelve minutes, when Paul Galvin was sent off following an altercation. There was plenty of time for Armagh to capitalise on their extra man, but a Darren O'Sullivan goal five minutes later ensured that there would be no nervy finish to this game. This Kerry team had finally beaten Northern opposition, defeating Armagh 3-15 to 1-13. Jack O'Connor wasn't too interested in that fact, however.

There was a lot of satisfaction in beating Armagh on their merits, because that was a good Armagh team . . . They played fantastic football in the first half of that game, and I often go back and make reference to that game. They played copybook football for, I suppose, twenty-five minutes of that game, and our full-back line was under serious pressure. If you talk about systems . . . I often admire the way Joe Kernan set out that team and maybe picked bits and pieces out of what he was trying to do, and he created tremendous structure within the team. And of course there was great shape to the way Armagh played their football at the time . . . They had a deadly duo inside in Clarke and McDonald who had a a telepathic understanding; and you had Oisín McConville kind of playing out a bit off them; and you had John McEntee going for the half-forward line, then out as a third midfielder, so they had a lot of good things going for them.

But for Mike Frank Russell, beating Armagh 'was a monkey off our back, and we lay the Armagh ghost to rest.'

Cork were Kerry's semi-final opponents, a third meeting of the season between the counties. It was one point each after six minutes; Cork led by three to one after fourteen minutes and four to two after eighteen. But Kerry were in front by the half-hour mark. After Cork made it five points apiece in the thirty-second minute, Kerry took over once more. It was Kerry 0-8, Cork 0-5 at half time.

The Kingdom still led by three going into the fourteenth minute of the second period. Two quick scores saw them pull away from their opponents. That made it twelve to seven. By the twentieth minute it was fourteen to eight. Cork brought it back to fourteen to ten, but Colm Cooper closed the game out for the Kingdom, and Kerry won both halves by eight points to five.

Mayo were once more their all-Ireland opponents. For the final Declan O'Sullivan was restored to the line-up. Eoin Brosnan, who had started all seven previous matches that season, was the one to make way.

Two Mike Frank Russell points inside six minutes gave Kerry a two-nil lead. Two goals in two minutes then left the Mayo folk dumbfounded. Declan O'Sullivan scored the first of those and Kieran Donaghy the second. Only eight minutes gone and already Kerry were ahead by eight points, 2-2 to nil. Seán O'Sullivan and Aidan O'Mahony tagged on further points to make it 2-4 only twelve minutes into the decider.

Mike Frank Russell knew at that early stage that Kerry were already closing in on all-Ireland number 34.

> The game was over after a quarter of an hour. I just think we were at the peak of our powers . . . It was probably fascinating to watch as a supporter as well.

Mayo's first score was a goal in the seventeenth minute. Paul Galvin and Kieran Donaghy pointed for Kerry before Colm Cooper got in on the goal-scoring act. It was now 3-6 to 1-0, with nine minutes to go to half time. A Séamus Moynihan point followed on the half hour to make it 3-7 to 1-1. Kerry had a twelve-point advantage, one that Mayo ate into with a point followed by two quick goals. When half time arrived the score was Kerry 3-8, Mayo 3-2. Mayo's mini-comeback only served to lend respectability to the score.

Kerry weren't done yet with the goal-scoring, however, as Eoin Brosnan sent home their fourth in a victory of 4-15 to 3-5.

When the Kilkenny hurlers dismantle an opponent, they're rightly hailed for their achievement and for their clinical attitude. However, when Kerry do something similar, many dismiss their victory. Phrases such as 'Ye beat nothing' and 'a soft all-Ireland' are commonplace when reference is made to the victories of 2006 and 2004. Paul Galvin takes offence at such terms.

> It's a very flippant way to describe winning an all-Ireland . . . You don't win soft all-Irelands . . . We were on fire both days; we played very, very well on both days, and it probably made it look like it was easy, but there's no such thing. And anybody who suggests that it's easy is probably somebody who never played the game . . . All-Ireland finals aren't won in one day over seventy minutes: there's a long, long campaign that started early in the year, and you go through many different stages of the year where you are tested and tested to your last.

The journalist Dónal Keenan believes that no side could have lived with Kerry on all-Ireland final day in 2006.

> The dismantling of Mayo—people might say that Mayo didn't turn

up . . . I don't think it was just Mayo capitulated. I just think Kerry did what they did to Dublin this year [2009], they literally just blew them away, and when they blew away they just kept blowing them away. So I think that entire performance was very special.

For Diarmuid Murphy it was

fantastic; we're over-joyed with it now. It's just been a great day for everybody involved. It was a very strange first half. It was kind of hard to put your finger on it. We were well up, but we knew they were going to come back, and they made it tough for us there at the end of the first half. This year we've had a very tough year . . . But the harder it is the better it feels when you win it then.

Aidan O'Mahony agrees.

An excellent day. You could see after the final whistle what it meant to players in the dressing-room here. After the Munster final people were only writing us off, and we showed today there's great team spirit there . . . A team performance, every player played out of their skin.

For Colm Cooper it had been

a bit of a roller-coaster season, but today we really showed what we were capable of doing, and I'm delighted for everyone involved . . . Strangely enough, I didn't feel any bit of nerves before the game, and usually coming into an all-Ireland final—or a game like that—you would. But I tell you I was very relaxed this morning with all the boys, and I didn't put any extra pressure on myself, but I thought there was a good performance in me, and, thankfully, I got some of that out today . . . The boys showed great character, and the management showed great character, and we changed a few things around and we haven't looked back since.

Seán O'Sullivan had never heard support like it.

They're mad hungry, Kerry fans, and, yeah, they expect the best, because we are the best county. We have the best record, and they expect any time a Kerry team comes up here, you know, to win; and, look, that's the pressure you're under being a Kerry player; but to the fans I will say, Thank you, ye have been great all year.

Séamus Moynihan was

in heaven, in heaven. Dreams come true, after all. This time last year, twelve months ago, I never felt so depressed in my whole life [after losing to Tyrone]. Football and sport is funny: if you stick at it long enough and hard enough and put in the effort, it always comes around; and fair credit to this team, we took the hits all year.

For Ger O'Keeffe

it was a tough year . . . I suppose things didn't go very well for us at the start of the championship . . . We won the league and we played very well against Laois and Galway in both second halves; we kind of went into hibernation then, at that stage, and we struggled against Waterford and Tipperary. And then we didn't play well against Cork . . . The two games we played against Cork I think are the reason why we won the all-Ireland today . . . Cork are an extremely good side . . . We got a great challenge from them this year and last year, before the Tyrone match . . . We just didn't compete at the upper level that Tyrone set and the standards for last year. This year, now, we moved up our training dramatically over the last couple of weeks, and everything was with a focus. We had a weekend in Cork . . . the team really gelled together, and everything was really going well, so we knew there was a big performance in the team.

And for Declan O'Sullivan

it's fantastic, you know, especially after last year. We have seen both sides of the coin, and you treasure these days all the more after tasting defeat, and it's a fantastic day for Kerry.

When the moment arrived, the Kerry captain, O'Sullivan, invited Colm Cooper to lift the Sam Maguire with him. With O'Sullivan sidelined,

Cooper had captained the side for the games against Longford, Armagh and Cork. Cooper was surprised and honoured by the gesture. 'It wasn't planned. Declan just came up to me and said he'd like if I went up for it with him. I was just delighted.'

Kieran Donaghy was humbled by the homecoming.

The homecoming feels very special. It all happened so quick for me, you know, and all of a sudden I'm down in Denny Street [Tralee], where I had been in 1997, 2000 and 2004 . . . and all of a sudden there was councillors saying, Come on, Kieran, and say a few words . . . and I'm out there talking to fifteen thousand to twenty thousand people. That was a great honour and a great privilege.

| HISTORY ON THE LINE

A 2-15 to 0-4 defeat of Waterford began 2007 for Kerry. Eoin Brosnan had two goals in the first half.

The Munster final was against Cork. With the teams level at one point apiece, two Declan O'Sullivan scores put Kerry three to one in front after eleven minutes. James Masters responded with two points for Cork, and the game was tied in the middle of the half. Cork opened up a lead of seven points to four by the twenty-fifth minute. It was nine to six to Cork in first-half injury time. Eoin Brosnan made it a two-point game at the break, Kerry 0-7, Cork 0-9. Kerry drew level, then went in front eight minutes into the second period through a Colm Cooper penalty.

Kerry built on that goal to move six ahead. With a quarter of an hour of the second half gone, Kerry led 1-12 to 0-9. Cork, though, drew level through four unanswered scores: three points and a goal. The scoreboard showed 1-12 each. Mike Frank Russell edged Kerry back in front, but James Masters replied. It was tied at 1-13 entering the final minute. Cork were in on goals but somehow shot wide in an incident in which they could just as easily have been awarded a penalty for a foul. A let-off for Kerry, and the game seemed to be heading for a replay.

Kieran Donaghy feels that he made the most of the opportunity that then presented itself.

I remember Marty Morrissey saying, watching it afterwards . . . Who's going to have the gumption to kick a winning score? It didn't flash through my head about, you know, trying to be a hero or trying to kick or anything, you know, I wouldn't be one to kick points, really. I just remember Fitzgerald Stadium the way the wind was going that day, it was coming nicely . . . and I kind of remember

it was on my right side, and it was perfect for me . . . that I'd kicked
a lot of times out at training . . . I knew how to kick that ball in and
I got it . . . The Cork fellows probably didn't expect me there . . . They
were running around after Franny [Russell] and Brian Sheehan,
probably because they would be the notable kickers . . . but I threw
it onto the right, and once I kicked it I knew it was over.

Regulation time was up, and Kerry were ahead by 1-14 to 1-13.
Approaching the third minute of injury time, Kerry added the
insurance point, through Seán O'Sullivan.

Kerry were Munster champions, but the title nearly cost them,
further down the line. As provincial champions they spent six weeks on
the sidelines while the various rounds of the qualifiers took place. Mike
Frank Russell feels that the break worked against them.

Monaghan came with a game plan, and, you know, I think the fact a
lot of people forget that . . . we were inactive for a while . . . but
thankfully I think our strength and depth that day, our subs coming
off the bench that day, pulled us through, and we got the wake-up
call that we needed.

Monaghan looked the sharper early on in the quarter-final. They were
leading two points to one entering the eighth minute when a penalty for
the northerners put daylight between the sides. Kerry recovered to draw
level, 0-5 to 1-2, after twenty-two minutes. Monaghan had three points
in a row and led 1-5 to 0-5 after twenty-eight minutes. They wouldn't
score for the remainder of the half, and Kerry drew level in the
meantime. At the turnaround it was Kerry 0-8, Monaghan 1-5.

Kerry managed only one point in the first twenty minutes of the
second half, by which time Monaghan had scored four. Ahead by 1-9 to
0-9, Monaghan were fully deserving of their advantage as a rusty-
looking Kingdom looked like relinquishing their all-Ireland crown. But
a lifeline arrived in the twenty-third minute. A Declan O'Sullivan goal
drew Kerry level at 1-9 apiece. Rather than kick on from that, however,
Monaghan went back in front by two points. With five minutes to go,
Kerry trailed 1-11 to 1-9. They then showed just why they are regarded as
the standard-bearers. Two points by Bryan Sheehan had Kerry level,
then Tomás Ó Sé followed suit. Kerry were ahead for the first time

against Monaghan, and that final point of the day saw them over the line, 1-12 to 1-11.

Kieran Donaghy takes nothing away from Monaghan's efforts.

> Yeah, scraped home, very tough. I remember scratching my head after that game . . . We were defending champions, and we were trying to retain Sam for the first time in twenty years, and I remember thinking afterwards that actually we were very lucky to win it . . . If Monaghan had actually gone about it more, and put us to the sword when they had the chance, they would have won, they had us for the taking that day . . . We were rusty. We had a six-weeks lay-off, which is wrong for any provincial winners to have to wait . . . Whatever way, they're going to have to change it, they're going to have to do something about it; but, saying that, we were kind of saying to ourselves [before the game], it doesn't matter about six weeks . . . The press were making a deal out of it, but we were saying, we're going to be fine, we're going to be fine. But I remember that game, Monaghan started at a ferocious pace, we weren't able to keep with them . . . and struggling the whole way through, and only for Brian Sheehan coming on, kicking two big points, and Tomás Ó Sé driving up the field to get the winner . . . we were in serious trouble, and our dreams of retaining an all-Ireland and being the first Kerry team in a while to retain an all-Ireland would have gone by the wayside.

After disposing of Monaghan, Kerry faced a semi-final against Dublin. Kerry were three points to nil in front after three minutes. Their next score didn't come for another twenty-two minutes. In the meantime, Dublin posted four scores of their own. Bryan Sheehan levelled the game at four points each after twenty-five minutes. Dublin proceeded to go two in front. The final five minutes of the half saw Kerry put over three points to Dublin's two. It meant that, at the short whistle, Dublin led by the minimum, eight points to seven.

Kerry's burst of scoring at the opening of the second half proved fatal to the Dublin challenge. A Declan O'Sullivan goal and three points, without reply, put Kerry ahead by 1-10 to 0-8 after seven minutes of the second period. Dublin had the next point, but Tomás Ó Sé and Eoin Brosnan soon put over for Kerry. It was now Kerry 1-12, Dublin 0-9. The

Kingdom endured a seventeen-minute scoring drought while the Dubs tagged on five points. With a little more than five minutes remaining it was a one-point game, Kerry 1-12, Dublin 0-14. Two points provided Kerry with some much-needed breathing space. The game was by now relatively safe, Kerry leading by 1-14 to 0-14, entering the final minute. Dublin managed two late points before the goal-scoring hero Declan O'Sullivan pointed to give Kerry a 1-15 to 0-16 victory.

It was Kieran Donaghy's first championship outing against the men from the capital. He can still remember the atmosphere of that afternoon.

> Normally you're playing semi-finals with fifty or sixty thousand there, but it was my first time ever playing the Dubs in the championship, and the atmosphere was outstanding . . . I knew after that game what the fellows in the seventies must have felt like, and in the eighties, going up to play the Dubs, the crowd and everything that goes with it, the razzmatazz of playing the Dubs in the capital; and that was a huge game for us . . . We played some excellent football for long periods, and played some bad football for periods when Dublin came back into it . . . We've been here before, and the Dubs hadn't got over that stage yet . . . and we knew how to get that step above them, and, thankfully, we did.

For the first time in the history of the association Kerry and Cork were to meet in the all-Ireland final. Never in the course of a rivalry spanning more than a hundred years was so much at stake. The counties had contested all-Ireland semi-finals on three occasions already during the decade. Each time—in 2002, 2005 and 2006—Kerry prevailed. Despite this statistic there was an element of confidence about Cork. It was felt that the semi-final stigma was not in play and that this was a one-off, that what had happened previously could be discarded.

The journalist Seán Moran was among those who predicted a Cork victory.

> The 2007 all-Ireland final—it was peculiar because, it was a situation where the stakes between Cork and Kerry had never been higher. I felt—and it's a matter of public record rather than a shameful confession—but I believed Cork would win the 2007 final, and I

previewed it accordingly. One of the points I made was that, for a change in a Cork-Kerry clash—within the championship, Cork were playing Kerry with no history. This was the first time the counties had met in an all-Ireland final. Therefore Cork didn't really have any baggage with Kerry, and they had an opportunity to restate or redefine the relationship with Kerry . . . I suppose what I overlooked is that Kerry football in the era of the qualifiers has almost come to regard Croke Park as its home venue, and that Kerry football performances seem to take off in August, even in years when they haven't done well in Munster. They come to Croke Park in August and there seems to be some—I don't know—chemical reaction with the venue, and because of that in 2007 Cork came out and Cork seemed to feel that, not so much that they were breaking new ground but that they were retreading familiar ground; and that familiar ground did not have positive associations for them, because they were playing Kerry at a venue where they conspicuously failed to compete with them in previous years, and it was unfortunate. You could look at the match and say there were strokes of ill-fortune that befell Cork, and, as a result, they ended up further behind on the scoreboard than maybe they should have. But the fact was they were far more spooked by playing Kerry in an all-Ireland final, regardless of the fact that it was a fresh stage in which to play them. It was unusual and it was unfortunate. It was a pity, given the history and the traditions of the fixture, that their first meeting in an all-Ireland final was so one-sided.

Kieran Donaghy appreciated the pressure that came with such an occasion.

That was my hardest game ever in a Kerry jersey . . . Even Armagh in 2006, I was only a greenhorn, a rookie, I wasn't really paying attention to what they were saying; but I remember putting pressure on ourselves as players, and fans putting pressure on you, saying, 'Ye can't lose to Cork, no matter what happens,' and I remember just not being really able to sleep that night before the game and kind of saying, Ah no, am I going to be tired . . . am I going to play bad . . . No matter what they say, we have it over Cork . . . we have it over Cork, over the hundred years, the hundred and twenty-five years we've had it over Cork. And all the work by the greats, all their work, beating Cork all the years, would have gone by the wayside if they had beaten us in the big one, and that's how we felt. There was huge pressure on us, and I was always worried about it, because there was no pressure on Cork. We had beaten Cork already . . . They could come in and beat us and always have it over us, and we would probably never get to play them in an all-Ireland final again. That group of players would have it over this group of players; even though most of these players would have three, four or five all-Ireland medals; but that wouldn't be good enough, 'cause they'd say, We beat ye in the all-Ireland final, ye couldn't beat us in the big one. So the stakes were huge.

Mike Frank Russell too was aware of what was in store for Kerry if they lost.

It's kind of surreal, really, to be playing Cork in an all-Ireland final, you know. It's always been a Munster final, but the stakes were high this time—as high as they ever were. A lot of things were on the line . . . The history was on the line. We'd never have been let forget about it. Imagine having lost to Cork in an all-Ireland final—would have been unbearable.

For Declan O'Sullivan, ahead of all-Irelands,

as a player, you can't get involved; to a point, you almost have to be rude. You have to get into your own bubble, stay with your own friends, your own circle, and switch off, really. You can't get caught up in the build-up. Maybe that might be hard for supporters sometimes. Our motto is, if we win it there'll be plenty of time for that stuff after. Certainly in the build-up to games you have to put yourself away from all that type of hype.

The sides were tied on three points after a quarter of an hour. Not for the first time, Colm Cooper then imposed himself on the greatest GAA stage of all. In the eighteenth minute Séamus Scanlon launched the ball goalwards. Cooper was first to the ball, flicking it into an empty net. Even in the pressure-cooker of an all-Ireland final, Cooper was plotting as that ball travelled through the air.

> You might sense it more than hear it. I knew Kieran O'Connor was
> pretty tight to me, and when I was just shooting in and around the
> square I knew, I had a feeling that Alan Quirke was coming for it. So
> I just thought, if I could get any touch to it there was a chance of a
> score, be it a point or a goal. When the roar went up, you knew it was
> in the net. I suppose it's the little senses you get around the place,
> and there's no better place to get it than at Croke Park, I guess.

Cooper followed up with a point, and Kerry were ahead 1-4 to 0-3 just
shy of the twenty-minute mark. Cork out-scored Kerry by three points
to two between then and the interval, at which stage Kerry led 1-6 to 0-
6. The game was finely poised. Fans on both sides were set for a similarly
tight second half; but nothing could have prepared anyone for the Cork
farce that was to follow. As the Cork defence attempted to work the ball
out from their own square the goalkeeper, Alan Quirke, moved away
from his posts to give his team-mates the option of laying the ball off to
their unmarked netminder. That never happened: Donaghy stole the
ball and was left staring at an empty net.

> I suppose I used my basketball skill for one, you know, when Cork
> had a chance to really get the ball out. Ger Spillane looked at me,
> and I knew when he was coming at me, he was saying, 'I'm taking
> you on here, and I'm going past you.' But the focus was right after
> half time; we said they came out a little too easily in the first half in
> defence. Lynch and Canty and these fellows were bursting out, and
> we said we need to put a stop on them, and if Canty or Lynch comes
> out, try to put them on the back foot straight away. I remember
> Spillane coming at me, and I almost got into a defensive position
> and stance, and he put the ball out there, and I was lucky enough to
> knock it away. To turn around, then, and kind of say, How am I
> going to beat Alan Quirke here now? No goalie! . . . and I thought,
> I'm going to get a clatter here now in a minute. I can't see him. But
> I just saw him in the corner of my eye running in, and for a minute
> I was going to flake it and try and take the net off, but I said I'd better
> roll it in, because if I flake it it could hit the crossbar or a post, and
> I could drive it wide then, and I could be forgotten very easily and

always be remembered as the man that missed a chance like that. So I just rolled it in and went off celebrating, as I usually do.

Of his elation after scoring he added:

> I always give out to myself afterwards. I kind of say, That's an awful stupid way to go around celebrating. But when I score a big goal like that I can't control the emotions. Whatever happens happens, and it's ten or fifteen seconds afterwards I kind of gather myself afterwards and say, Calm down and back playing football.

Kerry were relentless in the next seven minutes, making it 2-10 to 0-6. A Cork point gave them a glimmer of hope, but that light faded soon after. Different circumstances from the first goal but a similar outcome, as Donaghy was presented with another gift of a goal after a high ball into the Cork square was misfielded. The Austin Stacks man, however, absolves the Cork goalkeeper of blame for this one.

> A lot of people blamed Alan Quirke for that. The Cork media blamed him, and the national media blamed him. But he actually called the ball that day. I stayed out of the way, 'cause I knew he was coming, and I said, This could fall somewhere, you know, and Shields jumped into him and hit Alan Quirke's hand, and the ball fell and I ran. I don't think it was that easy. I thought I did a nice little swivel, because if I picked it Noel O'Leary was flying in behind me, you know, and he would probably have blocked it or knocked it out of my hand, or given away a penalty. So I remember kind of saying to myself, running out to the ball—I could see him running at me, so I said, You have to swivel now and try to knock this in. But I thought it was a quality finish . . . I'll take it any day of the week.

Thirteen minutes into the second half, the game was over. Kerry had opened up a twelve-point lead, with Cork the architects of their own downfall. Kerry won by 3-13 to 1-9. In the dressing-room afterwards Paul Galvin revealed how he felt.

> Just a fantastic feeling, you know. A sense of relief, I suppose, too, because there was so much riding on this today for Kerry. Being it

was Cork and in an all-Ireland final, I felt everything we had achieved and everything that Kerry football stood for was on the line . . . a hundred years of being the greatest county in Gaelic football, dominating Cork for so long . . . If Cork had beaten us today we wouldn't have been let back into the county, in my eyes. I think it was that big, the stakes were that big for us. Everything, our reputations and our pride in Kerry football, was riding on seventy minutes. That's how I looked at it.

Some years later he still stands by that sentiment.

Yeah, I know a lot was made of that quote subsequently . . . I'll always feel that way any time Kerry play Cork—or any time Kerry play in an all-Ireland final, but more so against Cork. Because, you know, the fact of the matter is, if we lose, if we ever lost up there in a final or in a semi-final, we'd never hear the end of it. You know, Cork people in particular would say, 'Sure what about it? If ye beat us all those times, so what? We beat ye!' And they would always have it over us, and I just felt . . . there was a bit more than a game of football riding on those games.

Kieran Donaghy feels that Galvin's speech that day opened the squad's eyes.

He said, A hundred years of beating these . . . I won't even say—a hundred years of beating these fellows, and it'll be all forgotten if they beat us today. And I think that just hit home, and it drove a focus and it drove a determination into fellows, that, no matter what happens, we're not getting beaten. And I know we got a few lucky breaks; but, I think, overall, in general play we had enough of the ball to win the game.

Paul Galvin also revealed his hope that the win over Cork in 2007 might serve as the platform for further success.

We started talking about it [three in a row] in the dressing-room. That's what Kerry football is about. Maybe it's time for a new dynasty in Kerry football. The greats are the greats, but maybe we can create a new dynasty of our own, and that's the aim.

The journalist Jim O'Sullivan feels that

> no Cork player or no Cork supporter will look back on that game
> with any degree of comfort, because it was just one mistake after
> another. You could say it was their lack of experience, but I suppose
> they made mistakes. You could say it another way, that they weren't
> able to cope with the Gooch. Colm got the first goal; he certainly was
> on a bigger opponent, but, again, perfect timing. Everything about
> Colm is so spot on, and he just met the ball coming in. Cork
> conceded goals—I suppose that's what really killed Cork that day . . .
> Whatever chance they had of upsetting Kerry, they had no chance
> when they made such mistakes. They weren't strong enough, really.

The Kerry manager, Pat O'Shea, described at the homecoming how

> we'd been asked to do a very pressurised job. There was only one
> thing we could do: win an all-Ireland. We've done it for our own
> people: that's the most important thing of all. We represent a very
> proud county, and every time we put on a Kerry jersey we're
> conscious of that. When we crossed the county bounds, that was the
> most special feeling of all, 'cause we're back with our own people in
> Kerry. There was nobody ever more proud to lead Kerry back to this
> county . . . to send a message to our near neighbours in the county
> of Cork that there's only one football team in this country, and that's
> the Kingdom.

Even before Kerry went on to win the 2009 all-Ireland, Dónal Keenan
believed that the team of the 2000s had every right to be compared to
the greats of yesteryear.

> Absolutely, this Kerry team, over the last seven, eight, nine years, has
> been a great team. This Kerry team has had to put up with the
> qualifiers; it has had to put up with the re-emergence of the
> Northern teams: the Tyrones, the Armaghs—great sides in any era,
> this Tyrone team, or that great Armagh team that Joe Kernan
> coached . . . The great teams of the past, and I'm not degrading them

by saying they didn't have that problem, Kerry could win an all-Ireland by playing just three matches, and one of those might be against Sligo, as happened in '75. That doesn't happen any more, so it's a lot harder to win an all-Ireland now ... The brilliant under-age structures that have been put in place in the North are beginning to produce very, very strong teams, as we're seeing. So that's made it a lot harder ... This team is probably as good as the three-in-a-row team of the '80s. It's impossible to say they were as good as the other team, because the other team was so good. But you look at the players that have come through, and you look at the quality of footballer; you take Séamus Moynihan—he would certainly have got on the great four-in-a row-team. Darragh Ó Sé would certainly have got a place in the great four-in-a-row team; the Gooch I think would have got his place in the great four-in-a row-team; he would possibly have been an even better player. There are other wonderful players ... I think history should be very kind to them, because I think they have been, probably, the team of the decade, themselves and Tyrone.

Kieran Donaghy finds it hard to separate his two finals.

I can't put one over the other, and I'll give you the reasons why: because 2006 was a very special one for me, because it was my first one, and I never thought I'd win one. My grandmother was in Croke Park for the first time in her life—she'd be very close to me—she was at the game in the wheelchair section, and I knew that going into the game. I wanted to win a medal, and I wanted to win it for my family, number one. I wanted to win it for Kerry, and that was great ... So I can't really weigh up and to say one is better ... They're cherished, and I hope I can get my hands on one or two more.

Donaghy was one of thirteen Kerry players who began each of that season's five championships games, and the Kingdom reaped the rewards of having such a settled side.

Pat O'Shea left the position of Kerry manager following defeat at the hands of Tyrone in the 2008 all-Ireland senior football final, and Jack O'Connor was lured back to the post he vacated in 2006. With Tyrone getting the better of Kerry not only in 2008 but also in 2003 and 2005, there were claims that a sense of unfinished business was partly behind O'Connor's return; however, he says that this is not the case.

> People will have that idea in their heads, but I needed a bit of time out of the game in 2006, because that was a very trying year, emotionally and psychologically—and physically as well. I was pretty spent at the end of that, and I just needed a break from the game. I wasn't trying to go out in a blaze of glory or anything like that—I just needed a break, and I got that break for a couple of years; and I think going back in with Kerins O'Rahillys and having a great run with them in the county championship in 2008 had a big bearing on me returning to the game with Kerry, because I got my appetite, big time. When the opportunity came to get involved with Kerry, then . . . I was determined this year to delegate a bit more and just stand back and have my input, just coming in with my input a bit more strategically and sporadically. So that's the way it was, and I think maybe it did work a bit better than the last time.

Éamonn Fitzmaurice joined Jack O'Connor in the Kerry set-up for 2009. Ger O'Keeffe was the other selector. O'Connor believes that Fitzmaurice has the potential to one day take the top job in Kerry football.

> He was a fellow I always admired when he was playing, and he was a great leader, and a great leader with his club . . . There's no doubt about it, Éamonn has the material to be a future Kerry manager . . . I kind of was saying that to him, that this was a great way to dip his toe in the water at this level, and I think he has enjoyed the year, but he was a huge part of it, because himself and Ger really got along in the training, along with Alan and Pat, and I thought we had a great set-up . . . And there was no fellow standing on the sideline looking in: we were all involved in it. And I think that's important for the players, that we would all play together, and we would all take the flak together and the praise together.

Silverware arrived early in 2009 for Kerry, with the side beating Derry in the National Football League final.

Tadhg Kennelly made his senior championship debut for Kerry in the Munster semi-final against Cork. Jack O'Connor hoped that the introduction of such new blood would rub off on the players who had tasted all-Ireland defeat the previous season.

> We felt that the team needed a kind of a new impetus, because when you're beaten in an all-Ireland you can't go back with the same team anyway, because you just need to try something different . . . and Tadhg was a big part of that, and he just brought a great freshness and a great enthusiasm to us—a bit like Kieran Donaghy did in 2006. He was a breath of fresh air around the place and obviously had a huge role to play in the final as well.

In the semi-final Cork quickly led, two-nil. The Walshes, Tommy and Donnchadh, drew the Kingdom level. Tommy then limped out of the game. He was barely off the field when Cork struck for the only goal of the match. They went four in front on twenty-four minutes. Donnchadh Walsh and Darragh Ó Sé, the sub, had Kerry points, halving the deficit by the twenty-ninth minute. On the half-hour mark Kerry forged an attack once more. A penalty to the Kingdom, and Colm Cooper was presented with the opportunity to put Kerry in front. He missed. There was to be only one more score in the half, a Donncha O'Connor free for Cork, who led at the break by 1-5 to 0-5.

The gap was extended to 1-9 to 0-7 by the twenty-third minute of the second half. Kerry seemed dead and buried, but an eight-minute spell yielded five points for them. It's hard to believe, but Kerry had drawn level with three minutes remaining, 0-12 to 1-9. The search was on for a winner. Injury time produced what seemed to be the deciding score, Colm O'Neill pointing for Cork. But Kerry would have one last chance to save the day, and Bryan Sheehan's fifth point of the afternoon earned them a share of the spoils.

The replay was a nightmare for Kerry, except for a ten-minute spell at the beginning of the second half. Kerry had gone in at the short whistle down by nine points to four. It should have been a lot more, as Daniel Goulding struck a post and Pearse O'Neill blasted wide when through on goal. Paul Galvin of Kerry and Noel O'Leary of Cork received their marching orders on twenty-five minutes, following an off-the-ball incident.

The opening salvos of the second half were Kerry's, five points bringing them level. However, one minute later Kerry's hard work was undone when they conceded a penalty, which Cork converted. The Kingdom never recovered from that, and Cork went on to win, 1-17 to 0-12.

Jack O'Connor feels that Kerry's success in the National League contributed to their downfall.

> What was going wrong? I felt myself that we hadn't the volume of work done that Cork had done . . . We came back late from the holiday and started training just two weeks before the league, so the fact that we won the league then meant that you really hadn't much opportunity to do many blocks of work during the league. Then you had [local] club championship at the end of the league, and you had basically a couple of weeks to prepare for Cork . . . A good share of their players would have been playing college football as well, so they would have been well ahead of us early in the year . . . We felt after the game in Páirc Uí Chaoimh that we would have to restructure the team, and that's what we set about doing through the qualifiers.

Darren O'Sullivan feels about the Cork game that

> they gave us a good hiding on the day, which highlighted a couple of our problems. But the fact of the matter is that, without playing well, we still managed to pull them back early in the second half. Yeah, we kind of lost our way a bit. They got a penalty. After all the hard work it was hard to pick yourself up again. If they hadn't scored the penalty we might have gone on to win that game, not being at our best, not being at our physical peak.

With this defeat mirroring the events of 2006, Paul Galvin didn't give up hope that they could also turn around this campaign. Galvin sensed that the Kingdom could still challenge for the end-of-season honours.

> Our training probably was just gearing up at that stage of the summer and that we would improve; but it was obviously a hard call to say that we might win an all-Ireland in the way we did. But you

always hope, and you always have a great chance when you're with Kerry . . . but we had done something similar, very similar, we were in a very similar situation in '06, having got well beaten by Cork in Páirc Uí Chaoimh, and we pulled it around, so that was what we were focusing on. And, you know, that was always there in the back of our heads, that maybe, maybe, maybe we could; so we just clung to that.

Jack O'Shea was not too perturbed by the Munster loss to Cork. He questions the merits of winning provincial championships.

It's actually nearly beneficial at the moment not to be provincial champions, because you can kind of get your act together and get your team rebuilt and on the road . . . I feel the provincial finalists should be played against one another, as they always were—the two winners go through to the semi-final. I think the two losers—now at the moment they lose out, they don't get any second chance—I think they should be brought back in and they should play the two teams that come through from the back-door system. So I think instead of the back-door system, teams coming down to four, I'd bring it down to two, and then, along with the provincial finalists, make up your quarter-finals and then have your semi-finals accordingly.

Defeat to Cork meant that Kerry were now forced to take the scenic route to Croke Park. Jack O'Connor took the opportunity to knock on the door of a familiar face—Mike McCarthy—in a bid to tempt him out of retirement.

Mike agreed to come back when I met him two days after the replay in Páirc Uí Chaoimh. The timing was right. He was a big plus to the team because he has a great football brain, and he just gave us a huge bit of solidity in the number 6 slot, a bit like Moynihan had done back in 2006 when he came out there.

(Tomás Ó Sé, in an interview with the now defunct Dublin-based INN)
    Just as in 2006, a loss in the Munster championship to Cork was followed by a qualifier against Longford. Kieran Donaghy was placed at full-forward in his first championship appearance of the season. A

foot injury had caused him to be sidelined since the National League final.

The game against Longford was level at one point each heading into the eighth minute, when Tommy Walsh netted. Kerry had the next four points, moving into a 1-5 to 0-1 lead after seventeen minutes. Longford doubled their tally before the Kingdom took over again. With eight minutes to half time, Kerry were leading 1-10 to 0-2. Longford had two points before the end of the half, and Kerry now led 1-10 to 0-4.

The second half should have been academic. Tommy Walsh pointed one minute after the restart to make it 1-11 to 0-4. Kerry would score just once more. Longford kicked three points before Tommy Walsh had that final point for Kerry. Longford failed to take their opportunities and only added four more points. Kerry had progressed by 1-12 to 0-11. Kieran Donaghy lasted forty-five minutes against Longford, going off injured.

If Kerry were unconvincing against Longford they were downright lucky against Sligo the following week. They led early, three to one, but Sligo levelled before the twentieth minute. It was then four all. Paul Galvin had Kerry leading by seven points to six before the only goal of the game arrived.

Sligo led at half time, 1-6 to 0-7. Kerry were responsible for six of the eight scores obtained in the first ten minutes of the second half. Leading by 0-13 to 1-8, Kerry seemed to be on their way to victory. But they had only one more point against Sligo, who themselves could only manage two more. Bryan Sheehan had Kerry's final score, a point with nine minutes to go. That gave the Kingdom a two-point lead, 0-14 to 1-9. Three minutes from time, that most dangerous of leads was in danger. Sligo were awarded a penalty. David Kelly stepped up to take the kick. Immortality beckoned if he could score the goal to knock Kerry out of the championship.

The headline-writers paused in anticipation of the sports story of the year. Kerry's season may have been on the line in those few moments, but their goalkeeper, Diarmuid Murphy, says that he didn't feel too much pressure. He made the save.

> The pressure is on the kicker, really . . . He's supposed to score, and my attitude was, if this guy is going to put it into the top corner or the bottom corner at speed, well, then, fair play to him . . . I just

waited for a shot and then reacted accordingly.

Sligo did manage to halve the gap before the end, but Kerry survived—just about—on a score of 0-14 to 1-10.

Kerry were criticised in all quarters following each of their qualifiers, but Tomás Ó Sé, speaking to INN, felt that the players knew they were doing what had to be done.

> We had a meeting after we lost to Cork, and things weren't going well throughout the games; but, having said that, they were tough qualifier games we had, I don't care what anyone says. We felt we weren't too far off clicking. Now, we were very lucky against Sligo . . . We're lucky we got over that, and we kept on plugging away.

As the qualifiers progressed, Kerry brought in the services of some familiar faces. Jack O'Connor turned to his former selector Johnny Culloty, among others, for help.

> Well, Tony O'Keeffe and Séamus Moynihan came in midway through the year, just to be kind of an eye up in the sky, up in the stand . . . Their input was very valuable, and sure Johnny will always be one of the main advisers, I suppose, because his knowledge of the game and his interest in the game is unbelievable . . . Johnny is a fantastic judge of a player . . . You could liken him to a racehorse trainer, the way he can judge a player, and even young lads coming through, he has a tremendous interest in the development of young lads; and he would pick out a college player there for you and he would say, That fellow is going to make it, and your man won't make it . . . So I would always have great faith in Johnny's judgement . . . He has been a great adviser and a great support for me down through the years.

In the wake of the Sligo victory it emerged that Colm Cooper and Tomás Ó Sé had, as Tadhg Kennelly put it, broken the squad's self-imposed drinking ban. The news that they were facing discipline broke on the Friday before the Antrim match. 'Kerry stars carpeted' read the front page of the *Irish Examiner*. Those members of the county board and the team management who could be contacted that Friday refused to comment. Speaking later in the year, Jack O'Connor said he knew that the matter had to be dealt with, although he was not pleased that the story made the headlines.

> It was a decision you don't want to make. It was one of those things that you'd rather not have to deal with it; but we had a certain set of guidelines on the panel, and a certain set of rules, so we just felt that the situation needed to be addressed; and, to be fair, the lads handled it well, and they took it on the chin. It was just unfortunate that the media made a big hullabaloo about it, and sure, like everything else, we wanted to keep it as quiet as we could. But it got out there anyway, and sure at the time it kind of tied in with the conspiracy theory that we were going badly, and we were in chaos, and we were throwing in the towel. So the media latched on to that and made a big deal out of it. You'd have to say that going into the Antrim game the following week that many people didn't give us a chance of surviving much further.

Cooper and Ó Sé were left on the bench for the outing against Antrim. Their absence was not felt early on, as Kerry took a four-point lead in the first fifteen minutes, thanks mainly to a Tommy Walsh goal. Antrim wiped out that 1-2 to 0-1 deficit by the nineteenth minute. It was 1-3 to 1-2 in Antrim's favour as the clock ticked towards the half-hour mark. Tommy Walsh then pointed, Kerry's first score for more than a quarter of an hour.

Cooper and Ó Sé's punishment ended after thirty-one and forty-four minutes, respectively: the pair were summoned from the bench to aid in Kerry's fight to remain in the championship. For Jack O'Connor,

> the one thing that you can't afford to be, as an inter-county manager, is to be vindictive . . . We knew that if we were going to go anywhere this year we needed those two players, and they both played a big part when they came on in that game. Colm kicked three or four points, and Tomás set up the important goal there in the second half for Paul Galvin . . . After that . . . we wiped the slate clean.

Antrim led 1-4 to 1-3 at half time. They went two in front when the game resumed. Colm Cooper had three frees in a row, to nudge the Kingdom ahead. Paul Galvin made it 1-7 to 1-5 after thirteen minutes of the second half. With ten minutes to go Antrim and Kerry were level, at 1-8 each. The deciding moment was just around the corner. A Paul Galvin goal meant that Kerry were now three ahead. With five minutes remaining that gap was reduced to two, Kerry 2-9, Antrim 1-10. While Antrim failed to trouble the scoreboard again, Kerry consolidated their position, finishing winners 2-12 to 1-10.

Kerry were the underdogs for their quarter-final with Dublin, and understandably so. No-one could have predicted what lay in store on that holiday Monday in Croke Park. Kerry were travelling more in hope than in expectation. For Darren O'Sullivan,

> when you're getting that bit of criticism, eventually it does take its toll. It can be a bit draining when you're listening to the same thing over and over—how the team's finished, and they definitely won't win it this year. It can dent your confidence, and you do start to doubt yourself. But I think the game [against Antrim], and the way we finished, the way certain fellows were going around, carrying themselves in that game, gave everyone a lift.

The Kingdom's fears heading into the Dublin game were immediately banished, Colm Cooper goaling thirty-six seconds into the proceedings. That goal set the scene for the afternoon. Dublin were startled. Kerry were relentless, defying the experts and critics with one of their greatest displays of all time. Kerry led by seven points only a quarter of an hour in. The gap was doubled in the next twenty minutes, and Kerry went in at the break with a 1-14 to 0-3 lead. Jack O'Connor considers those thirty-five minutes to be the greatest display of his tenure.

> It was, without a doubt, the best. You often said that the 2006 final, the first twenty minutes of that, was serious football . . . But this was really sustained stuff . . . Any team that kicks 1-14 in the first half of a game, they have to be doing an awful lot of things right, and especially from where we were coming from. And the fact that we were being written off quite a lot coming into the game meant that we were really motivated and fired up; and I suppose that showed in the football that we played.

Diarmuid Murphy feels that the build-up had worked a treat for the Kingdom.

> All the pressure was on Dublin. There was fierce pressure on them. I remember reading an interview on the morning of the game . . . The impression was that this is kind of half done and dusted, and they are moving on, like, before the game was played at all. And I thought the pressure was really gone off us on the day, and we played well. I knew there was a big performance in us on the day, and whether that was good enough or not to win the match is a different thing entirely, because a lot depended on what Dublin did. But they didn't play on the day at all, and our lads played really well, especially the first twenty-five minutes, and I think that's the best we have played as a group.

With the game now in the bag, the Kerry supporters were able to sit back and enjoy the second period. Kerry outscored Dublin, 0-10 to 1-4, in the second thirty-five minutes, winning 1-24 to 1-7.

The Kerry captain, Darren O'Sullivan, knew that the side needed to remain focused. Dublin, he felt,

> just didn't perform today. They were unlucky with a few efforts, but we'll just have to worry about ourselves from now on, and we're just delighted to get into the semi-final. Now, we have been favourites going into a lot of games, but we're not going to worry about that, we never do; it's all about preparing for the game as it comes, and that's what we're looking forward to now.

The first score of the semi-final against Meath came three minutes after the throw-in. O'Sullivan scored from the penalty spot after Colm Cooper had been up-ended in the Meath square. O'Sullivan slipped as he kicked the ball; but all that mattered was that the ball found the back of the net. Cooper pointed in the tenth minute. Cian Ward put over Meath's opener just before the quarter-hour mark. A low-scoring first half ensued, with Kerry tallying 1-3 and Meath 0-4.

Kerry introduced Tommy Walsh twenty minutes in, a decision that would reap almost immediate rewards. Jack O'Connor believed that they had to draft him in.

We had to change tactics half way through the first half and put in Tommy Walsh, because we needed an aerial route . . . It changed the game, basically.

Once again Kerry's first score of the second period was a goal, this time coming only one minute after the break. The scorer was Tommy Walsh. That goal had a devastating effect on Meath, and from that moment on the result was never in doubt. Kerry were now ahead by 2-3 to 0-4, and they kept up the pressure. Only five minutes into the second half Kerry had extended their advantage to 2-5 to 0-4. The match petered out after that, a goal in injury time for Meath making for a final score of 2-8 to 1-7. After the game Jack O'Connor

really felt that the game very much panned out the way I thought it would. I thought it was going to be a dog-fight; I thought it was going to be tough; and I thought that Meath were going to give a great account of themselves, especially with the rain. There was no easy ball being won by forwards there, and that's the way you want a semi-final to pan out. That Dublin game was never—that's not the real world—we kept saying that to the boys all the week, that that's not the real world. I just think that they lost heart. But Meath were never like that, Meath have never been like that . . . They kept plugging away till the end.

Tadhg Kennelly's all-Ireland dream lived on. He was seventy minutes from realising that dream.

I suppose the Dublin game, we got everything our way, and we knew playing against Meath, it was going to be a physical game, especially with the conditions, a wet, greasy ball. It wasn't going to be easy football, but we knew if we kept going we had the footballers and the physical players out there to match them, and we knew we would break them. I suppose we were lucky in a way that we got a goal at the start of the second half, but we changed our game plan a bit . . . Because it wasn't a day for putting in a nice, special ball, like we did against Dublin.

Declan O'Sullivan agrees.

The semi-final was great in terms of preparation for the final. Conditions were bad. Cork were after beating Tyrone in a great semi-final, so pundits were really buying in to that. Cork were in great form, and, as I say, we struggled a bit to get through Meath. We always felt that we played within ourselves against Meath. We were happy to get over that, and the big day was coming for the final. It's all about getting to the final and playing well there.

Cork, having dismantled Tyrone in the last four, were to be Kerry's opponents in the decider. Unlike so many other matches, Kerry actually went into the 2009 decider as underdogs. It's a rarity, but it's a tag that Jack O'Connor relished.

It was a great feeling, to be honest with you, because it kind of meant that we weren't under as much pressure as Cork were, and we felt, ourselves, that even the semi-final game with Meath was the ideal type of result and an ideal performance, in a way, because again we weren't very fluent . . . We felt that we were in quite a good place, that we were in an all-Ireland final under the radar and exactly where we wanted to be, and we still had one or two positions that we were playing around with, so that's always a good thing going into a final.

Tommy Walsh's goal-scoring appearance off the bench in the semi-final saw him promoted to the starting-fifteen for the decider. Donnchadh Walsh was the one to miss out.

The beginning of that all-Ireland final has been much discussed, mainly because of an incident in the opening minute. Tadhg Kennelly in his autobiography revealed that

my theory was that I really wanted to set the tone for the game for our side. We wanted Cork to know that we were a totally different animal to the one they'd faced three months earlier. As we got to our positions, I looked across at Galvin, who nodded, and then positioned myself on the line ready to race in when the referee put the ball in the air. My eyes were almost rolling around in the back of my head. I was like a raging bull . . . After a few strides I knew I'd timed it right. Cork's Nicholas Murphy had just turned slightly towards me which opened the way for my shoulder to catch him perfectly on the chin. Cop that. It's different this time, boys.

Kennelly later issued a statement.

> The controversy arising from the incident involving Nicholas Murphy in the All Ireland final and an account of which was published in the *Sunday Independent* has devastated both me and my family. I have been publicly vilified and I want to tell the truth. I admit I have made a mistake and a big one. I should never have allowed the piece regarding the incident with Nicholas to be described in the fashion in which it was. I gave an interview to the Australian ghost writer, Scotty Gallon, just a couple of days after the all-Ireland. I didn't read it over as I should have and the first account I saw of the incident was on last Sunday morning. Scotty used an expression, 'cop that,' to describe my feelings immediately after I connected with Nicholas. I said no such thing. I'm sure Nicholas can confirm that . . . What really happened was this: It was my first All Ireland final and I was very emotional . . . I admit I did intend to get physically stuck in right from the start. I didn't plan to tackle any particular Corkman but I did intend to shoulder charge an opponent immediately the opportunity arose . . . On my solemn word I did not and would never intentionally go out to hurt another footballer . . . Let me also clarify: Paul Galvin had absolutely nothing to do with my plan . . . I sincerely apologise to all Kerry supporters and the Kerry management team for any bother I might have caused.

After the incident Cork went into a lead of three points to one. They extended that in the tenth minute with the sole goal of the afternoon. Kerry were in trouble, trailing by five points after ten minutes. The Kingdom goalkeeper, Diarmuid Murphy, feels that patience and experience were crucial for their survival.

> I think we have a lot of experience in our team, and we had a game plan set out before the game; and we said, Look, no matter what happens here we're going to stick to our game plan. And that's how it turned out . . . Nobody panicked, everybody just stuck to the game plan, and everybody had faith in the next guy alongside him, that if

we keep sticking to this, things will come for us.

Two points by Colm Cooper reduced the gap to three by the quarter-hour mark. Donncha O'Connor for Cork made it 1-4 to 0-3 after seventeen minutes. For the next thirteen minutes the game belonged to Kerry. From being four points down they were two to the good after half an hour. Each side had two points in the closing minutes, leaving the half-time score at Kerry 0-11, Cork 1-6.

Without the expected backlash from Cork, Kerry took it to their opponents in the opening minutes of the second period. Their lead had been extended to four after forty-four minutes, 0-13 to 1-6. The Kingdom then had Diarmuid Murphy to thank for staying in front by that margin: Murphy brilliantly kept out a piledriver from Daniel Goulding.

There was widespread surprise when Tadhg Kennelly was called ashore in the fifty-second minute and Donnchadh Walsh was introduced in his place. A run of three Cork points in a row brought the gap down to the minimum by the fifty-fourth minute, Kerry 0-13, Cork 1-9. Cork would not score again. Kerry meanwhile pulled away once more. Tomás Ó Sé went upfield to fire over his second point of the match. That Kerry point in the fifty-ninth minute was the last of the game. The Kingdom, for the second time in three seasons, had beaten Cork in the all-Ireland final. It ended Kerry 0-16, Cork 1-9.

Tadhg Kennelly finally had his all-Ireland medal, emulating his brother and his father.

> My father inspired me, simple as that—inspired myself and Noel [Tadhg's brother] throughout our career. Everything I ever did or still do is for my father, and the whole year itself was dedicated to my father and to winning an all-Ireland medal.

Darren O'Sullivan's speech after the match will always be remembered for his phrase 'Tá Sam ag teacht abhaile.'

> It was a bit of a blur. I was very excited at the time, and then when I started walking up the nerves started to kick in. I remember looking out and I trying to get things sorted in my head, what to say and what not to say.

Not for the first time, the Kingdom had proved their doubters wrong. Paudie O'Mahony, the former Kerry goalkeeper, has high praise for the efforts of Tadhg Kennelly.

> He was definitely the saviour this year ... God forgive me for talking about Tim Kennelly's death, but I remember the day that Tim died, you know, because Tim and I were close friends—and I met Tadhg that day ... He was so upset and sad, and I said to myself, As sure as God this guy is going to come back to Kerry to prove to Tim and to his mother, Nuala, that there's life in the old dog yet. And he came back and won his all-Ireland with Kerry. He was definitely the key this year to change the forwards' outlook.

The format of the championship is called into question with each campaign. Tomás Ó Sé is proud of Kerry's achievements at the provincial level, but he does believe that the system needs tweaking.

> Fellows are saying, We have it easy down our way, and, I mean, we've done it both ways. We've won Munster championships and then we've gone on to win the all-Ireland; and then we haven't won Munster championships and have gone on to win the all-Ireland. And each time we do it fellows seem to have an argument that it's suiting us . . . I mean, ideally, we would like to win a Munster championship. I don't care what anybody says, there's pride in winning a Munster championship or Leinster championship or Ulster championship or Connacht championship. I mean, the alternative is to scrap those competitions, which would be a huge step for the GAA to take, so I don't know are they willing to take that ... When you do win a Munster championship, people say, You're going to be fresh going into an all-Ireland quarter-final. I don't buy into that at all. I would prefer to have games every two weeks . . . I like the way there was the qualifier matches, very close to each other.

Paul Galvin was subsequently named Footballer of the Year. His return to form in 2009 coincided with the Kingdom's rise to the top table once more. For both Kerry and Galvin 2008 was a year to forget, Galvin playing a bit part as Kerry lost to Tyrone in that season's decider. He was Kerry's captain in 2008, but his tenure ended early following the notorious incident in which he knocked the notebook from the referee's hand during the championship opener against Clare. Galvin says that being skipper in the future isn't an issue for him.

> I don't know, it kind of came upon me that time a few years ago. It came out of nowhere, because we weren't expected to win a county championship, and it was never an ambition of mine, and it just happened to fall onto my lap, and obviously it didn't work out very well, but it's not something I think about. It's over now, and it's not something I will think about going forward. Being captain isn't an ambition of mine, never was an ambition of mine. It was a fantastic honour, and it took a lot of hard, hard work, but we won a county championship more so than I became captain of Kerry . . . My county championship medal is what I think about and focus on. I don't think about captaincy and how it turned out or how it might, it's not an issue for me, certainly not. If it happened, it happened, and I'd go about it and see what happens, but certainly it's not something I think about or lose any sleep over.

For Kerry fans, at least, getting the better of Cork in an all-Ireland final is arguably their holy grail. Jack O'Connor, however, doesn't see it quite that way.

> No, I wouldn't say that, nothing about ultimate achievements. You could look back on the year and you could say there was an awful lot of highlights . . . We took on a lot of satisfaction as a team . . . Going up to Omagh and beating Tyrone in the league up there . . . that was a good achievement, because Tyrone are never easy to turn over . . . We played a lot of good football, especially in the first half of that game . . . The Dublin game was a big highlight.

This Kerry team is yet to defeat Tyrone in the championship, but, like all great sides, the team of the present era will be judged on what it's won, not on who they beat along the way. Paul Galvin has no complaints that beating Tyrone is still not on Kerry's cv.

> Not for me, anyway . . . I mean, fair play to them, they beat us, and they were a great side, and I have a lot of respect for that Tyrone side

... We struggled against them, and it's a great challenge for us, going forward, and hopefully we'll meet them, and maybe next year or the year after. But that's a great challenge for us to face, down the line ... Cork were just as big a challenge—probably a bigger challenge, actually—this year than Tyrone, because they were just playing so very, very well ... We really had to pull out all the stops to beat them.

Declan O'Sullivan is fully aware of the level that any side needs to attain to remain at the top.

It's getting tougher every year, really. I think the main thing this year that we learnt is that you have to time your run. We could see that from Tyrone last year. They started off very slowly. They were being written off. Once you come to July, August, that's the time you need to be getting yourself primed and getting a good run for maybe six, eight or ten weeks. I think we did that this year. It's a long year ... so you have to be very careful of burn-out. Obviously you have to introduce new players, and you saw that with Mike McCarthy walking away from it there. I think he had enough. Coming back to it this year, he was as fresh as ever. Freshness and sharpness plays a huge part coming to the end of the year ... The one thing I really enjoyed after winning all-Irelands is going back into the dressing-room with the players, and the warm-up area, around in a circle, the manager and a few of the fellows having a few words, having the Sam Maguire in the middle of the group. It's a very special feeling. All the hard work throughout the year was definitely worth it in those moments.

INDEX